ADOBE® CREATIVE SUITE® 4

DESIGN PREMIUM

W9-ADW-676

WHAT'S ON THE DISC

Here is an overview of the contents of the Classroom in a Book disc

Lesson files … and so much more

The *Adobe Creative Suite 4 Design Premium Classroom in a Book* disc includes the lesson files that you'll need to complete the exercises in this book, as well as other content to help you learn more about Adobe Creative Suite 4 Design Premium and use it with greater efficiency and ease. The diagram below represents the contents of the disc, which should help you locate the files you need.

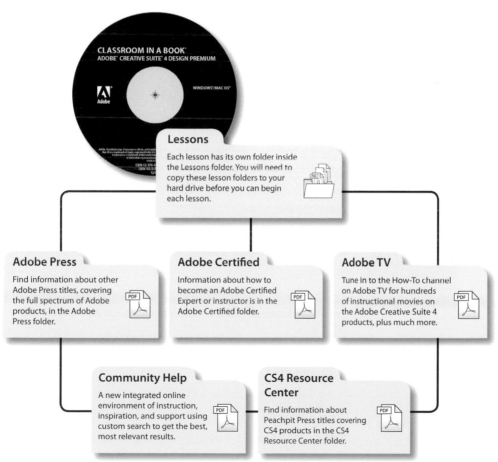

Lessons
Each lesson has its own folder inside the Lessons folder. You will need to copy these lesson folders to your hard drive before you can begin each lesson.

Adobe Press
Find information about other Adobe Press titles, covering the full spectrum of Adobe products, in the Adobe Press folder.

Adobe Certified
Information about how to become an Adobe Certified Expert or instructor is in the Adobe Certified folder.

Adobe TV
Tune in to the How-To channel on Adobe TV for hundreds of instructional movies on the Adobe Creative Suite 4 products, plus much more.

Community Help
A new integrated online environment of instruction, inspiration, and support using custom search to get the best, most relevant results.

CS4 Resource Center
Find information about Peachpit Press titles covering CS4 products in the CS4 Resource Center folder.

CONTENTS

FEATURE TOUR

PART II: THE PROJECTS

1 SETTING UP BASIC ASSETS

2 CREATING A BROCHURE

4   CREATING INTERACTIVE FLASH DOCUMENTS

GETTING STARTED

Adobe® Creative Suite 4 is a unified design environment that delivers the next level of integration in creative software. This software is the ultimate toolkit for today's designer. Express yourself in exciting new ways and deliver rich creative experiences across print, web, and mobile media. New features and tighter integration among suite components simplify creative and production tasks, enabling you to work more efficiently than ever before.

This Classroom in the Book introduces you to the key elements and applications of the Adobe Creative Suite 4 Design Premium edition.

About Classroom in a Book

Adobe Creative Suite 4 Design Premium Classroom in a Book is part of the official training series for Adobe graphics and publishing software developed by Adobe product experts. Each lesson in this book is made up of a series of self-paced projects that give you hands-on experience using the following Adobe products: Adobe InDesign® CS4, Adobe Photoshop® CS4 Extended, Adobe Illustrator® CS4, Adobe Flash® CS4 Professional, Adobe Dreamweaver® CS4, Fireworks CS4, Adobe Acrobat® 9 Pro, Adobe Device Central CS4, and Adobe Bridge CS4.

Adobe Creative Suite 4 Design Premium Classroom in a Book includes a CD attached to the inside back cover. On the CD you'll find all the files used for the lessons in this book, along with additional learning resources.

Prerequisites

Before you begin working on the lessons in this book, make sure that you and your computer are ready.

Requirements on your computer

You'll need about 500 MB of free space on your hard disk for the lesson files and the work files that you'll create as you work through the exercises.

Required skills

The lessons in this book assume that you have a working knowledge of your computer and its operating system. Make sure that you know how to use the pointer and the standard menus and commands, and also how to open, save, and close files. Do you know how to use context menus, which open when you right-click / Control-click items? Can you scroll (vertically and horizontally) within a window to see contents that may not be visible in the displayed area?

If you need to review these basic and generic computer skills, see the documentation included with your Microsoft® Windows® or Apple® Mac® OS X software.

Installing Adobe Creative Suite 4 Design Premium

Before you begin using *Adobe Creative Suite 4 Design Premium Classroom in a Book*, make sure that your system is set up correctly and that you've installed the required software and hardware. You must purchase the Adobe Creative Suite 4 Design Premium software separately. For system requirements and complete instructions on installing the software, see the Adobe Creative Suite 4 Design Premium Read Me file on the application CD or the Adobe Creative Suite Support Center on the Web at www.adobe.com/support/creativesuite.

Make sure that your serial number is accessible before installing the software; you can find the serial number on the registration card or CD sleeve.

Copying the Classroom in a Book files

● **Note:** The files on the CD are practice files, provided for your personal use in these lessons. You are not authorized to use these files commercially, or to publish or distribute them in any form without written permission from Adobe Systems, Inc. and the individual photographers who took the pictures, or other copyright holders.

The CD attached to the inside back cover of this book includes a Lessons folder containing all the files you'll need for the lessons. Each lesson has its own folder; you must copy the folders to your hard disk to complete the lessons. To save room on your hard disk, you can copy only the folder necessary for each lesson as you need it, and remove it when you're done.

Copying the Lessons files from the CD

1 Insert the *Adobe Creative Suite 4 Design Premium Classroom in a Book* CD into your CD-ROM drive.

2 Browse the contents and locate the Lessons folder.

3 Do one of the following:

- To copy all the lesson files, drag the Lessons folder from the CD onto your hard disk.

- To copy only individual lesson files, first create a new folder on your hard disk and name it Lessons. Then, drag the lesson folder or folders that you want to copy from the CD into the Lessons folder on your hard disk.

4 When your computer has finished copying the files, remove the CD from your CD-ROM drive and put it away.

Additional resources

Adobe Creative Suite 4 Design Premium Classroom in a Book is not meant to replace documentation that comes with the program, nor is it designed to be a comprehensive reference for every feature in Creative Suite 4 Design Premium. For additional information about program features, refer to any of these resources:

- Each Adobe Creative Suite 4 Design Premium application comes with Help built into the application. You can view it by choosing Help > *[Application Name]* Help, or by pressing the F1 key / Command+?.

- Browse the support pages and links to additional learning resources on the Adobe website (www.adobe.com). This option requires that you have Internet access.

- Adobe TV is a free online video resource for expert instruction and inspiration about Adobe products (http://tv.adobe.com).

- Community Help (http://community.adobe.com/help) is an integrated online environment of instruction and support using custom search to get the best, most relevant results.

Adobe Certification

The Adobe Training and Certification Programs are designed to help Adobe customers improve and promote their product-proficiency skills. The Adobe Certified Expert (ACE) program is designed to recognize the high-level skills of expert users. Adobe Certified Training Providers (ACTP) use only Adobe Certified Experts to teach Adobe software classes. Available in either ACTP classrooms or on-site, the ACE program is the best way to master Adobe products. For Adobe Certified Training Programs information, visit the Partnering with Adobe website at http://partners.adobe.com.

ADOBE CREATIVE SUITE 4 DESIGN PREMIUM

Delivering innovative ideas in print, web, and mobile design

Design with familiar tools, including Adobe InDesign CS4, Photoshop CS4 Extended, Illustrator CS4, and Acrobat 9 Pro software, knowing you can translate your work smoothly into virtually any medium. With animation in Adobe Flash CS4 Professional software made easier than ever, Adobe Fireworks CS4 software included for prototyping websites, and Adobe Dreamweaver CS4 software enhanced for standards-based web production, now you can deliver content in your favorite media.

This overview discusses some of the key advantages of the Creative Suite 4 Design Premium:

- Working faster and more creatively with images and graphics

- Breaking down barriers between print and electronic publishing

- Creating easy animation using skills you already have

- Prototyping website designs without being a code wizard

- Designing, previewing, and testing mobile content efficiently

- Connecting to the power of the online community using Creative Pro Online Services

The next chapter, "Feature Tour," introduces each of the Creative Suite 4 Design Premium component applications. The lessons in the second part of this book will cover specific aspects of using the applications in much more detail.

With today's exciting array of media and delivery channels, there's no such thing as a single, all-purpose workflow. No matter what your route to a final creative product, Creative Suite 4 Design Premium lets you use your existing skills to go beyond what you already know, while letting you reuse your creative assets no matter what media you're working in.

Versatile workflows for multiple media

Exciting new tools in Creative Suite 4 Design Premium software let you imagine daring creative possibilities, in the confidence that you can make them real. User-inspired enhancements and simplified workflows help you achieve more efficiency in everyday design and production tasks. Improved integration and more interface consistency between Creative Suite components allow you to draw on your existing expertise to venture into new creative territory: begin where you're most at home (usually Photoshop, Illustrator, or InDesign) and then switch easily to Flash, Dreamweaver, Fireworks, or Acrobat 9 Pro software for refinement, production, and high-quality output for print, Web, or mobile.

The Design Premium suite also provides access to online services that enable you to collaborate by sharing your screen right from within your design software and to learn from an extensive community of Adobe experts by searching Adobe-endorsed technical content directly from within Design Premium.

The second part of this book provides a hands-on tour of some of the most compelling new and enhanced features in Design Premium, focusing on various points within a complex cross-media creative project based on a fictitious movie called Double Identity. You will step through a workflow that allows you to experience the seamless integration across the various components of Design Premium, first working with assets in Photoshop and Illustrator, then layout in InDesign and creation of a SWF file for viewing in Adobe Flash player. Next you will learn how to take your content to Flash Professional to add interactive content. You will work with a website mockup in Fireworks, and then take it into Dreamweaver for final production. Finally, you'll see how to test your content for mobile devices using Adobe Device Central CS4 software.

Working faster and more creatively with images and graphics

Whether for a printed annual report, a corporate website, an interactive brochure, or a mobile entertainment site, vivid images and graphics help tell compelling stories. New tools in Adobe Photoshop and Illustrator let you work smarter and more imaginatively, no matter where the artwork will be used.

As graphic design extends beyond paper to an ever-widening variety of computers and other electronic devices, the opportunities explode for doing novel things with images and vector graphics. New versions of Photoshop and Illustrator offer exciting ways of working both more creatively and more efficiently, no matter where and how the final artwork will be used.

Brand new in Photoshop CS4 Extended is a powerful feature for scaling images intelligently based on their content. Also included are tools for editing, enhancing, and manipulating 3D images directly. For example, you can paint directly on a 3D model with the full range of Photoshop image-editing tools—just as you would in a 2D image—and see the results immediately. You can create a print-quality product shot from a 3D model, and then scale, align, and light it so that it fits perfectly into a composite image or place a 3D logo into a Flash animation and rotate it along a motion path.

In Illustrator CS4, let the new Blob Brush tool inspire novel ways of sketching, and work more efficiently by using multiple artboards to develop related pieces of artwork within a single file.

Enhanced user interface

Creative Suite 4 introduces several interface enhancements that provide you with more familiar work environments as you move among Design Premium components, or even between Macintosh and Windows versions. Not only do InDesign, Photoshop, Illustrator, and Flash offer these enhancements, but the interfaces in Dreamweaver and Fireworks have also been redesigned for greater consistency with other Design Premium software. *(See the illustration on the next page.)*

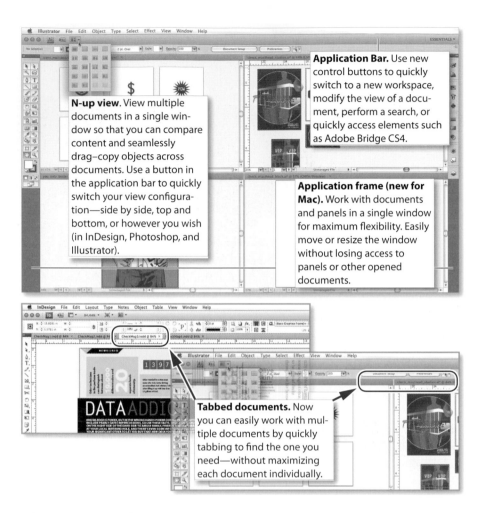

N-up view. View multiple documents in a single window so that you can compare content and seamlessly drag–copy objects across documents. Use a button in the application bar to quickly switch your view configuration—side by side, top and bottom, or however you wish (in InDesign, Photoshop, and Illustrator).

Application Bar. Use new control buttons to quickly switch to a new workspace, modify the view of a document, perform a search, or quickly access elements such as Adobe Bridge CS4.

Application frame (new for Mac). Work with documents and panels in a single window for maximum flexibility. Easily move or resize the window without losing access to panels or other opened documents.

Tabbed documents. Now you can easily work with multiple documents by quickly tabbing to find the one you need—without maximizing each document individually.

Enhancements specific to Adobe Photoshop CS4 include:

Intelligent image scaling

Imagine that you have an image which is ideal for a new project—say, an article on surfing for Check Magazine—except the proportions are wrong. Your challenge? To fit it into a specific location in a layout without distorting people or losing important background elements. Up to now, solving this kind of problem involved numerous time-consuming, cumbersome tasks.

But no more—Content-Aware Scaling is a revolutionary new feature that lets you resize and recompose images simultaneously. As its name implies, the feature automatically analyzes the image as you adjust it and intelligently recomposes it to preserve the most visually interesting areas. If you need fine-grained control over the results, you can use selection tools to define critical visual elements before you scale.

Content-Aware Scaling automatically identified and protected important image elements, such as people, from unwanted distortion, even though overall aspect ratio was not maintained. For even more precise results, you can use a simple alpha channel to preserve selected image areas during scaling.

Fluid canvas rotation and ultra-smooth pan, zoom, preview, and painting tools

Photoshop CS4 includes several enhancements which harness the power of your computer's graphics processing unit, greatly improving your ability to work at any magnification with perfect clarity, to smoothly navigate even the largest images with no stutter or delay— and even to rotate the canvas so that you can work at exactly the angle that's optimal for the task at hand.

Before scaling, note that the first image below is a rectangle roughly 4 inches by 3 inches, with a gap between the two surfers on the left and the one on the right. After Content-Aware Scaling, the second image is nearly square, the gap between the surfers has been closed, and the proportions of the human figures have been preserved.

Breakthrough 3D editing and compositing

The previous version of Photoshop Extended introduced exciting new features for editing 3D images. Now, Photoshop CS4 Extended takes 3D editing to a new level, enabling you to work as directly with 3D images as you do with 2D images. Rotate, roll, drag, slide, scale, and paint—without using dialog boxes or specialized texture layers. Leverage all of the image-editing tools in Photoshop to create 3D images that will add new dimensions to your print, web, and mobile designs.

• Revolutionary 3D painting and compositing
• Adjustments panel
• Masks panel
• 3D object and property editing
• Fluid canvas rotation
• Auto-blending of images
• Smoother panning and zooming
• Content-Aware Scaling
• Auto-alignment of layers
• Extended depth of field
• Enhanced motion graphics editing
• Better Raw image processing
• More powerful printing options
• Industry-leading color correction
• Integration with other Adobe software
• Improved Adobe Photoshop Lightroom workflow
• File display options
• Extensibility

The 3D model of the getaway car used in the Double Identity movie makes use of 2D artwork that wraps around its 3D contours.

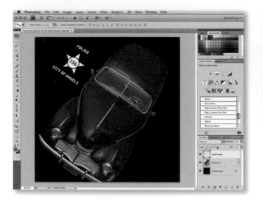 

Enhancements specific to Adobe Illustrator CS4 include:

Multiple artboards

The highly anticipated multi-artboard feature in Illustrator CS4 enables you to share graphical elements, symbols, styles, and interface settings easily from one artboard to another, allowing you to work efficiently and maintain consistency across many parts of a complex project. Create up to 100 artboards of varying size in a single file, and then place only the artboards you want in other Design Premium components.

The Illustrator file below shows one file with different artboards: it contains a poster, two postcards, a small print ad, a mobile scene navigator, and a web banner ad—all sharing a common color palette, symbols, styles, and more.

Blob Brush tool

The new Blob Brush tool allows for intuitive, freeform drawing, much like drawing with pixels in Photoshop or with natural-media tools. The Blob Brush tool provides natural, multi-stroke sketching and fast, easy editing of the resulting paths, and can be used in conjunction with the Eraser tool and the Smooth tool introduced in Illustrator CS3. Combined with a pressure-sensitive tablet and stylus, these features enable natural gestures with which illustrators and artists will feel at home.

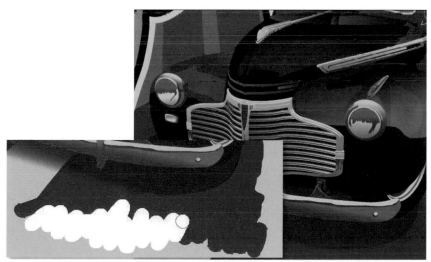

Breaking down barriers between print and electronic publishing

Top new and enhanced features in Adobe InDesign CS4

- Live Preflight
- Custom Links panel
- Conditional text
- Cross-references
- Interactive document design with SWF file export
- Page transitions in SWF and PDF files
- Export to Adobe Flash CS4 Professional
- Smart Guides and Smart Spacing
- Spread rotation
- Smart text reflow

Although publishing continues to move beyond print, designing pages and working with type is still at its heart. As a premier layout hub, InDesign not only offers new and enhanced tools for creating pages but also provides more output paths in more directions—for example, via XFL to Flash, via SWF to the web, and via PDF to virtually anyone in the world.

Adobe InDesign CS4 blazes new paths between the realms of print and electronic publishing. With new features and workflows for interactive onscreen documents added to its already powerful print design tools, InDesign enables you to create sophisticated, engaging layouts for onscreen audiences as easily as for print audiences.

Enhancements specific to Adobe InDesign CS4 include:

Customizable Links panel

Find, sort, manage, and organize all of your document's placed files in the newly redesigned Links panel. Each object in the Links panel is represented by a thumbnail image, so no more guessing by filename. Click any thumbnail to view even more detailed information, or click the page number to go directly to that file in your document. With consolidated access in a single panel, you can easily specify and then scan the link attributes most critical to your workflow—scale, rotation, resolution, and more—whether you're creating content for print or Web.

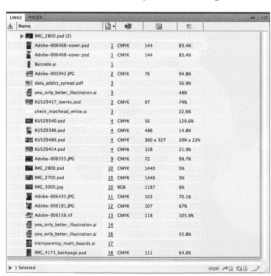

No matter whether your InDesign layout includes two dozen linked assets or two hundred, the new Links panel makes it much easier to manage all the details. What's more, you can use the Panel Options dialog box to select only the link attributes most appropriate for a particular project or medium, thereby streamlining the Links panel and avoiding information overload.

Support for Illustrator CS4 multiple artboards

Remember the multiple artboards Illustrator file that contained posters, ads, and other Double Identity campaign components—all bound for different destinations? A new integration feature in Design Premium enables you to open a multi-artboard file and select only the artwork you want to place in your InDesign layout—even matching the artwork bleed with the layout bleed.

The multi-artboard place feature also works in Photoshop CS4 and Flash CS4 Professional, making it very easy to work within a single Illustrator file on variants of artwork for produced for different media types.

Support for 3D Photoshop images

With support for 3D Photoshop images in InDesign CS4, you can place a 3D image just as easily as a 2D image. What's more, InDesign preserves the resolution of the original PSD file—if the 3D image is print-quality resolution in Photoshop, it will still be so when printed from InDesign.

Of course the 3D image can still be easily edited in Photoshop. The streamlined handling of 3D images in Photoshop and InDesign enables you to more easily tackle practical design problems and pursue new creative possibilities.

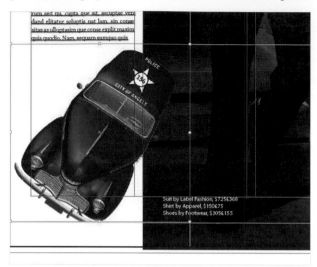

Immediate error detection and correction with Live Preflight

Enhanced preflight in Adobe Acrobat 9 Pro

You can control costs, reduce errors, and deliver premium customer service using extensive preflight and print production features that are now better than ever in Acrobat 9 Pro. Provide preflighting instructions and custom PDF export presets to ensure that your PDF files conform to specific production requirements. Then automatically validate files and easily fix issues from faulty hairlines to transparency handling, black conversion, spot color mapping, and more.

Preflight while you design, for better results, greater time savings, and lower production costs. Continuous preflight testing alerts you to potential production problems in real time—directly within the InDesign layout. Create a custom preflight profile that allows you to immediately identify and correct errors during the design phase instead of waiting until the document is ready for print or another output medium. When an error is detected, quickly navigate to the problem area, fix the problem, and keep working on your document. Create different custom preflight profiles for different workflows and share them with project teams to ensure that all files are checked using the same set of parameters.

Of course, Live Preflight isn't only for preparing InDesign files for print—you can create custom preflight profiles for layouts that will be output to SWF or PDF files for posting online. Incredibly efficient and effective, Live Preflight makes it possible to achieve the highest standards of quality, even under the most impossible deadlines.

Interactive buttons

Another way that InDesign CS4 removes barriers between print and screen is with new features for adding dynamic navigation elements to page layouts: Create interactive buttons, apply page transitions, and add hyperlinks in an InDesign layout and export it in PDF or SWF format to quickly produce a compelling onscreen publication. You can even lay out one version for print and another for screen by placing interactive elements on a separate layer.

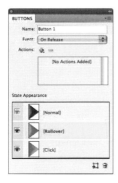

InDesign export in SWF format

By exporting an InDesign layout in SWF format (or PDF), you can produce engaging, dynamic documents—interactive presentations, magazines, brochures, catalogs, and more—without compromising design quality or mastering a new authoring environment.

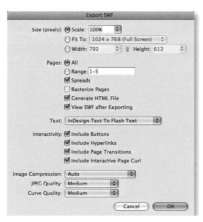

XFL support for InDesign-to-Flash workflows

Tight integration between InDesign CS4 and Flash CS4 Professional enables designers to produce compelling interactive documents. A new interchange file format developed by Adobe—called XFL—is the key to this integration. After creating a publication in InDesign CS4, you can export individual pages or the entire InDesign file to XFL format. When you open the XFL file in Flash, each page maintains visual fidelity to the original InDesign layout, and text and graphics remain editable. In Flash, you can add animations and interactions, or you can hand the XFL file off to a developer for more complex ActionScript® programming.

Whether you take the project all the way yourself or collaborate with a Flash expert, you can use your existing knowledge of InDesign as a design foundation to create truly rich, interactive documents that are a pleasure to interact with online. The illustration below shows the white cross changing to an interactive link in a Flash project.

The new integration of InDesign CS4 with Adobe Flash CS4 Professional using XFL enables you to combine the extensive strengths of both tools to create highly sophisticated digital publications using an efficient, straightforward workflow.

Discovering easy animation using skills you already have

Whether it's in a web banner or a dynamic presentation, motion catches the eye. Flash CS4 Professional makes animation much easier in two ways. You can start with familiar tools such as InDesign, Illustrator, and Photoshop, and then import your work into Flash CS4 to add motion effects, navigation elements, and more. A new object-based animation model makes it much simpler to create basic animations—even if you don't know a tween from a timeline. If you're already Flash savvy, you'll find making and modifying animations faster and more flexible than ever before. With a significantly streamlined interface and new ways to create animations, Adobe Flash CS4 Professional enables you to deliver engaging dynamic content to audiences everywhere—across browsers, desktops, and devices.

Enhancements specific to Adobe Flash CS4 Professional include:

Easy-to-create animation

In previous versions of Flash, creating even a basic animation involved numerous tasks such as converting objects to symbols and working in the Timeline to manually place keyframes and adjust tween spans. The object-based animation model new in Flash significantly simplifies this process, because you apply motion tweens directly to objects instead of keyframes. (A motion tween is an interpolation of steps between keyframes.) What's more, Flash automates a number of steps, including converting objects to symbols and creating motion paths composed of editable Bezier curves. In fact, you can create animations without ever touching the Timeline.

Top new and enhanced features in Adobe Flash CS4 Professional

- Object-based animation
- 3D transformation
- Inverse kinematics with the Bones tool
- Procedural modeling with the Deco tool
- Motion editor
- Motion presets
- Authoring for Adobe AIR
- Metadata (XMP) support
- XFL support
- H.264 support

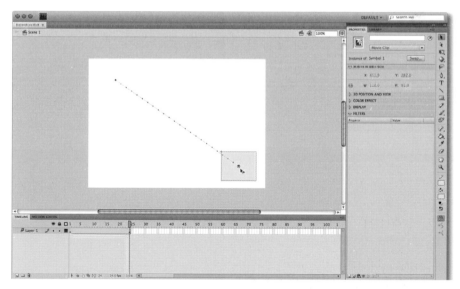

It really is that simple: No need to touch any code, or even the Timeline. Instead, you work directly with objects on the stage. Now let's see how easy it is to modify an animation using this object-based model.

Object-based animation editing

Not only is creating an animation simple, so is editing one. The motion path is an easily edited Bezier curve, with each point representing a frame in the Timeline. You can manipulate these components to modify the animation.

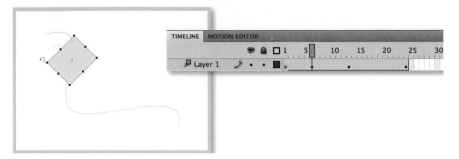

In Flash CS4 Professional, you no longer have to create keyframes manually. What's more, a single frame can include multiple keyframe attributes. For example, you could set an object to fade in, grow, and rotate using a single keyframe in a tween instead of using three separate tweens.

Prototyping and designing websites without being a code wizard

Top new and enhanced features in Adobe Fireworks CS4

- Improved performance
- New user interface
- CSS export
- Adobe PDF file export
- Enhanced type handling
- Workspace improvements
- Adobe kuler™ integration
- Adobe ConnectNow integration
- Adobe AIR™ authoring
- Style panel upgrades

Even if your heart is in print design, you're probably finding yourself drawn into the ever-expanding creative possibilities of delivering content on the web. Design Premium enables you to cover the gamut, from print to web, starting with what you know and venturing as far as you want to before handing off to a web developer.

Newly added to Design Premium, Adobe Fireworks CS4 enables you to develop beautifully designed prototypes for websites, application interfaces, and interactive designs. Easily open Photoshop and Illustrator assets in Fireworks, editing text as necessary, to mock up a range of design approaches—without writing any code at all. Add interactivity such as links, buttons, and animations to create a functional prototype. Save it as an interactive PDF for client review, and then export it as a CSS-based layout for further development in Adobe Dreamweaver. In Dreamweaver, easily fine-tune Photoshop content by placing Photoshop images as Smart Objects, tightly linked to their source files. Efficiently preview your work as you go using built-in Live View instead of switching to a web browser.

Enhancements specific to Adobe Fireworks CS4 include:

Importing content from Photoshop directly into Fireworks

Most designers like to work out website design concepts in the familiar environments of Photoshop or Illustrator. Now, with the addition of Fireworks CS4 to Design Premium, you can open a Photoshop web page comp, add interactivity, export it as a CSS-based layout, and continue in Dreamweaver—in one smooth, continuous process. Let's begin by opening the Photoshop comp.

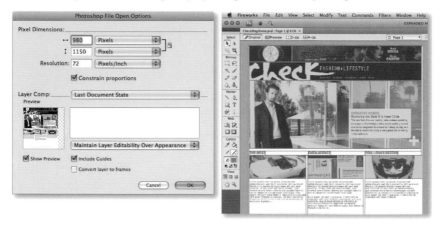

You'll find that just being able to open Photoshop images directly in Fireworks is already a great convenience but there are two other very significant ways in which Fireworks CS4 is integrated into Design Premium CS4. Firstly, Fireworks recognizes and converts Photoshop slices into Fireworks slices. Secondly, Fireworks CS4 now incorporates the Adobe Text Engine—the same technology used in both Photoshop and Illustrator. This means not only that Photoshop and Illustrator text opened in Fireworks is fully editable, but also that designers enjoy the same type quality and precision in Fireworks as in other Adobe design applications.

Creating high-quality interactive PDF comps for client review

It's one thing to perfect a design onscreen. It's another to present the design to a client for approval. In the past, designers were often forced to choose between sending their clients low-resolution JPEG images or multiple folders of HTML and image files. Neither strategy was optimal. Now, for the first time, Fireworks enables you to export a prototype as an interactive PDF file—no matter how many pages it includes.

Imagine the time this new workflow will save: Now you can package an entire site design into just one interactive PDF instead of distributing a cumbersome folder of HTML files and images or posting them on a server for review. The PDF document maintains hotspot-linked pages, resulting in interactive onscreen comps that are viewable by anyone with Adobe Reader 9 or Adobe Acrobat 9 software.

Defining CSS rules in Fireworks for use in Dreamweaver

Built-in HTML components allow you to quickly prototype functional parts of a web page in Fireworks that will translate to usable components in Dreamweaver.

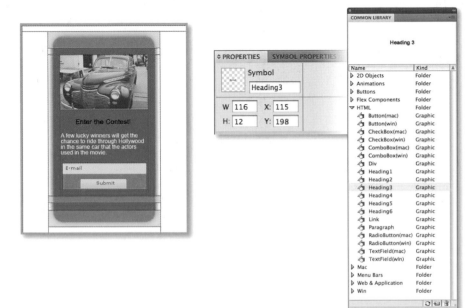

One advantage of CSS layouts is that components can be set to resize dynamically to accommodate differing amounts of content. In the past, setting up a CSS rule was tedious, but now Fireworks automatically does the work for you.

Adobe InContext Editing enables content authors to edit their own web pages without additional software installations while freeing them up to design more. The new online InContext Editing service lets anyone who can use a browser update content quickly and easily. Design your editable pages in Dreamweaver CS4 to retain total control over the look and feel of your sites. Then, simply designate the parts of the page you want your clients to be able to change; all other sections of the page are locked and editable only by you. Easily set CSS styles to ensure that user-entered content is properly and consistently formatted. Dreamweaver gives you the tools to create the perfect website, and hosted InContext Editing lets your clients keep the site up-to-date.

Enhancements specific to Adobe Dreamweaver CS4 include:

Photoshop Smart Objects

Compelling web pages often include images developed or enhanced in Photoshop. New in Dreamweaver CS4, the Smart Objects feature makes the Photoshop-to-Dreamweaver workflow really flow. Now you can simply insert a PSD file into a Dreamweaver CS4 web page to create a Smart Object, tightly linked to its source file. A badge on the Smart Object tells you its status—green means in sync and red means out of date. Just click an icon in the Properties panel to update the image without opening Photoshop.

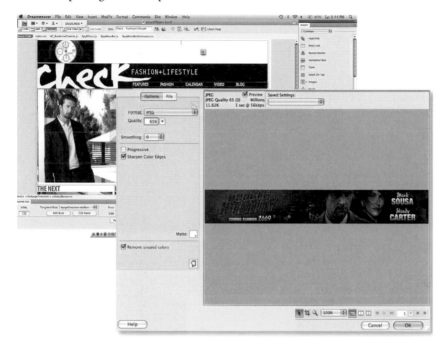

In addition to preserving optimization settings, Dreamweaver also maintains any new scale settings you apply. This means you could insert multiple instances of a PSD file—say, a company logo—each at a difference size; if the source file is modified, each individual instance is updated, while preserving its Dreamweaver dimensions. Dreamweaver lets you create dynamically linked Smart Objects. If a source file changes, a badge shows that the Dreamweaver version is no longer current.

To update the image, simply click the Update icon in the Properties panel.

Live View

If you've worked with Dreamweaver in the past, you know what it took to preview a page in progress—choose Preview In Browser, switch to your web browser, wait for the page to appear, review the page, and return to Dreamweaver. How many times an hour do you do this? Live View, a built-in preview feature in Dreamweaver CS4, turns this critical but cumbersome quality-control process into a single click.

Efficiently designing, previewing, and testing mobile content

Top new and enhanced features in Adobe Device Central CS4

- Browse a dynamically updated online library of device profiles
- Simulate performance and automate testing
- Easily upload content to multiple locations
- Communicate your ideas with high-quality video
- Improved video support and integration
- Organize your work with mobile projects

Before Adobe Device Central, testing content for mobile devices was tedious and time consuming, requiring that content be repeatedly exported, tested on target devices, and returned to Flash for editing. With Adobe Device Central CS3, developers could test directly from their desktops, simulating different devices and viewing conditions. Now, Adobe Device Central CS4 offers even more powerful testing tools, including the ability to take snapshots of content under different conditions and automated testing through scripts that can include multiple devices.

Enhancements specific to Adobe Device Central CS4 include:

Preview and test mobile content

With just a few clicks, and without handling any device except for your own keyboard and mouse, you can see how mobile content will appear and behave under a variety of real-life conditions. So much faster than loading your content onto multiple devices and heading outdoors to find some sunshine!

Taking snapshots

The ability to preview your content in so many ways is convenient, but how do you communicate the results to your client? With Device Central CS4, you can take snapshots of your content at any point in your testing routine.

Device Central generates CSS, which allows you to easily customize the resulting HTML page. You can then post the HTML page online where your client can easily view it.

Automated testing

Taking a snapshot of your content simulated on a single device is very convenient, but chances are you want your content to look great on a wide range of devices, not just one. Yet testing on multiple devices can be extremely time-consuming. With Device Central CS4, you can record a testing routine that incorporates a variety of settings, and then run that routine on multiple devices.

You can even include automated snapshots within a routine. The Automated Testing progress window shows the progress of the testing sequence you recorded on the selected devices. When testing is complete, the Log panel displays a list of the devices tested, along with any snapshots taken or errors detected. *(See illustration on next page.)*

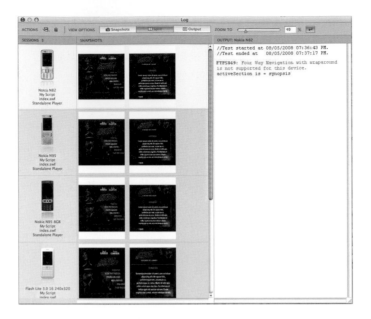

If you've experienced the tedium of manually running the same testing sequence on device after device after device, you'll appreciate the remarkable ease of being able to record one script, select virtual target devices, and let Device Central do the work for you.

Using Creative Pro Online Services

New online services that can be accessed from within Design Premium components let you search for help from the online community, share your screen with colleagues or clients in a few quick clicks, get color inspiration from your peers, manage day-to-day web content updates more easily and efficiently, and more. (All Creative Pro Online Services require an Internet connection.)

Adobe Community Help. Get the power of an online search engine within Design Premium, but with more targeted results, thanks to Adobe Community Help. Searchable content includes the in-depth, product-specific Help that Adobe has always delivered, plus additional Adobe and third-party content moderated by experts at Adobe and in the design and production communities.

Acrobat.com. Use Acrobat.com services with Acrobat to store and share large documents, collect form data, and review documents with anyone, anywhere. Thanks to the connection between one of the Acrobat.com services, Adobe ConnectNow, and Creative Suite 4 Design Premium, you can meet live over the web to share your screen, present creative concepts and ideas, and brainstorm with up to two online guests for no additional service charge. To share your screen with colleagues and clients, choose File > Share My Screen from Adobe CS4 components, such as Photoshop CS4 Extended or Flash CS4 Professional, or choose File > Collaborate >

Share My Screen from Adobe Acrobat 9 Pro. Guests can then see your desktop on their screens as you work. You can exchange ideas using the chat pod, add a live video or audio feed, or use the online Whiteboard feature to enable guests to comment on content. You can even temporarily hand over control of the screen to a guest to collaborate on a file.

Share your files with colleagues, clients, and peers without the hassle or limitations of e-mail attachments. Go to Acrobat.com, where you can conveniently upload, transfer, store, and share your files. You receive 5GB of free storage, with no individual file size limitation except that for total storage space. Acrobat.com also includes Adobe Buzzword®, an online word processor that allows you to collaborate on documents with others.

Additional Acrobat.com services, such as Share, Create PDF, My Files, and Adobe Buzzword, are accessible via Acrobat 9 Pro, an Adobe AIR version of Acrobat.com (included with Creative Suite 4 Design Premium), and your web browser. (Broadband Internet connection required.)

Adobe kuler. Explore, create, and share color themes with Adobe kuler. Kick-start your creative projects with color inspiration from the online kuler community. Browse thousands of themes sorted by newest, most popular, or highest rated; or search themes by tag word, title, or creator. Themes can be downloaded and moved to your Swatches panel with a single click. Or use an interactive color wheel that supports standard harmony rules to develop your own color themes that you can save, move to your Swatches panel, and upload to share with others. (Internet connection required for community functionality.)

InContext Editing. Make your web page content available for online editing by others when you use Adobe InContext Editing. Offer your colleagues, clients, or end users an easier way to make simple edits without impacting the design integrity of your web pages—and without help from you or additional software on their computers. Use the InContext Editing toolbar in Dreamweaver to set up your web pages, and then use the preview of this online service to enable content changes by others. (This service is currently available as a preview technology on Adobe Labs, and accessible from within Adobe Dreamweaver CS4. During this preview, you can use it at no additional charge. Further information about its availability will be posted to Adobe Labs and *www.adobe.com/dreamweaver* when appropriate.)

Adobe Bridge Home. Visit Adobe Bridge Home—an online channel available in Adobe Bridge CS4—and stay up to date with what's new from Adobe and the design, web development, and video and audio production communities at large. Watch the latest video tutorials for your Creative Suite 4 software, listen to a podcast interview with a leading designer, or learn about the next training event in your community. Discover tips and resources that can help you work smarter and faster, making the most of your Design Premium software.

The Adobe Creative Suite 4 Family

Adobe® Creative Suite 4 software combines shared productivity features such as visual asset management and access to useful online services with essential creative tools that let you design content for print, the Web, film and video, and mobile devices. You can choose between several editions of the Adobe Creative Suite to meet your specific needs.

Adobe Creative Suite 4 Design Premium

Exciting new tools in Creative Suite 4 Design Premium software let you imagine daring creative possibilities, in the confidence that you can make them real. User-inspired enhancements and simplified workflows help you achieve more efficiency in everyday design and production tasks. Improved integration and more interface consistency between Creative Suite components allow you to draw on your existing expertise to venture into new creative territory: begin where you're most at home (usually Photoshop, Illustrator, or InDesign) and then switch easily to Flash, Dreamweaver, Fireworks, or Acrobat 9 Pro software for refinement, production, and high-quality output for print, Web, or mobile.

Adobe Creative Suite 4 Design Standard

For design and production professionals focused on print publishing who do not need the full-fledged Web, interactive, and mobile design capabilities of Dreamweaver, Flash, and Fireworks, or the advanced video, animation, and 3D editing tools in Photoshop Extended, Adobe offers Adobe Creative Suite 4 Design Standard software. Design Standard combines full new versions of InDesign CS4, Illustrator CS4, Photoshop CS4, and Acrobat 9 Pro with Adobe Bridge CS4, Adobe Version Cue CS4, and Adobe Device Central CS4.

Adobe Creative Suite 4 Web Premium

Adobe Creative Suite 4 Web Premium sets a new standard in design flexibility, technical efficiency, and creative potential for web-related tools. Adobe Creative Suite 4 Web Premium includes the advanced coding and design capabilities of Adobe Dreamweaver CS4, the powerful new object-based animation model of Adobe Flash CS4 Professional, and the unrivaled editing power of Adobe Photoshop CS4 Extended. Add the increased graphic power of Adobe Illustrator CS4, the extended design and export options of Adobe Fireworks CS4, the intuitive audio features of Adobe Soundbooth CS4, and the integrated mobile authoring of Adobe Device Central CS4, and your creative possibilities expand exponentially.

Adobe Creative Suite 4 Web Standard

For web design and developer professionals focused on web publishing who do not need the full-fledged design capabilities of Illustrator and Photoshop, or the advanced video, animation, and 3D editing tools in Photoshop Extended, Adobe offers Adobe Creative Suite 4 Web Standard software. The Web Standard suite combines full new versions of Dreamweaver CS4, Flash CS4 Professional, Fireworks CS4, and Acrobat 9 Pro with Adobe Bridge CS4, Adobe Version Cue CS4, and Adobe Device Central CS4.

Adobe Creative Suite 4 Production Premium

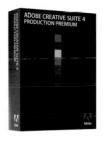

Adobe Creative Suite 4 Production Premium is designed for creative professionals who need to craft world-class video, audio, and interactive media: on-air, online, on-device, and invariably on deadline. Together, After Effects and the other components of Production Premium CS4 offer a tightly integrated, cross-platform toolset for pre- and post-production including video and audio editing, still and motion graphics, visual effects, and interactive media, as well as DVD, Blu-ray Disc, and mobile authoring.

Adobe Creative Suite 4 Master Collection

Adobe Creative Suite 4 Master Collection is your premier solution for professional creative work. The Master Collection combines the best of Adobe Creative Suite 4 Design Premium, Web Premium, and Production Premium editions with advanced productivity features, so you can create content for virtually all media with one value-packed offering.

Common Features

The components of Creative Suite 4 work with a full range of services including Adobe ConnectNow for online meeting collaboration, Adobe kuler™ for expressive color-set creation, and Adobe InContext Editing for client website modifications.

FEATURE TOUR

Adobe Creative Suite 4 Design Premium applications overview

This overview introduces the key elements and applications in the Creative Suite 4 Design Premium. The lessons in the second part of this book will cover specific aspects of using the applications in much more detail. The following applications and subjects will be covered in this overview:

- Adobe InDesign CS4
- Adobe Photoshop Extended CS4
- Adobe Illustrator CS4
- Adobe Flash CS4
- Adobe Dreamweaver CS4
- Adobe Fireworks CS4
- Adobe Acrobat 9 Pro
- Adobe.com hosted services
- Adobe Device Central CS4
- Adobe Bridge CS4

 You'll probably need one hour to read through this overview section.

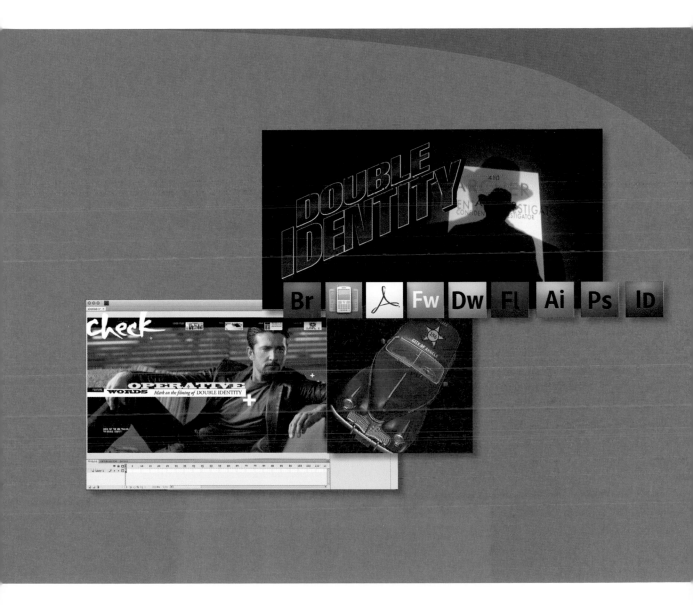

In this overview, you'll be introduced to the key elements and exiting new features in the applications of the Creative Suite.

Adobe InDesign CS4

Now you can create compelling print content, immersive Flash® publications, and interactive PDF documents—all with beautiful typography and stunning design. Adobe InDesign CS4 delivers all the tools you need to create sophisticated layouts for both traditional and online media. InDesign CS4 breaks down the barriers between online and offline publishing. With its new features and workflows for creating interactive documents integrated seamlessly with its already-powerful page design tools, you can create sophisticated and engaging layouts for onscreen audiences as easily as for print audiences.

Exploring the new interface

InDesign CS4 sports a number of user interface improvements that are reflected in most of the other Creative Suite 4 component applications, providing a consistent user experience.

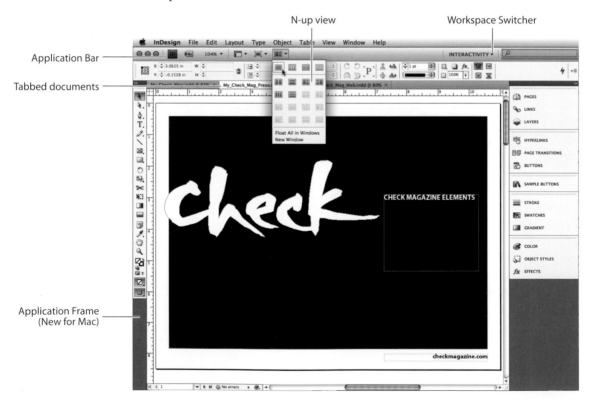

Application Bar: Use the new control buttons below the main menu to quickly switch to a new workspace, modify the document view, search online Help, and more.

Tabbed documents: Work across multiple documents and manage them with ease just by clicking their window tabs. Drag a tab downward to make the document float in its own window; drag its title bar back to the tab area to dock it back into tabbed mode.

Application Frame (New for Mac): All documents and panels are wholly contained within a single application frame, eliminating background distractions. Resize the frame and all the contents are resized as well, including the panels.

Workspace Switcher: Reduce the clutter in the interface and focus on the job at hand by selecting one of the new task-based workspaces or easily customize your own menus and panel arrangements and save them as workspaces that can then be shared.

N-up view: When you need to see and compare multiple layouts (or multiple views of the same layout) at the same time, choosing one of the N-up views from the Application Bar instantly handles all the tedious window resizing and positioning.

Creating a dynamic SWF presentation for client review

Using InDesign CS4, you can design and export interactive SWF (Shockwave Flash) files without needing to learn Adobe Flash CS4 Professional.

Adding interactive buttons

The creative concepts you've already developed can be part of your presentation without any reworking, since you can place native Photoshop and Illustrator artwork directly into your InDesign document. By quickly adding some interactivity to the layout, you'll be able to efficiently deliver an engaging SWF presentation that's innovative and fun.

With the new Buttons panel in InDesign CS4, the process of creating dynamic buttons tied to actions has been simplified and streamlined. You can turn any object on the page into a button or get a head start with one of the dozens of sample buttons included in the Sample Buttons library, some of which come complete with transparency effects and rollover behaviors.

The new Buttons panel lets you set events, actions, and states at the same time in a single screen—no more disruptive dialog boxes!

Setting up and testing hyperlinks

Creating hyperlinks in an InDesign layout file is now a simple and straightforward process, thanks to the redesigned and enhanced Hyperlinks panel. Build hyperlinks that quickly navigate to an external URL, open another file with supplementary information, launch an e-mail client, or jump to a page or section of a page within the same file or even in another document. Finally, you can test the hyperlinks right there in the layout before you even export the file.

Use this field to quickly create a URL hyperlink destination, bypassing the New Hyperlink dialog box.

Go to the destination of the selected hyperlink or cross-reference

Go to the source of the selected hyperlink or cross-reference

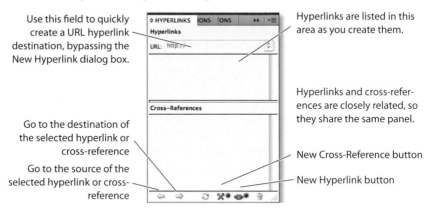

Hyperlinks are listed in this area as you create them.

Hyperlinks and cross-references are closely related, so they share the same panel.

New Cross-Reference button

New Hyperlink button

Creating animated page transitions

You can now add animated page transitions directly in InDesign. Users will see the transitions as they change pages (or screens) in the PDF and SWF files you export from the layout. Even before you export, you can preview page transitions in InDesign as Flash animations and experiment with different speeds and transition directions. You have a choice of twelve page transitions including Curl, Wipe, Dissolve, and Split Window.

New icon in the Pages panel

A small Page Transition Applied icon (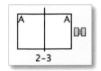) appears to the right of a spread's thumbnail in the Pages panel if a transition has been applied to it—a handy way to quickly check which spreads have (or lack) transitions.

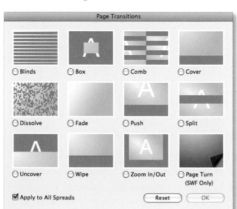

The Page Transitions dialog box is a Flash panel running inside of InDesign. Use it to compare transitions side-by-side—just move your cursor over any thumbnail to see an animated preview.

Exporting to SWF

With all your navigation buttons, page transitions, and hyperlinks in place, you're ready to export your InDesign layout to SWF format. You can specify custom settings for the SWF file in the Export SWF dialog box (Choose File > Export, and then choose SWF from the Format menu in the Export dialog box).

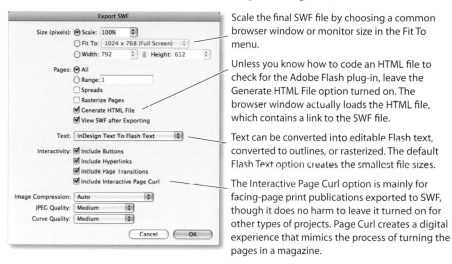

Scale the final SWF file by choosing a common browser window or monitor size in the Fit To menu.

Unless you know how to code an HTML file to check for the Adobe Flash plug-in, leave the Generate HTML File option turned on. The browser window actually loads the HTML file, which contains a link to the SWF file.

Text can be converted into editable Flash text, converted to outlines, or rasterized. The default Flash Text option creates the smallest file sizes.

The Interactive Page Curl option is mainly for facing-page print publications exported to SWF, though it does no harm to leave it turned on for other types of projects. Page Curl creates a digital experience that mimics the process of turning the pages in a magazine.

The HTML file generated during the export will open in your default browser, and the first screen—or page—of your SWF file that it references appears in the browser window. Dynamic elements breathe life into your online publications and presentations, digital magazines, digital brochures and catalogs, and more. With InDesign CS4 you can produce high-impact, interactive SWF documents without mastering a new authoring environment or compromising your page design.

Designing a print magazine

InDesign CS4 is full of exciting new features and enhancements that will help designers accomplish more—in less time and with fewer clicks.

Moving and transforming objects precisely with Smart Guides

Accurately arranging elements in a layout is a fast and fluid process with Smart Guides. You can quickly align, space, rotate, and resize objects in relation to other objects or to the page itself without using panels, menu commands, or even ruler guides. The Smart Guides appear when the object you're transforming with the mouse matches nearby objects, so you can easily snap the object to the guide when you need precision alignment. Smart Guides disappear when you release the mouse button, leaving you with an uncluttered layout.

As you drag an item around on the page, Smart Guides extend to other elements on the page, indicating that an edge or center of the item you're dragging is aligned with the edge or center of another object visible in the layout. You'll also see a Smart Guide appear when the object is aligned with the boundary or center of a column, gutter, or margin.

As you drag the photo of the man upwards, a green horizontal Smart Guide appears when the photo's vertical center aligns with the vertical center of any object visible in the window, such as the photo of the woman to its right. Since you want to align the top edges, you can ignore this guideline and continue dragging.

Release the mouse button when a Smart Guide appears that connects the top edges of the two images. The two items are now precisely top-aligned, and the Smart Guide disappears.

You can change the Smart Guide color in Preferences > Guides & Pasteboard.

As you resize a frame, a horizontal Smart Guide (⊢⎯⎯⎯⎯⎯⎯⎯⎯⎯→|) appears below it (or vertical Smart Guides appear to the left), letting you know when the horizontal or vertical measure of the frame you're resizing matches the equivalent measure of another visible element in the window.

Smart Guides appear when the width or height of the item you're resizing matches that of another object visible in the window.

When the white space between an object you're dragging (the image of the car in the illustration below) and an adjacent object is exactly the same as the space between two other objects in the window (the two images on the left), you'll see Smart Guides (⊢⎯⎯⎯⎯→| ⊢⎯⎯⎯⎯→|) appear, indicating equal distance between the objects. That's your cue to release the mouse button if you want the spacing between items to be even.

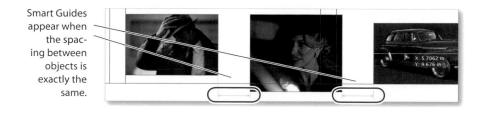

Smart Guides appear when the spacing between objects is exactly the same.

As you rotate an object with the Rotate tool, a Smart Guide () overlays the object, dynamically indicating the current angle of rotation. When the rotation amount matches the angle of another object visible in the window, the same Smart Guide appears on the other object as well.

When the object is rotated the same amount as another object in the window, Smart Guides appear on the other object as well, and the color of both guidelines changes to the Smart Guides color.

The intuitive and interactive Smart Align, Smart Spacing, Smart Dimensions, and Smart Rotation abilities of the Smart Guides feature all help you to quickly layout and arrange items on the page without extensive use of panels, menus, and ruler guides.

Customizing the Links panel

The production of complex documents requires effective management of linked content. The redesigned Links panel provides comprehensive and consolidated access to link attributes and metadata, including scale, original and effective resolution, layer assignment, copyright information, workflow status, and more. You can customize the panel to display the metadata and attributes that are most critical to your workflow for every linked asset.

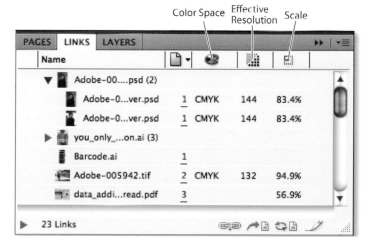

With the new information in the Links panel, critical data about your placed files is available at a glance.

Adding all the information that InDesign knows about linked files to the main Links panel would be impractical—you'd have to make the panel wider than your document to see all the columns! That's where the new, integrated Link Info pane comes in handy.

Clicking the Show/Hide button (circled) toggles the LInk Info pane below it open and closed.

Thumbnails in the Link Info pane (which appear if the option is activated in Panel Options) are larger than those in the main Links panel, making it easier to identify a selected link, even if it's not currently visible in the document window.

Clicking a linked page number in the Links panel is an efficient way to go directly to the link in the layout.

The Link Info pane lists all of a selected link's metadata and attributes by default. Information listed here varies according to the type of file selected.

The integrated Link Info pane is a convenient way to view all the metadata and attribute information for a linked file in a tidy scrolling list. Use the Panel Options dialog box to specify which information appears in columnar format in the main Links panel display (typically, just the few items critical to your workflow) and which appears in list view in the Link Info area. The same information can appear in both locations, if you like.

Redesigned from top to bottom, the Links panel gives you the power to manage and filter link information to meet your specific needs.

Rotating spreads onscreen

● **Note:** The Rotate Spread feature is a view option only; it will still print or export in its original orientation.

Many layout projects, such as invitations, calendars, and other folded pieces, require certain panels or pages to be rotated in the layout 90 or 180 degrees so that when the project is printed and folded, the page elements all read the correct way. The new Rotate Spread feature (View > Rotate Spread) allows you to rotate spreads onscreen in 90-degree increments, meaning you no longer need to stand on your head or upend your monitor to properly kern upside-down text.

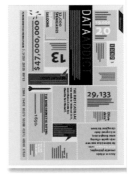

The page thumbnail in the Pages panel will display a Rotated Spread icon (↔), indicating that this spread has been rotated. Spread rotation is another example of user-inspired enhancement in InDesign CS4.

Enhanced table editing

You can now edit table text in the Story Editor window as well as the layout window. Writing and editing in the Story Editor allows you see the entire story, including table text, in one scrolling window, even if it's threaded through multiple frames and pages in the layout. Text appears in the typeface, size, and line spacing that you specify in Preferences > Story Editor Display, without layout or formatting distractions. Overset text in frames—and now, in table cells—is visible in the Story Editor window, so it's easy to copyfit. Any edits made in the Story Editor window are immediately reflected in the layout window.

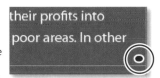

The small red dot at the end of a cell (circled at left and in the close-up at right) indicates overset text. This was an irksome problem to fix in previous versions of InDesign, but one that's easily solved now that you can edit overset table text in the Story Editor in InDesign CS4.

The Story Editor appears in a floating document window on top of the layout, and the text content of the table is fully visible and editable. Cell content is separated by dashed lines.

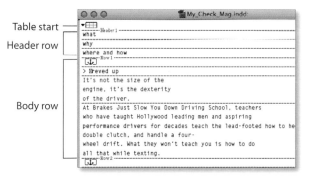

Table start
Header row
Body row

In the Story Editor, each table row is indicated in blue text. Each cell in that row is marked by a dashed line, and the contents of the cells appears between the lines. Anchored graphics in a story or table always appear as symbols (⊞) in the Story Editor.

Additionally, you can now embed inline notes in table cells, allowing you to include "Post-It"-like instructions to colleagues who will be working on the same table in the layout.

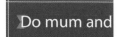

A note icon in your user color appears in the table cell, and anyone who works on this file can click the icon to open the Notes panel and read your message. (Notes are also visible in the Story Editor window.)

When table cells contain small, dense, or highly formatted text, it's much easier to edit the content in the Story Editor instead of the layout view. The ability to add inline notes to table cells means that you can insert your comment in the same location as the text to which it refers.

Adding cross-references to streamline layout and production

You can now streamline long document production and improve technical accuracy with the powerful cross-reference controls located in the new Cross-References dialog box.

Cross-references let you easily create a dynamic link to other text in the same file or in a different layout document such as another in a book set up as individual InDesign files. Cross-references can show the current page number of a specific text string you select as the referenced item, or pick up text and/or page numbers automatically based on a specific paragraph style applied to text throughout the document or book.

When Paragraph is selected in the Link To menu, InDesign lists all paragraph styles used in the layout in alphabetical order. To select the text string you want to reference (or its page number or paragraph number), first select its paragraph style from this list. InDesign lists the first few words of every paragraph in the layout with that style applied on the right.

Change the appearance of the cross-reference in this section. Selected settings become the default appearance for subsequent cross-references you create in this layout.

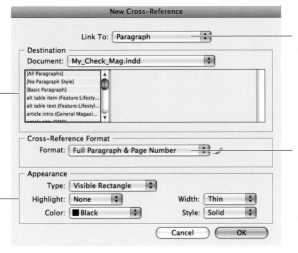

The default Link To: Paragraph option lets you create a cross-reference to any text in the layout. Choosing Text Anchor results in a list of specific Text Anchor destinations you've already created in the Hyperlinks panel.

Choose the type of cross-reference you'd like to insert from the Format menu. To edit a format or create your own, or to specify a character style for all cross-references of this particular format, click the Pencil icon to the right of the menu.

When edits to text or modifications to page design change the location of a referenced item (for example, moving a referenced figure number from one page to another, or editing the text in a referenced section title), the cross-references can be updated to reflect the changes.

Using the new cross-references feature in InDesign makes it simpler to write, produce, and manage long documents. The flexibility and power of the Cross-Reference Formats dialog box allows you to add and customize formats for your specific needs.

Cross-reference source

Referenced text

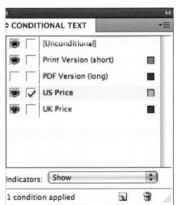

By cross-referencing a feature title in the TOC (left) to the actual title text on the feature spread (above), the TOC text will automatically update whenever the actual title changes.

Using conditional text for multi-channel publishing

You can use the new conditional text feature in InDesign CS4 to generate multiple editions or versions of a publication from the same source document, such as student and teacher editions of the same textbook or geographically localized versions of a product manual or retail catalog.

Some users have managed to accomplish this already by using different layers to hold edition-specific text frames. With the conditional text feature, you can apply and combine conditions within the same text frame (text flow), which means that creating these types of document is much easier than before.

You could use conditional text, for example, to show either US or UK pricing, allowing you to create two regional versions of your magazine from the same source document without using layers or duplicate text frames.

After the US Price condition is applied to the selected text, the text sports a green wavy underline, which is the indicator for that condition. You can modify a condition's indicator by double-clicking the condition name in the panel.

When you toggle the visibility of a condition, InDesign hides any text to which that condition was applied—throughout the document. Hide the UK Price condition, for example, to create the US version of your magazine, and then export it to a press-ready PDF or package it (File > Package) for handoff to a vendor.

Another scenario where conditional text expands your publishing options is to create long and short versions of the same article in a single source document. The long version might require two additional pages, so you'll only use it in the PDF edition of the magazine, where paper costs are not a concern. The short version is for the print edition. With color-coded conditional text indicators in the story, you can see which text has which condition (if any) applied. When the visibility of the long condition is toggled off in the Conditional Text panel, the additional two pages of text for the long condition will not show.

As you show and hide the short and long versions of the article, the new Smart Text Reflow feature (see margin note) adds and removes pages as needed. To enable this feature for the story, you need to change the default preferences for Smart Text Reflow.

The new conditional text feature in InDesign CS4 is a welcome addition for anyone who needs to create multiple versions of the same source document for different audiences.

Checking and correcting errors as you design with Live Preflight

The new Live Preflight feature alerts you to potential production problems as they occur while you're laying out pages, allowing you to immediately identify and correct them, thereby avoiding costly production errors.

Live Preflight is turned on by default for all new documents, and it uses a default preflight profile named Basic. This default preflight profile checks for missing or modified links, missing fonts, and overset text frames. If any of these conditions exist, the total number of errors in the document appears to the right of a red circle in an unobtrusive section of the document window's status bar. The Live Preview panel enables you to quickly locate the errors in the layout.

You can easily create custom Live Preflight profiles to catch other potential problems, such as image resolutions that are too low, stroke widths that are too thin, unwanted spot colors, and out-of-date cross-references. Custom profiles can be shared with other design and production team members to ensure that all files are checked using the same set of parameters.

If none of the conditions that the Live Preflight profile checks for are present, the circle in the document window's status bar turns green and the text reads No Errors.

Eliminating small errors in the layout as you work can help you avoid larger, more time-consuming changes after you've completed your entire document. With Live Preflight, you can deliver a final publication that's ready for print or online publishing in less time and with far greater document integrity.

Creating a rich interactive version of a print magazine

One of the most exciting new features in InDesign CS4 is its integration with Flash CS4 Professional. Publication designers and interactive design professionals can now collaborate to produce compelling interactive documents.

XFL—an entirely new interchange file format developed by Adobe—is the key to this integration. After creating a publication in InDesign CS4, you can export individual pages or the entire InDesign file to the XFL format. When a developer opens the XFL file in Flash CS4 Professional, each page maintains visual fidelity to the original InDesign layout, and all text and graphics remain editable. The Flash developer can then add sophisticated video, audio, animation, and ActionScript® programming to even the most complex page designs, resulting in a truly rich, interactive document that is a pleasure to view and read online.

Designing for Flash in InDesign

Each issue of Check Magazine will be delivered as a print, PDF, and Flash-based digital publication. The latter uses the same content and branding as the print magazine, but is optimized for editability in Flash CS4 and designed to be viewed onscreen in a radically different layout.

You can use the familiar drawing tools in InDesign to add visual elements (such as the large white plus symbols in the illustration on the right), that will become interactive links in the finished Flash version.

Small text and image frames going across the top of the pages will be turned into a navigation menu in the final Flash document. Smart Guides made it easy to align, space, and size the frames.

When embedding a Flash video clip, a poster image and custom playback controls can be created in InDesign.

The Flash team will later integrate the video into the page using the same playback controls as in the layout.

When the XFL file is opened in Flash CS4 Professional, all the text becomes editable Flash text, retaining the formatting in the InDesign layout.

With InDesign CS4, layout artists can create Flash CS4-ready page designs with the same powerful design and production toolset they use to create print, PDF—and now, SWF—documents.

Exporting the layout to Flash-ready XFL format

Converting an InDesign file to an editable Flash CS4 file is as easy as exporting a layout to PDF—actually, it's easier! A single Export command and choosing Adobe Flash CS4 Pro (XFL) as the export format is all it takes.

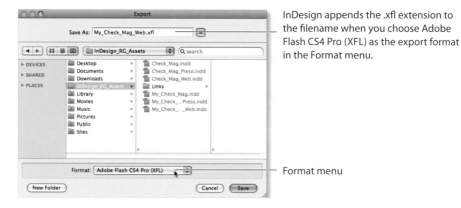

InDesign appends the .xfl extension to the filename when you choose Adobe Flash CS4 Pro (XFL) as the export format in the Format menu.

Format menu

After clicking Save in the Export dialog box, you can select conversion options and choose which pages to export in the Export Adobe Flash CS4 Pro (XFL) dialog box.

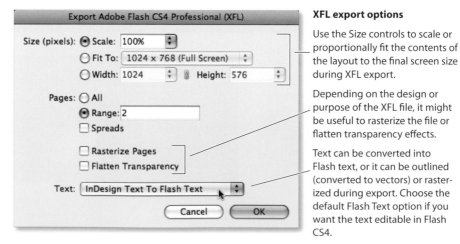

XFL export options

Use the Size controls to scale or proportionally fit the contents of the layout to the final screen size during XFL export.

Depending on the design or purpose of the XFL file, it might be useful to rasterize the file or flatten transparency effects.

Text can be converted into Flash text, or it can be outlined (converted to vectors) or rasterized during export. Choose the default Flash Text option if you want the text editable in Flash CS4.

At this point you could give the XFL file to your Flash developer to open in Flash CS4 to add videos, sound, tie it into a database, integrate ActionScript programming, and anything else that's on the team's to-do list.

Editing the InDesign XFL file in Adobe Flash CS4

The new XFL interchange format maintains the page geometry and editability of the InDesign layout page when it's opened in Flash CS4.

Page designs and text formatting are maintained when XFL files are opened in Flash CS4. Pages appear in the Flash "stage," which is analogous to page spreads in an InDesign file.

Stage area

Typography in Flash
One of the most exciting aspects of the new integration between InDesign CS4 and Flash CS4 is that you can use the powerful text handling and professional typography controls in InDesign to create beautifully typeset text, and then convert it to editable Flash text when you export the layout to XFL format. Even the text, strokes, and background colors in complex tables make it through the XFL interchange process intact.

The new integration of InDesign CS4 with Adobe Flash CS4 Professional provides an ideal combination of the fundamental strengths of each tool for creating highly sophisticated digital publications in a straightforward, streamlined workflow.

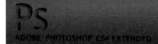

Adobe Photoshop CS4 and Adobe Photoshop CS4 Extended

Digital images are everywhere—from the photography studio to the X-ray lab, from the glossy magazine to your website. With two new versions and a heap of new features and enhancements, wherever you find great digital images, you'll find Photoshop.

Adobe Photoshop CS4 refines and redefines the professional image-editing experience, with faster, nondestructive ways to accomplish core tasks such as image adjustments and masks, and new tools and enhancements that enable you to work more easily, efficiently, and naturally.

Photoshop CS4 Extended starts with the complete set of features you'll find in Photoshop CS4, and then adds others designed specifically for professionals working with specialized image types and multimedia workflows. With breakthrough 3D editing and compositing features, richer motion-graphics capabilities, and enhanced image analysis functions, Photoshop CS4 Extended broadens your reach beyond traditional digital images.

Photoshop CS4 and Photoshop CS4 Extended feature a newly refined, tab-based interface in a single, integrated window, with self-adjusting panels arranged in docked groups. Tools kept exactly where you need them means greater efficiency, less clutter, and better results, faster than before.

Powerful new editing tools

Photoshop CS4 expands the photographers toolkit with new and enhanced editing features.

Live, nondestructive corrections with the Adjustments panel

Photoshop CS4 speeds workflow performance with the new Adjustments panel, cutting the time it takes to make nondestructive adjustments. There's no maze of dialog boxes to navigate—just go straight to the task at hand. The Adjustments panel features the new Vibrance adjustment, giving you greater control over color saturation while preserving delicate tones such as skin colors. On-image adjustments are now also available for Hue/Saturation and Curves. For even greater time-saving convenience, the Adjustments panel features a wide variety of modifiable presets for each type of image modification, including more than 20 new preconfigured, customizable starting points.

To create a live, nondestructive correction, start by selecting a correction type using the buttons at the top of the Adjustments panel, or by choosing a re-editable preset from the categorized list at the bottom of the panel.

When you choose an adjustment, the panel shifts to display the adjustment controls, and a new adjustment layer is automatically created in the Layers panel. You can re-edit the adjustment at any time.

Re-editable, feathered, density-controlled masks

The new Masks panel smoothes and speeds the creation and adjustment of both pixel and vector masks, making it easier than ever to apply effects selectively to precisely defined areas of an image. Now, with simple sliders, you can adjust the density and feathering of a mask, to control both the sharpness of the mask edge and how much of the adjustment effect you wish to reveal. The Refine Mask feature allows simple yet fine-grained control over the mask size and edges and the Color Range feature has been enhanced, letting you automatically create powerful and detailed masks based on single or multiple colors.

Left: The original photo.

Center: The Masks panel and Color Range are used to restrict the effects of a Black & White adjustment layer to everything except the tie.

Right: A new Vibrance adjustment layer is used to make the tie stand out even more from its monochromatic surroundings.

More refined, natural results with Dodge, Burn, and Sponge

The newly refined Dodge, Burn, and Sponge tools help preserve tonal quality while you spot-correct exposure and color saturation.

The Dodge tool lets you easily brighten the detail in specific areas of a photograph.

Enhanced productivity

Create stunning results faster with new tools and productivity enhancements.

Enhanced Auto-Align, Auto-Blend, and new 360° panoramas

360° panoramas
Choose 3D > New Shape From Layer > Spherical Panorama to convert a set of shots into a 3D scene that can be viewed from any angle.

The automatic alignment and blending technology in Photoshop CS4 enhances a wide variety of features, and will be particularly evident in the stitching of individual images into a panorama. Enhanced blending combines with new vignetting and geometric distortion corrections to bring you even better results—including the new option to create 360-degree panoramas, and to automatically detect and correct fish-eye lens distortion. *(See illustration on next page.)*

Enhanced Auto-Blend technology automatically masks and blends frame edges for better results on panoramas.

Extended depth of field

Extreme close-ups and wide apertures can severely limit depth of field. With Photoshop CS4, you can now use Auto-Align and Auto-Blend technology to create a breathtaking enhancement of any scene where lighting and depth of field are in short supply.

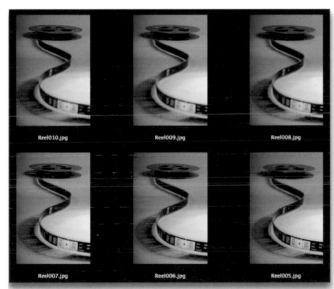

A range of shots, each with different exposure, color, and focal points (above), automatically becomes a single, color-corrected, expanded depth-of-field image with Auto-Blend Layers (right).

Fluid canvas rotation

Simply drag with the new Rotate View tool to spin the canvas to the orientation that works best for you.

Photoshop CS4 introduces a revolutionary new feature that lets you paint and draw as easily and naturally as sitting down at a drawing-board or an easel—by simply rotating the canvas, you can work at the angle and orientation that's suits you best, without affecting the orientation of the image itself. Canvas rotation is one of the many new enhancements in Photoshop CS4 that make use of OpenGL technology to leverage the power of the onboard graphics processing unit (GPU) in most modern computers. These new features combine to greatly enhance your ability to work at any magnification with perfect clarity, and to smoothly navigate around the largest images with no stutter or preview lag.

Workflow improvements

Take advantage of improved cross-application support.

Tighter integration with Photoshop Lightroom® 2

Photoshop CS4 makes your workflow easier than ever, with improved cross-application support.

Tighter integration between Photoshop CS4 and Photoshop Lightroom 2 means the non-destructive changes you make in one application will be recognized when you open the image in the other.

Background: Camera Raw 5 in Photoshop CS4.

Inset: Photoshop Lightroom 2.

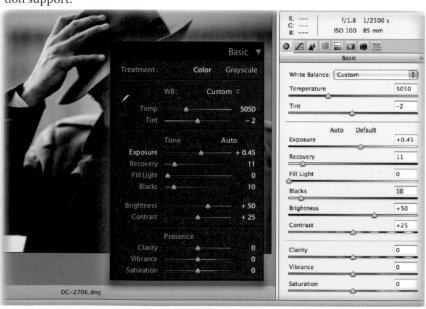

Professionals and advanced photographers can rely on the one-two punch of Adobe Photoshop and Photoshop Lightroom software as the complete digital photography solution.

Camera Raw 5 with localized, nondestructive adjustments

Camera Raw now enables you to make localized adjustments by simply painting effects directly onto an image, and then using sliders to control the change. Additional enhancements include Post Crop Vignetting and gradient-based localized correction. As always, the corrections you make to Raw, JPEG, or TIFF images are completely nondestructive, with the original files maintained in their pristine state.

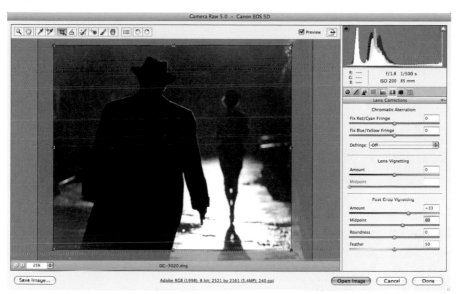

New Post Crop Vignetting lets you recreate artistic vignette effects In a photograph even after the original edge of the photo has been cropped away.

Extended features

Discover new dimensions in digital images with tools designed specifically to work with specialized image types and multimedia workflows.

Breakthrough 3D editing and compositing

With Photoshop CS4 Extended, you can now work with 3D models just as easily and powerfully as you can 2D images, without having to navigate through dialog boxes and special layer contents.

Left: The 3D car model with a 2D layer above it containing the police logo.

Right: After merging the 2D layer down, it becomes part of the 3D layer and is mapped onto the contours of the car roof.

Enhanced motion graphics

Photoshop CS4 Extended helps make the motion graphics workflow even more efficient, with enhanced preview of non-square-pixel images, 3D layer animation, and support for audio tracks.

Preview and export audio tracks, and view, edit, and export frame comments with the Animation panel in Photoshop CS4 Extended.

Volume Rendering

Volume Rendering is a new way to easily convert text, shape, or pixel layers into a volume. Artists can combine painted layers into entirely new and eye-catching volumes that can be viewed from any perspective. Motion graphics professionals can explore generating volumes from multiple text layers. Medical professionals can volume render a DICOM image stack (on the left in the illustration) into an anatomical image (on the right) that can be viewed and explored from all angles and depths.

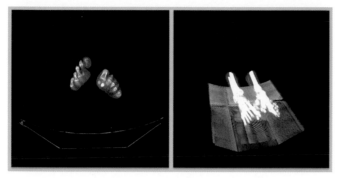

With Volume Rendering, the 2D images from a DICOM stack (left) become rich volumes (right) that can be examined from any orientation.

Easier data collection and analysis with the Count tool

Allowing fast, simple, point-and-click tallying of objects in scientific images, the Count tool is expanded in Photoshop CS4 Extended to allow for multiple counts, as well as resizeable labels and markers in separate colors for each count. This data is easily saved into the file for future reference, and can be collected in the Measurement Log panel for comparison and export to standard text files.

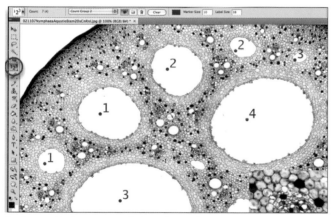

Perform multiple counts with the enhanced Count tool.

Adobe Illustrator CS4

Adobe Illustrator CS4 is a comprehensive vector graphics environment that is now tightly integrated with the other Adobe Creative Suite® 4 component applications. Discover the power of editing appearances, work efficiently with new guides and panels, and deliver across different media more easily than ever. Stay ahead of the pace of change with precisely the tools you need for mastering print, web, motion, mobile, and interactive content design.

With Adobe Illustrator CS4, you can explore new features that inspire fresh creativity, such as the Blob Brush tool and transparency in gradients. Use multiple artboards to enable new ways of working on a variety of design iterations or applications in a single file. You can also discover hidden gems—some of the deepest capabilities of Illustrator are now more accessible and easier to use. Work more efficiently with access to on-object controls, innovative Smart Guides, and new panel behaviors that enable smoother workflows. When you're ready to deliver, you can take your work anywhere, thanks to tight cross-product integration: send editable designs to developers for use in rich Internet applications (RIAs) and experiences, use Separations Preview for reliable print delivery, and collaborate easily on motion and video projects.

Interface enhancements and multiple artboards

Adobe Illustrator CS4 makes it easy to work efficiently with multiple deliverables: create postcard, a poster, and a T-shirt design—all in the same file! The following provides a brief overview of the new interface and workspace features such as multiple artboards.

Interface enhancements

The interface improvements in Adobe Illustrator CS4 can help you work faster and more efficiently. Tabbed documents, the arrange documents or N-up view feature, the Application Bar, the Workspace Switcher, and spring-loaded panels, offer more productive approaches to organizing and working on projects.

Choose a tiled view quickly from the Arrange Documents menu.

Drag the tab of any file over to the margins of your windows to drop into that location. Here, we're dragging the detective file over to the left margin of the application window.

Multiple artboards

Work with more than one deliverable at once. In one file, create separate artboards for a poster, a pair of postcards, and a T-shirt design. Artboards make it easy to copy elements between designs and use common styles and attributes that you can update all at once.

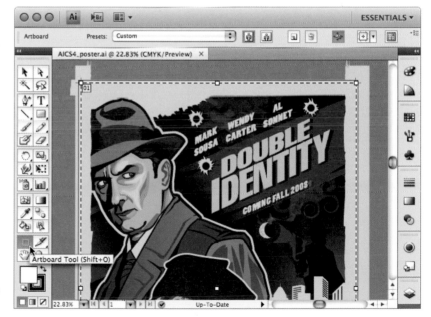

Create artboards of any size and tile, stack, or arrange them any way you wish.

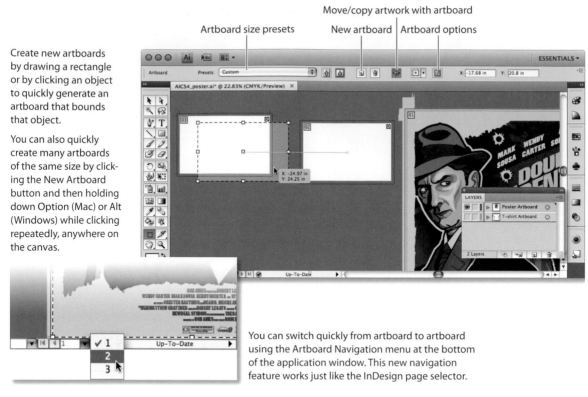

Create new artboards by drawing a rectangle or by clicking an object to quickly generate an artboard that bounds that object.

You can also quickly create many artboards of the same size by clicking the New Artboard button and then holding down Option (Mac) or Alt (Windows) while clicking repeatedly, anywhere on the canvas.

Artboard size presets

Move/copy artwork with artboard

New artboard   Artboard options

You can switch quickly from artboard to artboard using the Artboard Navigation menu at the bottom of the application window. This new navigation feature works just like the InDesign page selector.

The Blob Brush tool and Isolation Mode

Sketch naturally with strokes that flow together using the Blob Brush tool, and experience easy access to buried groups when editing and adding objects in Isolation Mode.

The Blob Brush tool

Do you remember the childhood joy of finger painting? Recapture that joy with a tool that provides amazing control while letting you sketch naturally and fluidly.

Together with the Eraser and Smooth tools, the Blob Brush tool lets you quickly experiment with and then perfect new shapes without once opening a panel, using Pathfinder tools, or expanding objects.

You don't have to be careful with your sketching

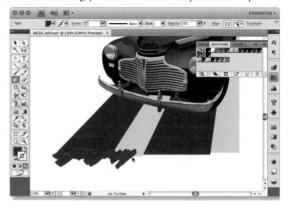

or worry about applying too much color. To reduce and refine your new shape, try using the Eraser tool.

Using Isolation Mode

Isolation Mode in Illustrator CS4 has been enhanced with clickable, iconic breadcrumbs and now supports more object types, including compound paths, gradient mesh objects, images, and clipping masks. You can isolate a single object and add new objects to a particular position in a stacking order.

Isolation Mode breadcrumb icon   Current isolated object

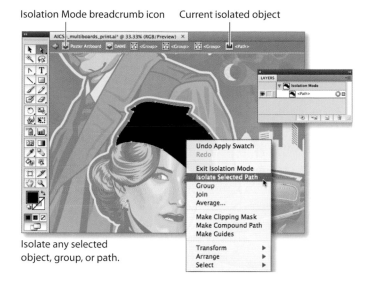

Isolate any selected object, group, or path.

Breadcrumb navigation is a powerful feature that not only shows you the levels of nested groups that an isolated object lives in, but now allows you to click each breadcrumb name to navigate through your groups, isolating each one as you go.

Use the clickable breadcrumb to navigate through isolated groups.

Use the Blob Brush tool to draw a highlight on the hat. Apply a gradient fill from the Swatches panel.

Gradients and transparency in gradients

Get creative with layered gradients that include transparent colors, and see how easy it is to apply and edit them, thanks to the new on-object controls.

Gradient controls right on your object

No longer do you have to use the Gradient panel to apply and edit gradient fills. You can now see exactly what's happening right on your object while you add colors, change angle, move gradient stops, and more.

Left: Move handles on the circle outline to change the dimension of your ellipse and to rotate the gradient.

Right: Edit gradient colors right on your object with immediate feedback.

Transparency in gradients

Make a gradient that goes from opaque white to transparent white to quickly create a transition fade.

Gradients can now include transparent colors—not just transparency of the gradient fill as a whole, but slider-controlled transparency of any individual color stop in any type of gradient.

It's unlikely that you'd submit T-shirt artwork with gradients to a silkscreen printer, but for iron-ons and decals, use of transparency in gradients is perfect. And the transparent cover-up is a super-fast way to accomplish a fade for quick comps and projects where you can deliver rasterized artwork.

One characteristic to note is that when you reduce the opacity of a color such as the green to 0%, you still see the green blend into the adjacent colors. This shows how you can create extremely interesting color mixes among objects layered on top of one another.

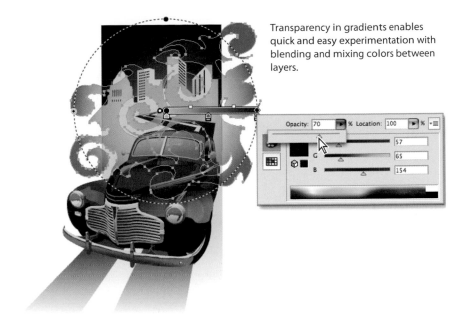

Transparency in gradients enables quick and easy experimentation with blending and mixing colors between layers.

Clipping masks and Smart Guide enhancements

Work with masking objects and edit masked contents, noticing how new Smart Guides help accurately position and align objects.

Clipping masks

Work with masks more easily, thanks to true WYSIWYG behavior. Now, when the clipping object or group is selected, you will see only the clipped area. Edit the masking object in Isolation Mode or choose to make it visible using the Clipping Path menu options.

Select the clipping path for editing

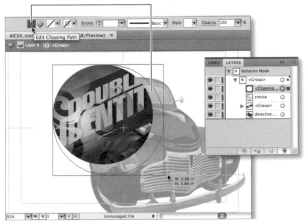

Edit contents of the group masked by the clipping path.

Smart Guides

Smart Guide options are set up in the Preferences dialog box.

You can experience the new Smart Guides and see the on-cursor readouts when you align artboards. Smart Guides also show rotation angle and relation to nearby objects according to the edge of your selection rather than the cursor position—continuously, while you transform your object.

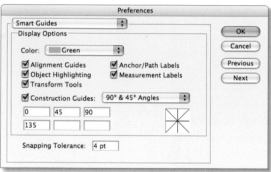

Appearance panel and Graphic Styles

Stay focused on your work with appearance editing right in the panel, quick and efficient use of styles across multiple objects, and easy control of advanced effects.

Appearance panel

Select multiple objects based on a single common attribute which can then be edited to update the appearance of all those objects at once.

The enhancements made to the Appearance panel are some of the most exciting advances for Illustrator CS4. The new tools enable even more work right on your objects, less interaction with multiple panels, and faster, more centralized access to controls. Note the new buttons for Add New Stroke, Add New Fill, and Add New Effect.

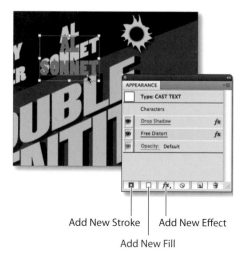

Add New Stroke | Add New Effect

Add New Fill

Flatter baseline

Graphic Styles

In Illustrator CS4, the Graphic Styles feature is better than ever. Previewing is greatly improved, and editing an individual element of a style is easy, thanks to Appearance panel enhancements. Find a new library of prebuilt styles that includes those that consist of effects such as drop shadows and blurs that can be added without replacing your fills.

View different styles with either text or square thumbnails in the Graphic Styles panel.

For a large preview, click the style while pressing the Control key (Mac) or right mouse button (Windows).

Thumbnails in either square or text view

Large preview

Separations Preview and color variations with Adobe kuler and Live Color

Deliver reliably to print using Separations Preview to check your colors, and quickly make variations using Adobe kuler and Live Color.

Separations Preview

Use Separations Preview to identify possible overprint problems before it's too late.

Overprint fill

Adobe kuler

Use kuler inside Illustrator to browse and search for Kuler themes. Download colors from the kuler community directly to your Swatches panel.

Quickly reduce the colors in your artwork for particular print projects, or experiment with creative recoloring.

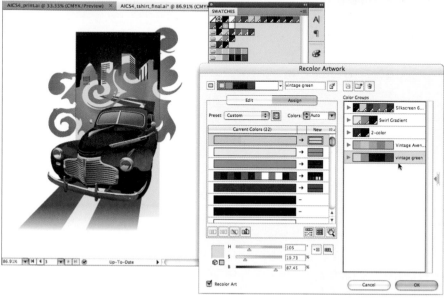

Live Color

Explore the many updates in Live Color, including the features in the Edit pane, where you can interactively shift the colors of your artwork.

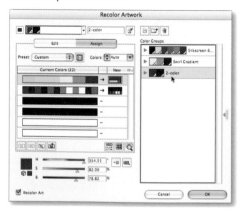

Adobe Flash Professional CS4

Adobe Flash CS4 Professional is the industry-leading authoring environment for creating engaging interactive experiences. Its user-friendly yet powerful new tools for animation and collaboration help you deliver rich dynamic content to audiences everywhere independently of browsers, desktops, and devices.

A refined and more efficient user interface

Tabbed documents make it easy to jump between open files. A single application frame provides a more efficient workspace and prevents documents from becoming hidden beneath panels. The Properties panel has been redesigned in a more efficient vertical format. Positioned at the side of the workspace, it now allows more space for the Stage. Workspaces allow users to quickly switch user interface layouts to better focus on specific tasks.

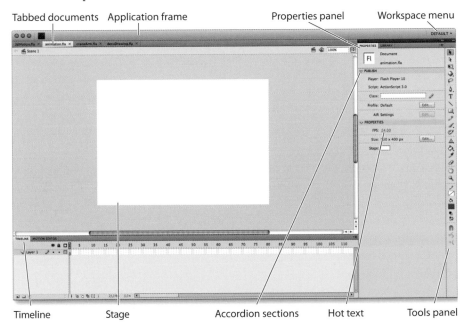

The default position of the Timeline is now below the stage, matching the workspace layout of After Effects. Accordion sections make it possible to show or hide information easily. Hot text allows you to simply click and drag on values to edit them, just as you can in Photoshop and After Effects. The Tools panel has been refined so that it doesn't distract from items on the stage.

Creating and editing an object-based animation

With the new object-based animation model in Flash CS4 Professional, motion tweens are applied directly to objects instead of to keyframes. This time-saving enhancement reduces processing steps and makes Flash more approachable for new users, while simultaneously providing advanced designers and developers far greater control of individual animation attributes.

With a single tween command, you can convert an object to a symbol if necessary, create a span, and move the playhead forward.

All that remains to be done to complete the animation is to move the symbol to another position on the stage. The symbol is tweened along the path you see on the stage—the motion path—as it plays through the animation. The dots along the motion path indicate the symbol's position at each frame in the timeline.

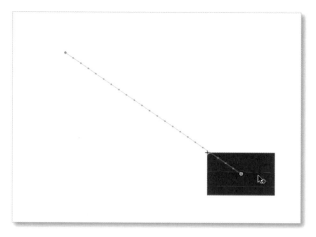

The motion path is an easily editable Bezier curve. Whenever you edit any property of a symbol—such as its position, rotation, or alpha (transparency)—at a particular point in time, a keyframe is created automatically for just that property. You no longer have to create these keyframes manually.

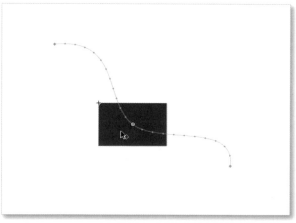

More importantly, a single frame in a tween can track multiple keyframe attributes individually. This enhancement means you can make adjustments to properties such as alpha (transparency) or rotation independently of each other.

Adding a professional touch with the Motion Editor

In the new object-based animation model in Flash CS4 Professional, keyframes take on a new and significant role. You can now exercise granular, independent control over important keyframe parameters, including rotation, size, scale, position, filters, and more, using the Motion Editor panel. Offering even more command over the creative presentation of your animations, the Motion Editor panel allows you to graphically control easing using curves.

Flash designers often need to tweak each attribute, separately and painstakingly, to ensure a smooth and professional result. This process can sometimes take almost as long as building the animation in the first place. To both save time and deliver a deeper level of granular attribute editing, Flash CS4 introduces the new Motion Editor panel.

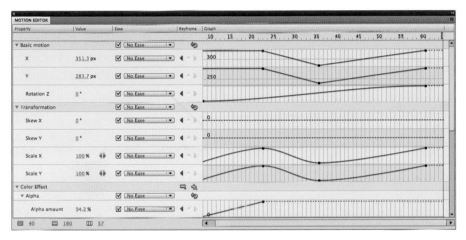

The Motion Editor panel displays all of the attributes and keyframes for a selected tween (or span), enabling the designer to tweak each keyframe attribute independently.

Each attribute (Basic Motion, Transformation, Color Effect, etc.) is listed along the left side of the Motion Editor panel. Bezier paths, representing motion, are mapped to frames along most of the right side of the panel. The points on each path represent keyframes in the animation.

By editing the Bezier path (as shown for the rotation attribute in the illustration) you control exactly how fast or slow the animation unfolds as it moves along the timeline.

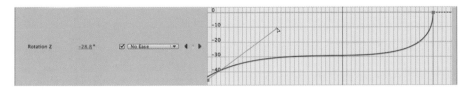

Quickly applying motion presets

Being efficient is a large part of being a successful designer or developer. To this end, Flash CS4
Professional provides a library of prebuilt animations to jump-start your projects. Motion presets
are a huge time-saver and are easy for anyone
to create and use. Users who spend a lot of time
on repetitive application of motion can increase
their productivity dramatically through the use of
motion presets. Motion presets can be shared or
distributed to an entire team of users, enhancing
team collaboration and consistency.

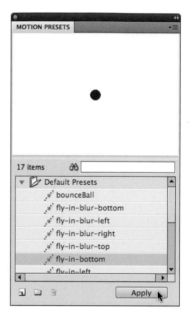

The new object-based animation model in Flash
CS4 allows animation attributes to be applied as
needed. It's also really easy to create your own
presets: just select any object that already has a
motion tween applied to it, and then click the
Save Selection As Preset button (▣) at the bottom left of the Motion Presets panel.

Adding sophistication with 3D transformations

Bringing perspective and dimension to your design can add an element of excite-
ment and fun to any project but until now, the ability to create 3D motion was available only to expert users via ActionScript or other sophisticated tools. Now, with
Flash CS4, you can animate 2D objects through 3D space with new easy-to-use 3D
transformation tools, greatly extending your creative possibilities.

Flash CS4 features two new specialized tools for applying 3D effects:

- The 3D Rotation tool allows you to spin and twirl your art within a 3D space.

- The 3D Translation tool provides visually intuitive x-, y-, and z-axis object
  manipulation.

You can have a lot of fun with the
incredibly easy-to-use new 3D features
in Flash CS4. Built for inexperienced
and advanced users alike, the new 3D
transformation tools make 3D motion
effects available to everyone.

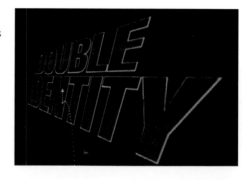

Defining interaction and distortion with the Bones tool

Those who live and breathe animation may be familiar with the term *inverse kinematics*, or IK, which is a method used to create chain-like motion effects with a series of linked objects or to quickly distort single objects. Much as the bones in the human body form a skeleton that moves and behaves in a defined way, the new Bones tool in Flash CS4 allows you to link a series of symbols or elements of a single shape together with "bones" that can be quickly and easily animated and controlled relative to one another.

Inverse kinematics with the Bones tool allows new users to work with advanced Flash functionality sooner, opens up new creative possibilities for experienced designers, and saves time for almost any user who would have previously had to use ActionScript to define complex symbol interactions and behaviors.

Creating cool pattern art with the Deco tool

If you think Flash CS4 is all about technical stuff that does nothing for the design side of the brain, think again. The Deco tool is a fantastic new addition that literally blossoms forth with symmetry and creativity as you turn any symbol into an instant design element. Whether creating patterns or kaleidoscope-like effects using single or multiple symbols, the Deco tool provides a new way to create and apply decorative motifs to your work.

The Vine Fill literally draws an organic vine and randomly attaches leaf and flower symbols. You can also specify custom symbols in the Properties panel.

When using the Vine Fill option with the Deco tool, the vine grows until it senses another object or border. If you select an object such as an oval shape, the vine fills only the inside of the shape (as shown in the illustration on the right). If you click outside the shape (for example, on the stage), the vine grows while avoiding other objects that get in the way.

The Grid Fill drawing effect fills any shape or background with a repeated pattern of the selected symbol. Designers interested in patterns, intricate drawing options, and rich textures and surfaces can now create and apply them to spaces or objects more easily.

Integrating high-quality H.264 video

Video content is fast becoming a first-class citizen on the Web. More that 75% of online videos are viewed using Adobe Flash technology, making Flash the number one format for video on the Web. As more companies make the decision to add video content to their online presence, designers and developers struggle to find that happy medium—video content that is high in quality but small in file size. With more and more people using their mobile devices to view video content, developers must be acutely aware of bandwidth issues—without budging an inch on quality. So it's no surprise that Adobe Flash Player 10 and Adobe Media Encoder, which is now integrated into Flash CS4, support H.264, which has become the standard in high-quality/low-bandwidth video content.

Now, developers can deliver high-quality video with more control than ever before. Adobe Media Encoder—the same tool found in other Adobe professional video products—now supports H.264 and is included with Flash CS4 Professional.

Publishing content as an Adobe AIR application

Adobe AIR, the technology that makes Flash experiences on the desktop possible, is now built into Flash CS4 Professional. By extending Flash beyond the browser with custom desktop experiences and branding opportunities, Adobe AIR introduces exciting new methods for delivering interactive content.

Adobe AIR applications can play directly on the desktop. You can choose to have your application appear within a standard application window or without any frames at all.

Adobe AIR allows you to leverage local desktop resources and data to deliver even more personal, engaging experiences. With the same skills you use to deliver to Flash Player, you can now reach even more audiences across more devices—web, mobile, and now the desktop.

Adobe AIR is a new cross-platform runtime application that offers an exciting new way to engage customers by presenting innovative, branded desktop applications.

Adobe Dreamweaver CS4

Build world-class websites and applications with Adobe Dreamweaver CS4. Manipulate pixel-perfect designs, craft complex code, or do both—with speed and grace. Dreamweaver CS4 creates leading-edge digital experiences that blend best CSS practices with web-standards compliant layouts for the web, digital devices, and desktop applications.

Designing, developing, and maintaining standards-based websites and applications

Adobe Dreamweaver CS4 software is the perfect tool for web designers, coders, and application developers at all levels. Enhanced coding functions make it a breeze to navigate through complex site pages during the design process. Improved layout tools expedite workflows from comp conception to client approval. Innovations throughout Dreamweaver CS4 help teams and individual developers alike reach new levels in performance and functionality.

Create next-generation web experiences that combine standards-compliant code with engaging interactive interfaces. New features in Dreamweaver CS4 provide direct access to the various elements—CSS, JavaScript, and other dynamic, rich media—that compose today's compound web page. Best practices in CSS design and Ajax-driven interactivity are within easy reach, with the enhanced user interface and advanced wizards. New technologies in Dreamweaver CS4 allow web designers to retain control of their content while distributing the site-maintenance workload.

Multifaceted and enhanced workspace

From the very first glance, you'll notice that Dreamweaver CS4 has undergone a major transformation. The striking changes are far more than skin-deep. Spring-loaded panels expand with a single click for quick access, and then collapse when no longer needed. Panels can now be iconified to maximize document workspace.

Dreamweaver CS4 is now more adaptable to the individual user than ever before. The new Workspace Switcher rearranges the Dreamweaver environment to best suit the way you work. Preset workspaces include options for coders, application developers, dual-screen users, and designers. There's even an option for folks who prefer the look and feel of the previous version of Dreamweaver. Additionally, you can save your ideal arrangement of the Dreamweaver environment as a custom workspace and recall it from the Workspace Switcher at any time.

The Workspace Switcher is initially populated with a range of options designed to fit the needs of web developers, hand coders, and visual designers.

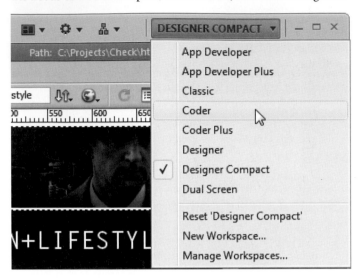

Once the workspace has been defined, you can make temporary changes to your design environment and then quickly return to your custom arrangement.

You can place as many docked panels next to each other as you like. You can also dock panels to the left of the Document window or below it. Within each docked group, only one panel can be open at a time; using multiple groups of docked panels enables you to keep more than one panel open simultaneously.

Rendering and coding enhancements

In addition to modifications that make Dreamweaver CS4 easier to use with other Adobe Creative Suite 4 applications, major upgrades to core functionality make Dreamweaver more suited to modern web development techniques. Web professionals today make frequent use of included or linked files—whether external CSS style sheets, JavaScript libraries, or server-side code—to create a compound document. In Dreamweaver CS4, users can work efficiently with all the underlying code while reviewing the final document in a real-world browser rendition, thanks to three new interconnected features: Related Files, Code Navigator, and Live View.

Stacking panels in iconic mode provides flexible accessibility to a variety of panels while taking up a minimum of workspace real estate.

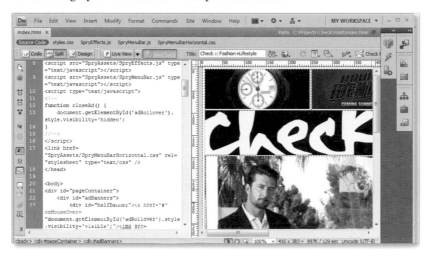

The Code Navigator window shows all the code sources related to the current selection. Each code source is linked, so you can go quickly to the relevant section. For immediate editing just click the link to jump to the relevant code. Changing the background-color value in the related styles.css file results in the color change shown in Design view.

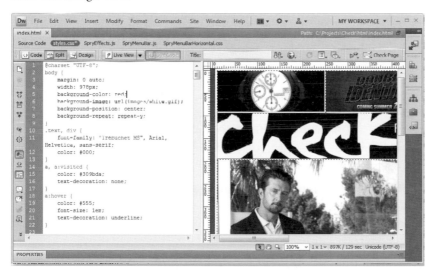

Another new feature, Live View, works hand in glove with Related Files and Code Navigator. Live View renders the current web page in real-world browser conditions, thanks to the use of the WebKit HTML rendering engine. Live View not only renders the page accurately, but allows the user to interact with it as with a standard browser.

You can toggle the Code Navigator off and on by clicking the Disable checkbox.

Live View can be invoked with Alt+F11 (Windows) or Option+F11 (Mac) or by clicking the button on the Document toolbar. You can use Live View in conjunction with Design View or Split View.

CSS best practices

Cascading Style Sheets (CSS) have become the de facto standard for building modern web pages. Dreamweaver CS4 is at the forefront in helping designers overcome the challenges of designing with CSS. This latest evolutionary step brings CSS rule creation and modification front and center in the Dreamweaver CS4 Properties panel.

The Properties panel (formerly known as the Property inspector) has been updated so that when text is selected, it splits into two view modes: HTML and CSS. Use HTML mode to set common properties like format, class, and link. You can also change the text into any type of list. All formatting controls have now moved to the CSS view of the Properties panel, including alignment, font-family, size, and color.

In addition to the formatting controls, a portion of the Properties panel in CSS mode is dedicated to CSS rules. A menu displays any currently applied CSS rule and also allows you to work with any other CSS rule in the current cascade. Additionally, you can quickly create a new CSS rule.

Even with the Properties panel in HTML mode, Dreamweaver CS4 writes web-standards compliant code, such as the <strong> tag for bold and <em> for italic.

In CSS mode, if there is no rule defined for the current selection, the Targeted Rule menu in the Properties panel displays <New CSS Rule>.

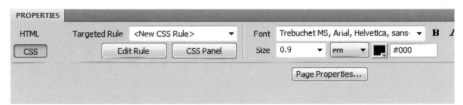

The New CSS Rule dialog box gives you control over the type of selector (tag, class, or compound) as well as the placement: embedded in the document or added to an external style sheet.

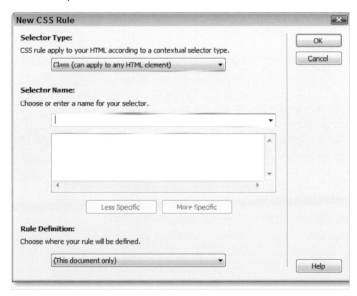

Dreamweaver creates and applies your CSS rule in a single step, adding the proper <span> tag with the new class attribute.

The new CSS mode in the Properties panel can also be used to modify existing styles quickly and easily. Once the color swatch is changed in the Properties panel, Dreamweaver updates the associated CSS rule and Design view immediately.

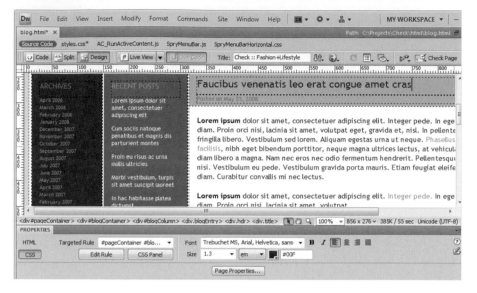

All the blog titles turn the same shade of blue as Dreamweaver updates the rule with the new color value. If you need to change CSS properties beyond what is available in the Properties panel, click Edit Rule to display the full CSS Rule Definition dialog box.

The New CSS Rule dialog box has been revised to give designers a much finer degree of control over the scope of their CSS changes. In Dreamweaver CS4, you can limit or expand the specificity of the selector to define your CSS rule so that it applies to just what you want—without writing a single line of code.

To make a change to the CSS of a link, you only have to place your cursor within the link—you don't have to select the whole tag.

Dreamweaver displays a plain-language translation of the selector in the adjacent text area. You can modify the specificity of the selector by choosing the Less Specific and More Specific options.

If you've made a selector less specific, you can still change your mind and click More Specific; Dreamweaver remembers the full compound selector for the current document selection.

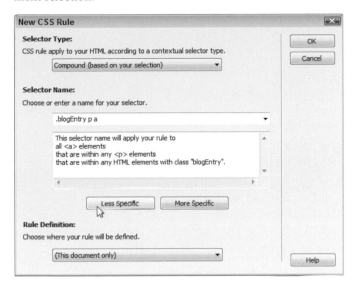

Photoshop Smart Objects

Integration between Photoshop and Dreamweaver has evolved to a new level of compatibility and functionality. For the first time, you can simply insert a Photoshop PSD file into a Dreamweaver CS4 page to create a Smart Object image. Unlike standard webpage graphics, Smart Objects are tightly linked to their source files. A small indicator on a Smart Object in Dreamweaver CS4 shows when the source and instance are in sync. When you make any changes to the source image, Dreamweaver notes that the files are out of sync; just click the Update from Original button in the Properties panel to immediately update your image without opening Photoshop. The sync indicator appears in the upper left of a Smart Object image; both parts are initially green.

Out-of-sync files are indicated with a symbol that is half green and half red.

In addition to honoring your optimization settings, Dreamweaver also maintains any rescaling. For example, from an original Photoshop image of a company logo, you could insert multiple instances in a website at a variety of sizes by using the scaling feature in the Image Preview dialog box. Should the source be modified, Dreamweaver rescales each inserted instance as previously defined.

HTML data sets

Dreamweaver CS4 combines accessibility with ease of use in the new HTML data sets feature. With this functionality, you create your data in a standard HTML table, a series of div tags, or even an unordered list, and then step through an easy-to-use wizard to integrate the data into a dynamic table on the page, complete with sortable columns, a master-detail layout, or other sophisticated displays using the Spry framework for Ajax. It's an easy way to create and integrate external data, with real-time previews of your data. Spry data sets also work with XML files to render information from RSS feeds and other sources.

All manner of data can be incorporated in an HTML data set, including a thumbnail, detail image, date, title, and location.

Here's what a completed HTML data set looks like. The columns of the table (Thumb, Picture, When, What, Details) correspond to data columns in a database; five of the six columns are shown in the figure above. Each table row represents a separate record. Notice that the image data is straightforwardly represented by HTML images. The HTML data set technique makes it easy for you to format your data with standard tags.

Once you select the data source file, Dreamweaver populates the Data Containers menu with all the available data structures identifiable by their ID, as for calendarList, shown in the image below.

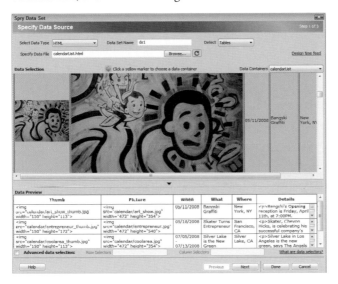

With the help of the wizard, you can determine how you want your data to be presented. There are four basic layouts: Table, Master/Detail, Stacked Containers, and Stacked Containers With Spotlight Area. You can also opt to create your own custom layout by choosing the fifth option, Do Not Insert HTML, and than inserting items from the Bindings panel.

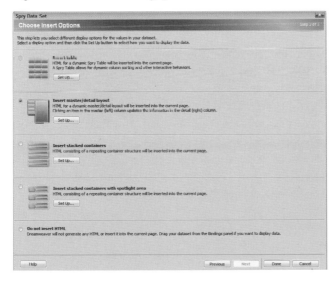

The four different insert options cover the full range of possibilities. Choose Insert table for basic information that is dynamically sortable and presented in a grid-like fashion. Master/detail layouts add two interconnected regions to the page. Stacked containers are like repeating rows of information in a single column, one data item per row. Stacked containers with spotlight area combine stacked containers with a single data field, typically a thumbnail image.

The master/detail layout design provides two areas for your data. The master area displays just a few key data points in a concise area, often in a list with thumbnail images. Selecting any of the master items in the list updates the data in the detail area, which provides more in-depth information and larger imagery. You can specify what data columns are displayed where using the Set Up option.

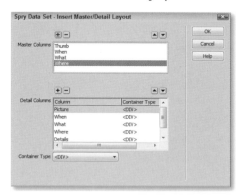

While in Live View, Dreamweaver reads in the current HTML file and outputs the data in the master/detail layout as selected.

When you make a quick modification to your data source, the modified record moves to the top of the page, because it now has the earliest date. The HTML data set is recognized as an interactive data source for your Spry master/detail layout—without the need to set up databases or XML files.

InContext Editing

The new online InContext Editing service from Adobe enables anyone who can use a browser to update content quickly and easily. Design your editable pages in Dreamweaver CS4 to retain total control over the look and feel of your sites. Then, simply designate which parts of the page you want your clients to be able to change; all other sections of the page are locked, and editable only by you. Easily set CSS styles to ensure that user-entered content is properly and consistently formatted. There are two aspects to the InContext Editing experience: establishing InContext Editing regions in Dreamweaver and editing the published pages in your web browser.

The InContext Editing category contains three items: Create Repeating Region, Create Editable Region, and Manage Available CSS Classes.

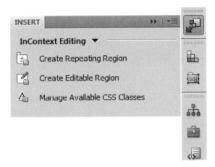

You can place an editable region around a selection, a tag, or a series of elements.

The Properties panel controls the ways in which the user can modify the text. As the designer of the page, you can restrict the editing options to retain control over its appearance. *(See illustration on next page.)*

If your selected content is not within a div tag, the Create Editable Region dialog box offers two ways to add the necessary code.

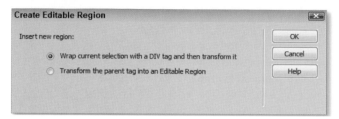

To further control the design properties of the editable content, you can ensure that users have access to only certain CSS styles. All the classes contained in selected external style sheets appear in a single Styles menu in the InContext Editing interface.

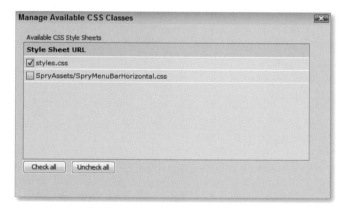

After publishing a file like this—and the included JavaScript and CSS files—the page will be editable from the browser, for anyone registered as an InContext Editing user.

SWF inserting

SWF media has long been a part of the Dreamweaver vocabulary; inserting SWF files has always been drag-and-drop easy. In Dreamweaver CS4, the simplicity of adding a SWF file to your page has now been enhanced behind the scenes with W3C-specified, XHTML-compliant code. Now when you add a SWF file to your document, Dreamweaver adds two external dependent files and in-page code that detects the player version and, if necessary, installs it quickly and unobtrusively. All the work is handled for you.

You can toggle the visibility of AP (absolute positioned) elements by clicking in the Eye column.

When an SWF file has been added to the page, you can easily review the content within Dreamweaver by clicking Play in the Properties panel. This Preview will give you a true sense of how all the elements work together.

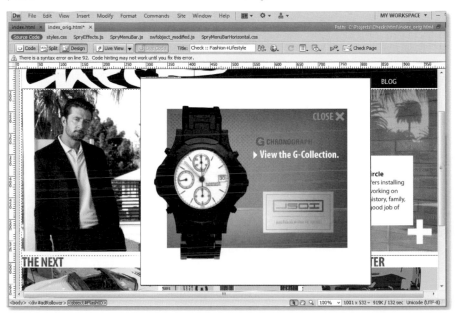

Behind the scenes, Dreamweaver copies the necessary files to your site to efficiently handle the web-standards compliant coding.

Adobe Fireworks CS4

Rapidly prototype websites, application interfaces, and interactive designs with Adobe Fireworks CS4. Use the enhanced Fireworks CS4 toolset to create everything from web graphics to multipage comps, faster and more accurately than ever before.

Fireworks CS4 is packed with new workspace improvements for web and application designers, including Smart Guides for faster object placement, more precise in-place symbol editing, and 9-slice scaling. Improvements to styles make single-source changes a reality, regardless of the number of times you've applied the style. Present comps to your clients, whether they are across the hall or across the country—there are numerous ways to share your designs, from PDF digital copies to the Adobe ConnectNow online service. You can even create Adobe AIR™ prototypes that go beyond your desktop to the web.

New user interface

The new look and feel of Fireworks CS4 is far more than just a designer-friendly overhaul. Fireworks now shares a common interface with other Adobe Creative Suite 4 component applications, from Photoshop Extended and Illustrator to Adobe Flash® Professional and Adobe Dreamweaver®. Maintain common workspace layouts and tools as you move smoothly between Fireworks and any other Creative Suite 4 component.

In Fireworks CS4, Adobe has improved the speed with which files are opened, saved, and closed. Now you can open multiple files in the time it previously took to open one. The new tabbed interface can display a large number of files in a very accessible manner.

Multiple-document handling has been vastly improved in Fireworks CS4. Initially, opened files are presented as a series of docked tabs. You can isolate any file by dragging its tab away from the group.

Designers working with a second display can easily drag a file from screen to screen. Even without multiple monitors, Fireworks CS4 offers numerous options for arranging your documents, including creating additional file groups. Reposition a single-file window by dragging the title bar; if you wish to move a file that is grouped with others, drag the file by its tab. Organize Fireworks CS4 file groups in whatever arrangement best suits your workflow, whether horizontal, vertical, or a combination of the two.

Performance improvements

In addition to the shorter load times, Fireworks CS4 is now much faster—and smarter—when saving documents. Today's Fireworks source files often contain large numbers of pages, layers, states, and symbols, resulting in very large file sizes. In tandem with overall speed improvements for saving large files, Fireworks CS4 now saves asynchronously, so you can continue working while the file is being stored.

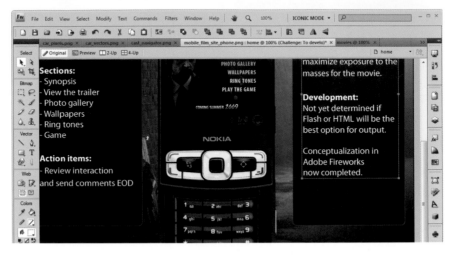

Note the asterisk that now appears after the file name in the tab, indicating that the document has been modified.

Workspace improvements

Enhancements to the standard guides now make it possible to gauge X and Y coordinates precisely. Simply pressing the Shift key while adjusting your guides enables you to view dynamically updated distances between the guides and the parallel edge of the canvas. Likewise, Smart Guides make it far easier to place objects in alignment with others already on the canvas, without resorting to the use of the Align panel. Even the Preferences panel has been updated to offer more options in the consistent Creative Suite interface.

Fireworks CS4 features a heads-up display of coordinates when moving guides and objects, to make accurate placement more fluid. You can use as many horizontal or vertical guides as you need to perfect your design.

When you hold the Shift key while moving a guide, Fireworks displays distances in pixels from the edge of the canvas to the next guide or between two guides. This feature is excellent for locating a midpoint.

The guide distance feature is also great for discovering the amount of space between two existing guides, particularly when determining values for proper CSS properties such as margins or padding.

Adobe AIR export

Adobe AIR uses proven web technologies to deploy applications to the desktop and across operating systems. Now you can preview and package your Adobe AIR interactive prototype directly from within Fireworks CS4, ready to be delivered to HTML and CSS, Flex, or Flash. Pages and states in Fireworks CS4 map accurately to an interactive Adobe AIR application experience, so you can quickly convert your click-through mock-up to a fully functional design prototype.

You can assign a variety of JavaScript functions, including those for Adobe AIR, to Fireworks slices.

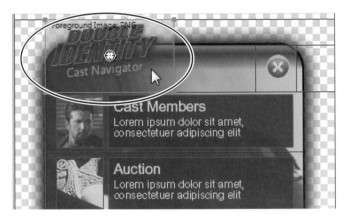

For Adobe AIR applications, you have the option of either applying the standard operating system windows or making the window transparent. You have also a full slate of options when creating your AIR package.

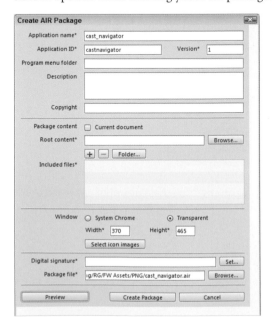

The upper left corner of the previewed Adobe AIR application not only serves as a handle for dragging, but also includes a built-in rollover effect applied in Fireworks CS4.

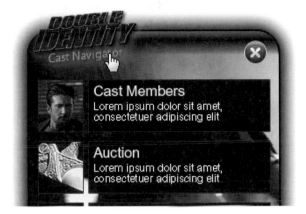

A completed prototype built in Fireworks CS4 could also include files from Flash or Dreamweaver, if desired. Your Adobe AIR prototype could be sent to the client to get the green light for the next stage of development.

PDF export

With Fireworks CS4, you can also deliver your fully functional design comps directly to your clients with the new Export To PDF feature. The PDF document retains hotspot-linked pages, providing an interactive electronic comp that is viewable by anyone with Adobe Reader® or Adobe Acrobat® software, with the benefits of all of their commenting capabilities.

All of the links in the exported PDF are functional, and accurately simulate the proposed project interactivity—even the Back button behavior found in typical web browsers.

Photoshop import and CSS export

Now you can design complete web pages in the robust graphic environment of Fireworks CS4, and then export web-standards compliant CSS-based layouts—complete with external style sheets—all in one step. Fireworks CS4 has the ability to integrate foreground and background graphics with the new slice types; you have the option to set background slices to repeat along X or Y coordinates (for gradient backgrounds) or not to repeat at all.

Fireworks displays the Photoshop File Open Options dialog box to help you optimize your file importing. If desired, you can choose to favor editability over appearance or vice versa, and opt to include guides or convert all document layers to frames.

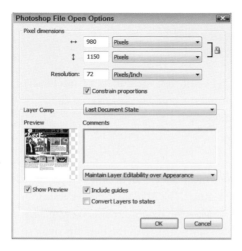

The new background slice attributes are set in the Properties pane. When exported, they are written to an external style sheet or a CSS rule embedded in the HTML file.

In addition to being able to set an overall background image, such as a watermark, you can also change the page alignment and create a separate file for your CSS rules. The code exported from Fireworks is web-standards compliant and displays faithfully on all modern browsers.

Style improvements

Styles are an important asset in any designer's toolbox, enabling consistent color, effects, and text attributes to be applied quickly and easily. The improved styles feature in Fireworks CS4 lifts this functionality to new heights. Now, when you modify a style, all elements to which the style has been applied are immediately updated. You can also separate individual instances from the style at the click of a Properties panel button.

Fireworks CS4 also supports multiple style sets. Designers can quickly switch between different style sets, whether standard or custom. The Styles panel, enhanced for Fireworks CS4, includes a pull-down menu which displays all open documents and their style sets for rapid editing.

The Styles panel has been revamped in Fireworks CS4 to make it easier to find specific styles and to share styles across documents. The pull-down menu at the top of the Styles panel provides access to a rich collection of styles. Whenever a style is applied in a document, whether from the Fireworks library of styles or another document, that style is added to the Current Document collection.

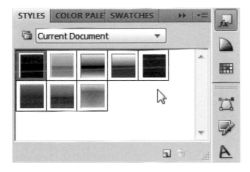

The Container Design style is applied to the selected path in this design. The Redefine Style button is to the right of the New Style button, which creates a fresh style based on the current selection. *(See illutration on next page.)*

Once you click the Redefine Style button, all applied styles are immediately updated.

Adobe text engine

The powerful typographical capabilities familiar to users of Photoshop and Illustrator are now implemented in the text engine of Fireworks CS4. The Adobe text engine improvements also enable you to bring Photoshop PSD files into Fireworks CS4 with fully editable text, and support ligatures and even text properties not previously available in Fireworks, such as strikethrough. Designers will appreciate the new ability to float text inside a path to quickly simulate text floating around an image in CSS layouts.

The Lorem Ipsum command is a handy tool for inserting a paragraph of placeholder text in a default set of properties, which can be modified through the Properties panel.

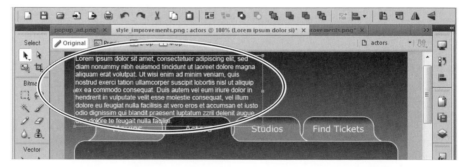

Before Fireworks CS4, designers had to use multiple text blocks to simulate text wrapped around an image. Now, all you need to do is select both the path and image and invoke a single command.

The Attach In Path command can be used to create complex text wrapping around any image or object.

New and enhanced commands

In addition to its robust core functionality, Fireworks is the beneficiary of a multi-faceted extensibility layer, as demonstrated by the numerous new commands and command panels that add functionality. In Fireworks CS4, new commands have been added—such as Demo Current Document, which creates a SWF slide show of all the current pages—and many user interface elements have been updated with improved consistency and functionality. Moreover, command panels can be authored in Adobe Flash Professional or Adobe Flex to further enhance the user interface. Two of the most powerful Fireworks utilities are the Path panel and the Auto Vector Mask.

The Path panel is filled with numerous time-saving, creative tools, like Convert Path To Fill, which allows you to change a vector path to a filled object—excellent for adding gradients to organic shapes.

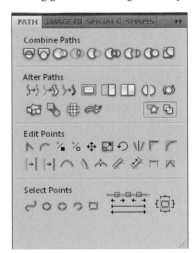

The Auto Vector Mask command was known in previous versions of Fireworks as Fade Image. The new name more accurately describes the applied operation, and the new user interface allows for real-time previewing. Each of the options in the Auto Vector Mask dialog box fades the applied object in a different direction or shape.

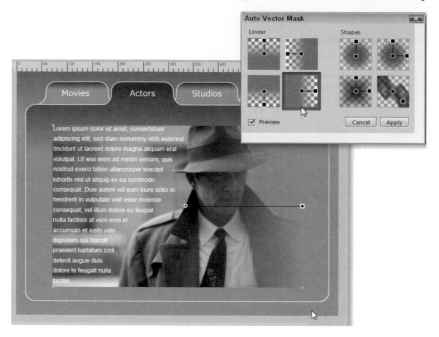

The image of the actor now appears to fade into the background on the right.

Enhanced symbols

Symbols have also taken a big step forward in Fireworks CS4. Now with in-place editing, you can precisely refine your symbol while keeping an eye on the larger picture on your canvas. Symbol properties are now more robust, with support for nested symbols. Additionally, editing one instance of a symbol now immediately updates all other instances.

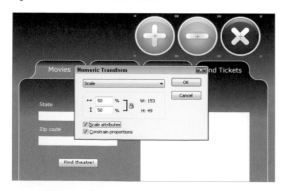

The Numeric Transform command is great for quickly rescaling or resizing symbols to precise values. The width/height ratio is locked by default—you need only to enter one of the two values to rescale proportionately.

Fireworks CS4 now supports nested symbols, so you can easily group common elements and use them over and over again.

The Symbol breadcrumb trail serves as both guide and interactive navigation; you can click any link to immediately jump to that location.

This image shows the new, darker gradient in the second Cancel button.

Note that the change applied to one instance of the symbol has been carried over to the other instance automatically. The updated symbols are now ready to be placed anywhere in the current document—or, with the new flexibility of the Styles panel in Fireworks CS4, any open document.

Adobe Acrobat 9 Pro

Communicating and collaborating more easily and securely with Adobe PDF

Whether you work in graphic design, web design and development, or high-end print production, the latest release of Adobe Acrobat—Acrobat 9 Pro—redefines the possibilities for collaborating and communicating with clients, realizing your creative vision, and controlling the quality of your output. With an array of new features as well as a range of enhancements to long-popular capabilities, Acrobat 9 Pro is the most powerful release of Acrobat software to date.

Creative professionals can speed up projects by using the intuitive collaboration features in Acrobat 9 Pro together with the exciting new Web-based services hosted by Adobe at Acrobat.com that enable you to create and store documents and collaborate online in a wide variety of new and exciting ways. In addition, Adobe Acrobat 9 and Adobe Reader now incorporate native support for Adobe Flash technology, enabling you to deliver richer, more compelling document experiences with PDF Portfolios that combine layouts, drawings, images, video, audio, and other elements into a single branded, interactive Adobe Portable Document Format (PDF) file.

In addition, using Acrobat 9 Pro you can now embed video, audio, and applications created using Flash Professional into your PDF files—your clients and others will need only the free Adobe Reader to see the content play back smoothly and to interact in the creative and collaborative processes.

Acrobat 9 Pro is also packed with innovative, timesaving production-oriented features for the creative professional—from the facility to view overprinted objects or convert colored text to solid black, to improved preflight and document comparison capabilities and enhanced color conversion. Acrobat 9 Pro also delivers layer control, intelligent Overprint Preview in both Acrobat and Adobe Reader and the ability to easily verify compliance with PDF standards—including newly adopted ones such as PDF/X-4p and PDF/X-5pg.

Acrobat.com: Hosted Services Ideal for Creative Professionals

With Acrobat.com, Adobe has launched a set of exciting new free online services that are helping creative professionals improve workflows inside and outside their organizations, across geography and firewalls. You can use Acrobat.com as a resource for a variety of activities, including sharing and storing files, communicating in real-time, and simplifying collaboration. In addition to using these free hosted services, Acrobat 9 users are able to work with Acrobat.com as a central location for document processes.

Using Acrobat.com, creative pros are able to gain access to a set of powerful, Adobe-hosted services that are constantly evolving and being enhanced: Adobe Buzzword for online word processing, Adobe ConnectNow for web conferencing, Share for sharing and storing files, My Files for file organization, and Create PDF for online PDF conversion.

The facilities at Acrobat.com are accessible directly from within Acrobat 9 Pro or Adobe Reader 9. Keep in mind that you don't need a heavy-duty IT infrastructure to enable you to take advantage of all of these capabilities—just Acrobat.com and Acrobat 9 Pro or Adobe Reader.

Easy access to all Adobe Acrobat 9 Pro features

Adobe Acrobat 9 Pro includes all the powerful capabilities users have come to rely on in the past, together with a range of new functionality and enhancements. The user interface is still organized around the different types of work you can do with Acrobat—creating PDF files and richly interactive PDF Portfolios, working with forms, reviewing documents, preparing files for output, and more. All of the most commonly used capabilities are instantly accessible from the taskbar buttons so you can get right down to work:

- Integrate an impressively wide range of content into a PDF Portfolio.

- Embed content created in Adobe Flash in your PDF documents.

- Create, manage, and analyze forms and collect forms data more easily and efficiently.

- Collaborate with clients or colleagues using the synchronized document view.

- Set up, initiate, and manage shared reviews with ease.

- Detect differences between document versions with greater ease and control.

- Enjoy the security of enhanced preflight checking, automatic correction, and an embedded audit trail of preflight results for high-end print production and digital publishing.

- Obtain full information about any selected object in a PDF file using the new Object Inspector.

- Be confident of accurate color conversion, including conversion of RGB and rich blacks to solid black and built-in Pantone libraries for converting RGB/CMYK colors to spot colors or mapping one spot color to another.

- Take advantage of support for PDF standards like PDF/X, PDF/A, and PDF/E.

- Enjoy greater control when creating layers and assigning objects to them.

- Launch faster.

Creating compelling content

Acrobat 9 Pro opens up new possibilities for developing and delivering engaging communications to peers, partners, and clients worldwide. New capabilities that support the rapid creation of rich and engaging PDF Portfolios set new standards for the range of information that can be packaged and communicated in a single PDF file. The examples below highlight just a few of the ways in which Acrobat 9 Pro can help you deliver more meaningful, memorable information.

PDF Portfolios: addressing business opportunities and changing user expectations

As a creative professional today, you need to create more dynamic, compelling communications, whether you're generating creative concepts, collaborating with colleagues, or exchanging information with clients. Already, digital audio, video, and interactive graphics are common in many interactions—both online and offline—dramatically altering people's perception of what now constitutes a high-quality, engaging experience. It's not surprising then that as expectations—and opportunities—change, creative professionals face tremendous pressure to make communication and collaboration across project teams and with clients more engaging and effective, particularly if the goal is to accelerate project completion and gain an edge over competitors.

With native support for Adobe Flash technology, Acrobat 9 Pro sets new standards for what it means to deliver rich multi-media content to the widest possible audience. Static documents can now be combined with a variety of dynamic content in a single, integrated, compelling PDF Portfolio replete with high-quality video, audio, web content, animations, and more. This means that you can better communicate your concepts to clients and present potential clients with tailored information that includes videos and audio testimonials, while motion designers can let review teams explore interactive content in PDF. And that's just the beginning!

With Acrobat 9 Pro, you can select from a variety of PDF Portfolio layouts to rapidly create communications that meet your objectives and grab the attention of intended audiences. Navigator layouts can be easily customized to include logos, company descriptors, contact information, and other details. Programmers comfortable with developing in ActionScript 3 have the option to build layouts of their own using Adobe Flex® Builder™ or Adobe Flash CS3 Professional.

Regardless of the approach, PDF Portfolios offer advantages to content creators and viewers alike, providing a clearer picture and more memorable insight into the topic at hand. Imagine being able to produce a creative brief that truly showcases motion and interactive projects with rich video, audio, presentations, and other materials that clients can view using just the free Adobe Reader. What a step up from using a mishmash of traditional files such as static screen grabs and text files that don't do the work justice. PDF documents have never been so lively and compelling!

Safeguarding your creative content

Acrobat 9 Pro now supports 256-bit encryption, the Advanced Encryption Standard (AES) approved by the U.S. government. By leveraging powerful security features in Acrobat 9 Pro, you can restrict others from performing specific actions on PDF files, such as opening, printing, or editing files. You can add two types of encryption to a document: password encryption or certification encryption. Password encryption lets you assign a password and specify security options to restrict the opening, printing, and editing of PDF files. Certification encryption encrypts a document so that only a specified set of users can access it.

Acrobat 9 Pro continues to support digital signatures in PDF, allowing anyone with Adobe Reader 8 or higher to approve a document by adding his or her digital signature to a PDF file using a digital ID. Document authors can also verify content in PDF files by adding a certifying signature. The status icons associated with a signed PDF document let users know if the signature is valid.

Creating your own PDF Portfolio

Acrobat 9 Pro brings together the best of PDF and Flash, making your communications come to life and helping you deliver exactly the information needed in an interactive way that both engages the viewer and makes sense.

You can choose from a variety of layouts for your PDF Portfolio. Customize the PDF Portfolio's appearance by selecting one of many layouts and options available in the Edit Portfolio panel located on the right side of the window. Take a look at the Choose A Layout options and try out the layout Basic Grid from the Basic Layouts menu.

The On An Image option allows you to choose a background image (such as a map or a product image) and place files on top of it.

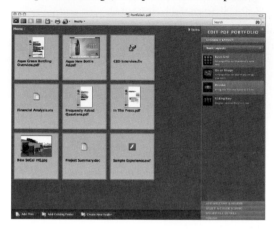

You can personalize your PDF Portfolio by adding logos, images, and welcome text. Acrobat 9 Pro supports a variety of image file formats, including JPG, GIF, and PNG. For each layout option, Acrobat gives you the flexibility to change font styles and sizes, logo image opacity, and even the background color for the entire header, enabling you to brand your PDF Portfolio or simply give it a professional edge.

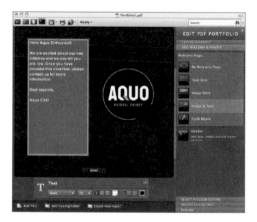

Acrobat 9 Pro automatically uses your choice as a base color, and then applies shades to the various PDF Portfolio elements, including text and backgrounds. You can even define your own color scheme—based on your corporate colors, for example—by choosing Customize Color Scheme and modifying each element separately.

You have a wide variety of options for organizing files within a PDF Portfolio. Once you're done, you can publish and save it to your hard drive or external media, send it via e-mail, or share it directly to Acrobat.com.

Collaboration made simple

Acrobat 9 Pro makes it easier than ever to collaborate on documents anytime, anywhere, regardless of what operating system your partners use or whether or not they are behind a firewall. The ability to synchronize document views online brings new immediacy to project teams and streamlines working on large, complex documents because team members can be literally on the same page, whether they're just down the hallway or thousands of miles away. There's no need for the IT department and no complexities associated with connecting with people behind firewalls. Everyone can see each other's documents and reconcile contradictory feedback in real time.

Eliminating guesswork by synchronizing document views

Anyone who has tried discussing specific content remotely by phone knows how difficult it can be. Simply getting a colleague on the right page, in the right section, and looking at the right text/font, color, image, or content often requires a lengthy conversation. Clearly, it would be easier if you could literally point others to the exact page or item in question. With Acrobat 9 Pro, review team participants can do exactly that—no matter where they are. Acrobat 9 enables you to zero in on content in a PDF file by synching your view within a document to what others see in the same file on their computers. Participants in the discussion need only Acrobat 9 or the free Adobe Reader 9 to co-navigate documents with colleagues and clients.

● **Note:** If you are using Acrobat 9 Pro on Microsoft Windows and you want to test shared document reviews, you can use your own internal server. This may be an internal SharePoint workspace, network folder, or web server folder (WebDAV) to which recipients have read/write access. The document and review comments are hosted on this shared location.

You can specify your recipients and allow either open or controlled access to your PDF file. The Collaborate Live panel adds another dimension by letting you chat live with the other review participants.

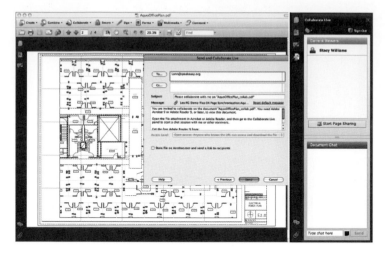

Conducting more effective shared document reviews

Initiating a shared review of a PDF document is quick and easy with the improved distribution wizard in Acrobat 9 Pro. The enhanced Tracker is the central dashboard for reviews. In Tracker, you can who the reviewers are, and who has already reviewed the document in PDF. For anyone who works with dispersed teams engaged in lengthy review cycles, this facility can eliminate much of the delay and confusion typically associated with traditional review processes. You even send reminders to reviewers and receive alerts within Acrobat when each project team member has reviewed and edited a document.

You can see a consolidated view of comments either by clicking the View Comments link in Tracker or by referring to the Comments Pane. Tracker notifies you that new comments are available and gives you the option you to accept them so they are copied to your file. Note that there may be a brief lag between the reviewer clicking Publish Comments and your notification that new comments are available. You can check for the latest comments manually by choosing Check For New Comments in Document Message Bar at the top of PDF file being reviewed.

Creating, managing, and analyzing forms—from start to finish

Acrobat 9 Pro includes everything you need to create high-quality forms, distribute them, collect responses, and track and export the results. If you don't already have a form, you can quickly create one by converting either an electronic document such as an InDesign file or a scanned document into a PDF file. The form field recognition capability in Acrobat 9 Pro speeds the process of creating reliable digital forms from existing documents.

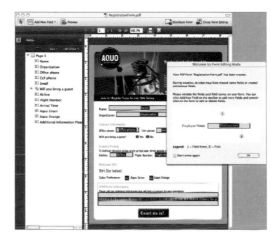

When you're ready to distribute the form, you can e-mail it to a list of recipients, upload it to a shared location and specify who you would like to have access, or distribute it via Acrobat.com. Finally, you can use the new response file interface—a PDF Portfolio that is automatically generated and populated with all the responses to the form—to view, sort, or filter data much as you would in a traditional spreadsheet application.

Comparing documents at a glance

For anyone who works with teams to review and revise documents, Acrobat 9 Pro overcomes the challenge of figuring out exactly what has changed from version to version down to the smallest detail. You can easily compare minute details such as tables, text edits and formatting, annotations, backgrounds, line weights, and images pixel-by-pixel between any two PDF documents, and immediately identify differences. Should you wish to compare changes to a creative comp created in an application that does not support a "compare" capability, Acrobat 9 Pro makes it easy. For example, you can convert two versions of an InDesign file to PDF and quickly see the differences—even though that's not possible in the native application. Acrobat 9 Pro delivers several enhancements to help you identify changes, with more visual cues and more detail about the content differences.

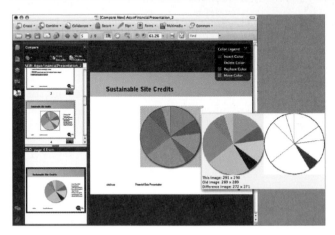

Unparalleled PDF workflows for professional creative production

The breadth of enhancements to Acrobat 9 Pro is extensive. Beyond improved collaboration, rich PDF Portfolios, Acrobat.com, enhanced forms and comparison capabilities, Acrobat 9 Pro delivers a full range of features that save time and automate common production tasks for the print professional, allowing you to deliver high-quality print output faster.

Overprint Preview

Intelligent Overprint Preview helps ensure that overlapping elements will display and print correctly. Overprint Preview does not need to be turned on manually as it did in previous versions—it is enabled intelligently, whenever it is needed.

By default Overprint Preview will turn on intelligently when it detects a PDF/X file. You can also set your preferences to have Overprint Preview activated automatically when any PDF file is opened. With Intelligent Overprint Preview, creative professionals can accurately view PDF files without worrying about activating a menu option.

Output Preview with Object Inspector

Output Preview lets creative professionals preview how files will output under a wide variety of conditions. New in Output Preview are options for viewing different types of objects and colors and a broad range of options for viewing the contents of a PDF in preparation for output, allowing you to simulate output results, identify problems, and fix them using Acrobat 9 Pro tools before output.

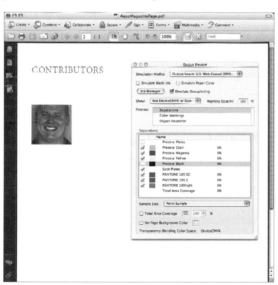

Top 10 features for print professionals:

- Intelligent Overprint Preview
- Enhanced Output Preview with Object Inspector
- Enhanced color conversion, including converting RGB and rich blacks to solid black
- Support for the latest PDF industry standards
- Enhanced preflight checking and corrections, including an embedded preflight audit trail
- New layers controls for assigning objects to layers and importing a PDF as a layer on a specific page
- Built-in Pantone color libraries
- Document Comparison
- Text editing enhancements
- Print dialogue enhancements

There's also the new Object Inspector, which provides details about an asset's resolution, sizing, color space, and other attributes. The new Object Inspector provides in-depth details about any object you click.

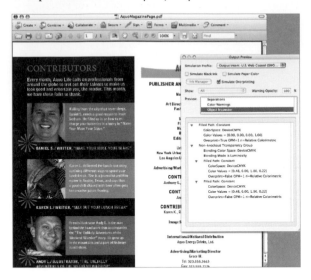

Color conversion

Acrobat 9 Pro incorporates enhanced color conversion capabilities, including improved handling of black/K. Whether converting rich CMYK or RGB to solid black—Acrobat 9 Pro can handle it all. Now it's easy to reliably convert RGB colors (including traditionally problematic rich black text) to CMYK, or vice versa. Acrobat 9 Pro accurately controls color conversions across selected object types or for every object within a PDF. You can save and load color conversion settings so your most often used settings are at hand when needed and can be distributed to others. Spot colors can also be converted in the PDF file using the Ink Manager in the Convert Colors dialog box.

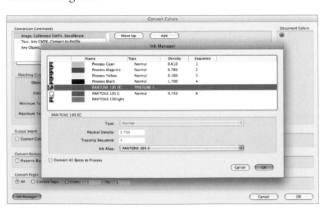

PDF standards verification

A new PDF Standards Pane provides details on compliance to standards such as PDF/A, the ISO standards for long-term archiving of electronic documents, and PDF/X, the ideal formats for high-quality, professional printing. Whenever you open a PDF file, Acrobat 9 Pro or Reader 9 automatically checks to see if it complies with a PDF standard. If the file does comply, Acrobat 9 Pro or Reader 9 automatically displays the PDF Standards Pane showing information on the file's compliance—there's no need to run a preflight profile to know whether or not a file complies with a specific standard.

Preflighting

Although the ability to preflight files has long been a feature in Acrobat Professional, Acrobat 9 Pro makes the process easier and provides more comprehensive capabilities. Via an enhanced, more intuitive user interface, print professionals can dig deeper into files when testing them, and track each PDF file's preflight status right within the file.

The new and enhanced preflight features in Acrobat 9 Pro can not only pinpoint issues, but can also fix them. Acrobat 9 Pro preflight automatically corrects common problems based on user defined rules, identifying and fixing incorrectly specified spot colors, embedding fonts, and much more.

You can use the search option in the preflight user interface to find just the right rule for checking for and fixing any common problem in a PDF file. You can select single checks and fixes—individual rules that are easier and faster to preflight than a complete preflight profile that contains many rules.

Single Checks allow you to quickly scan a PDF without making changes, to identify a wide variety of issues within the PDF—including transparencies, images below a specified resolution, overprinting, fonts that are not embedded, and more.

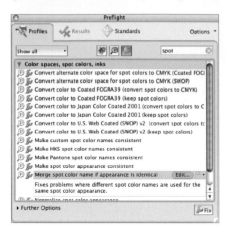

Now that Acrobat 9 Pro includes Pantone color libraries, another great spot color fix can be accomplished using preflight—converting objects in specific RGB or CMYK color values to a target Spot Color.

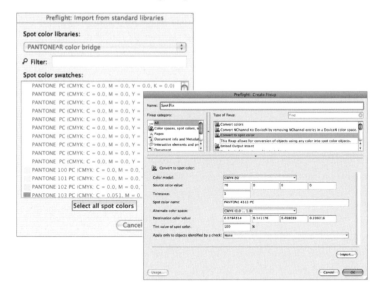

To help you review and troubleshoot your file for printing, Preflight can create layers to which it will assign any type of object so that you can easily see what's going on by turning layers on and off in the Layers panel.

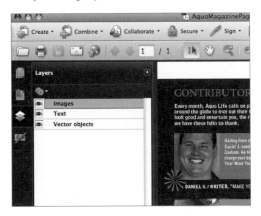

An end-to-end PDF workflow

A vital part of the PDF workflow is the Adobe PDF Print Engine, a next-generation printing platform that is based on the same PDF technology as Acrobat 9 Pro and Adobe Creative Suite software. It allows PDF files to be rendered natively throughout the workflow, eliminating the need to flatten artwork containing transparencies and enabling a complete, end-to-end workflow that uses common technology to generate, preview, and print PDF files.

The latest version—Adobe PDF Print Engine 2—enables end-to-end PDF workflow solutions for printing graphically rich content, including variable content for personalized publishing. For more information, visit http://www.adobe.com/products/pdfprintengine.

Acrobat 9 Pro delivers more robust JDF features than ever, including the ability to export and save JDF information to an HTML page and view it in a browser, effectively creating a viewable, printable job ticket. You can also use the Media Manager in the JDF pane to specify media weight options in pounds. Try it by choosing Advanced > Print Production > JDF Job Definitions.

Adobe Device Central CS4

Adobe Device Central CS4 simplifies the production of innovative and compelling content for mobile phones and consumer electronics devices. Save time by automating testing and emulating network performance of mobile content across a dynamically updated library of device profiles. Create mobile projects to manage assets, target device profiles, and export tasks from one central location. Record content as it plays and send high-quality movie clips to pitch ideas more easily to clients. Intelligent integration with Adobe Creative Suite 4 components means that Adobe Device Central CS4 can help creative professionals and mobile developers deliver engaging experiences to millions of mobile devices worldwide.

Tightly integrated across CS4

Adobe Device Central provides a consistent interface for previewing and testing mobile content—whether it's created in Photoshop CS4, Flash CS4, Illustrator CS4, or After Effects CS4 software. Quickly toggle between any of these Creative Suite 4 components and Adobe Device Central as you create, test, and fine-tune your creations. With a growing library of more than 450 devices, Adobe Device Central keeps you up to date in this fast-changing field. Benefit from improved video integration through support for FLV (Flash video) emulation, device specific compositions in After Effects, and mobile export presets for Adobe Media Encoder.

Simplified mobile workflows

Get started faster by understanding the differences in mobile device screen sizes and content types through a searchable online library of hundreds of dynamically updated device profiles. Organize and save your mobile projects for all media types with mobile project management. Easily publish mobile content to an FTP server or send to a phone via Bluetooth—without ever leaving Device Central—by using the export options provided by the mobile project's Tasks feature. Present mobile concepts for approval by creating and sending a video recording of your content, which executives and clients can easily play back.

Increased productivity

Save significant time by automating the testing of mobile content across any number of device profiles at the click of a button. Take snapshots at specified frames on various devices, and then view the snapshot log to visually identify any problems with the content quickly, or to show colleagues and clients what your content looks like on these devices. Go even further on the desktop with Flash Lite emulation and network simulation.

About Adobe Device Central

More and more, people are looking to their mobile devices—including cell phones, smart phones, and gaming systems—to find rich and engaging content. While designers and developers are familiar with web-based workflows, they are far less familiar with the challenges at hand for delivering mobile content. It is impossible to ignore the ever-growing reach of mobile content.

For anyone working in the field of mobile devices, the fragmented nature of the market landscape—with numerous new devices coming out each quarter—makes it difficult to stay up to date with new technical and design requirements. Unlike the desktop environment, where you need to deal with only two or three operating systems and a small number of releases, designers who publish content to mobile devices must deal with literally hundreds of different screen sizes, form factors, and a flurry of other requirements.

Adobe Device Central CS4 moves you beyond these problems to a simplified environment that focuses on three main areas: browse profiles, create new content, and test existing content.

Worldwide, more people access the Internet on mobile devices than on desktop computers.

The largest mobile device manufacturer sells one million handsets each day.

The number of people with Internet-capable phones outnumber the number of Internet-capable desktop computers by a ratio of almost four to one.

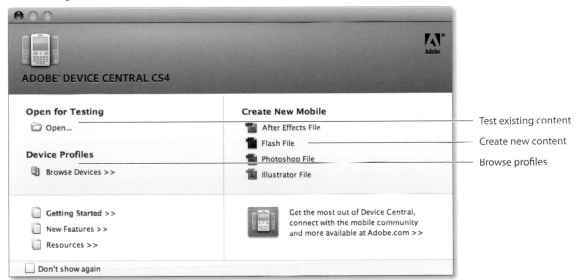

• **Browse profiles**—Adobe Device Central provides an online library of device profiles, each containing important information about screen sizes, network and carrier support, and important technical specifications such as memory limits and software support.

- **Create new content**—Device Central assists in the creation of content by acting as a front end to Creative Suite design components such as After Effects, Flash, Photoshop, and Illustrator. Using the information stored in the device profiles you have selected, Device Central creates new documents at the right sizes and specifications for mobile delivery.

- **Test existing content**—Device Central allows designers and developers to test content on a broad range of devices, delivering the facility to run content—and interact with it—and to perform complex testing routines simultaneously across multiple devices.

Exploring mobile devices

From within Adobe Device Central CS4, you have access to an online library of up-to-date mobile device profiles, where you can browse, group, and search profiles. You can compare multiple devices and create custom device sets for quick project access. Use the convenient and easy-to-use Search feature to search the device library using a wide assortment of criteria, and then save your search results for later use.

Each device profile provides detailed information about screen size, navigation type, sound availability, network options, and other relevant data that is important to consider when creating mobile content. When working with Flash content, you have even more options.

The three panels on the left of the Adobe Device Central window are used to access device profiles:

- **Device Sets**—a collection of profiles that you've grouped together. You can create groups of profiles that you use often for specific types of project, for particular clients, or even for specific content types.

- **Local Library**—device profiles that you've selectively added to your local computer so that they are available to you whether you have an active Internet connection or not. As you browse the online library, you can add devices to your local library by simply dragging them from one panel to the other.

● **Note:** The Online Library feature in Device Central CS4 requires an Internet connection.

- **Online Library**—device profiles that are stored in the Adobe database. These profiles are continuously updated with the very latest device information, ensuring that each time you launch Device Central, you will have access to the most accurate information available. Double-clicking on any device profile in the online library will add that profile to your local library. In addition, you can simply drag profiles from the online library into the local library.

Device Central provides a list of devices, with their details listed beneath them so that you can quickly compare capabilities and specifications across devices. Click on the disclosure triangle for each setting to view additional information (for example, the addressable screen size for each device). Scroll left and right to see additional devices.

Intuitive search capabilities

With so many devices to work with, it's important to be able to quickly find the profiles you need. Device Central CS4 features an easy-to-use Search capability to help you quickly locate a specific device, devices by a particular manufacturer, all devices that support a specific version of Flash Lite, and so on. The search feature is dynamic, so the list of matching devices automatically updates in the Search Results panel as you enter search criteria.

Device sets for a streamlined workflow

Speed up your workflow by creating your own device sets that you can call up at any time. By default, the device profiles available are grouped by manufacturer and sorted by name. Alternatively, you can group selected devices by carrier, supported content type, display size, supported Flash Lite version, or region. When working on a mobile project, you can create a custom device set containing any combination of devices. For example, you could create a device set that contains all available device profiles that have a particular display size and support a particular version of Flash Lite.

Creating mobile content

Intelligent integration with Creative Suite 4 components is a unique and powerful feature of Device Central CS4. You can preview and fine-tune your mobile content quickly, moving back and forth easily between Device Central CS4 and other Creative Suite 4 components.

For example, you can start a new mobile document in After Effects, Flash, Photoshop, or Illustrator, and then quickly switch to Device Central to specify your target devices and other relevant settings. Alternatively, you can start a new After Effects, Flash, Photoshop, or Illustrator mobile document from within Device Central CS4, and then edit and complete your mobile design in one or more of these authoring environments.

The consistent user interface, shared menus and functionality, and persistent mobile device sets mean that you can focus on your project and not on the settings when you're working on mobile content with any of the Adobe Creative Suite 4 component applications.

Manage files and more with mobile project files

To enhance your mobile design and development workflow even further, you can use mobile project files, which keep a collection of device profiles, source files, and publishing settings at your fingertips—all in one easy-to-manage place.

The project window consists of three sections:

- **Resource Files**—The source files needed for your mobile content.

- **Devices**—The device profiles for which your content is being developed.

- **Tasks**—Saved settings for Export services, allowing you to quickly upload content to devices.

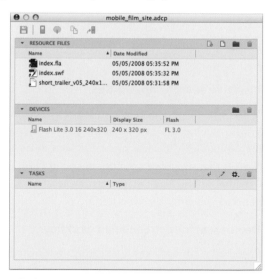

Previewing and testing mobile content

Before Adobe Device Central, it was difficult for Adobe Flash Lite developers to test files created for mobile devices. Testing content could take up to half of a developer's time as he or she struggled to manually export and test on target devices and then return to Flash to make necessary changes. Adobe Device Central CS3 gave developers the ability to easily test Flash Lite content, minimizing testing time on the actual device.

Now, with Adobe Device Central CS4, mobile developers have even more powerful tools at their fingertips. In addition to testing memory, device status and network conditions on a range of devices, Device Central CS4 makes the mobile workflow even easier and more efficient with the ability to emulate network performance, automate testing over multiple devices through recorded scripts, and even to automate the process of uploading final content to a device via Bluetooth or directly to an FTP server.

In the Emulator tab, where Device Central CS4 displays your Flash content on the selected device, you can perform a range of tests to verify that the content works as expected. More importantly, you can interact with the content just as you would with the device itself, allowing you to also test the usability of your content.

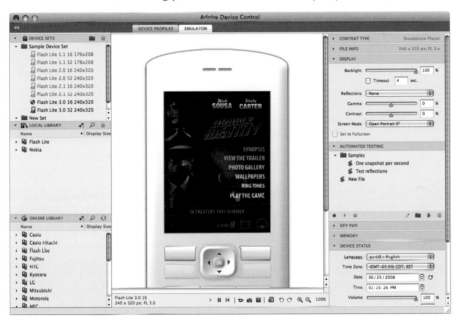

Note that in this testing scenario, the device shows how the content appears with no outdoor light reflecting on it. But that isn't always how a user will be viewing your content. Along the left side of the Adobe Device Central application are various panels that allow you to test your content with various parameters and settings.

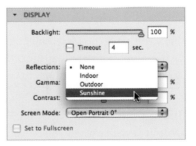

Taking snapshots

While it's wonderful to be able to emulate network performance for your content on an actual device using all of these settings, it's another challenge to explain to your client or manager how your content might appear in a range of conditions. Adobe Device Central CS4 features the ability to take snapshots of your content at any time throughout your testing routines, allowing you to share the results with others.

The Snapshots Log displays the device along with any snapshots you've taken. This provides a great way to compare various settings. In addition, Device Central makes it easy to share this information with others.

Automated testing

Taking a snapshot of your content as you test it against a single device profile is great, but you can understand that testing your content across multiple devices can be extremely time-consuming. Chances are that you want to make sure your content looks great on a wide range of devices, not just one.

Adobe Device Central CS4 introduces the facility to record a series of testing routines. You can even include snapshots within an automated testing routine, making it possible to review different portions of your content and making it easier to catch potential errors.

Once you begin recording a testing script, Device Central watches each click as you test your content, until you stop the recording—similar to the way Actions are recorded in other Adobe Creative Suite applications such as Photoshop or Illustrator.

You can then play the testing script back across multiple devices.

Once testing is complete, the Log window appears, displaying all of the devices tested, along with the snapshots that were taken during testing. You can quickly scroll through the snapshots to confirm that your content displays correctly as it plays on each device.

The Log window also tracks any Flash output (for example errors or trace messages). Output is visible when you're using the split or Output views. The output, if available, is displayed per selected device.

Publishing, collaborating, and pitching to clients

Testing content in Adobe Device Central CS4 allows both designers and developers to streamline their workflow. But testing doesn't stop at the desktop. You will often want to upload your content so that you can preview it on actual devices. This is usually done either by copying content directly to a mobile device (either via Bluetooth or via USB cable) or by uploading the content to a server via FTP.

Developers who need to test on multiple physical devices may find the process tedious to say the least. Using the Project feature in Adobe Device Central CS4, you can create Tasks, which store various publishing settings, allowing you to instantly upload or transfer your content as needed.

The task created for the illustration above copies the mobile content to the desktop, but you can just as easily create a task to upload content to an FTP server or directly to a mobile device via Bluetooth.

Capturing video

What do you do if you want to show clients how their content will look when it appears on a particular device? More importantly, what do you do if you're trying to pitch an idea to a client, or trying to bid on new business? Sure, taking a few snapshots, as we did earlier, might work. But to really show your content in the best way, it would be nice if you could show a potential client a video of your content as it is actually running.

Adobe Device Central CS4 gives you the ability to do just that. You can easily create a high-quality H.264 QuickTime video capture of your content, which you can then send out for review or to pitch an idea.

The Adobe Mobile & Devices Developer Center provides extensive online resources and information on mobile development using the Flash Professional authoring tool, tips and tricks, and code samples. Adobe also offers a free Mobile Developer Program with information and resources on Adobe mobile technologies and solutions, content development kits (CDKs), and discussion forums, as well as technical support (for an annual fee). To learn more about the Adobe Mobile Developer Program, go to www.adobe.com/go/mobiledeveloper.

Adobe Bridge CS4

Adobe Bridge CS4 is a powerful, easy-to-use media manager that's perfect for anyone who is visually oriented. Available in all editions of Adobe Creative Suite 4 software and with all professional Adobe creative applications, Bridge provides centralized access to project files, applications, and settings, as well as XMP metadata tagging and search capabilities.

Exploring the user interface

View and manage images more efficiently in a redesigned interface. You can customize the workspace to your liking and save the arrangement for reuse.

A. Backward/Forward navigation controls

B. Recent files and folders

C. Camera import

D. Web/PDF output

E. Path Bar navigation controls

F. Workspaces

G. Thumbnail quality controls

H. Ratings filter

I. Search Bar

J. Thumbnail rotation

K. Thumbnail size

L. View options

Starting Adobe Bridge

You can start Adobe Bridge directly as you would start any other application installed on your computer, or launch it from within any Adobe Creative Suite component (except Adobe Acrobat). Simply choose File > Browse In Bridge or click the Launch Bridge button (■) in the Application Bar.

Browsing files

Use Adobe Bridge, to browse, locate, and organize the assets you need to create content for print, the Web, television, DVD, film, and mobile devices. Bridge keeps native Adobe files (such as PSD and PDF) as well as non-Adobe files available for easy access. You can drag assets directly into your layouts, projects, and compositions, preview files, and even add metadata (file information), making your files easier to sort and locate.

You can use Bridge to rename, move, or delete files and to edit metadata, rotate images; and run batch commands. You can also view images and movies imported directly from your digital still or video camera.

Use the new Carousel View (View > Review) to quickly cycle through your assets, assign ratings and labels, flag rejects and create collections from the remaining candidates.

Multiple file format support

In Bridge, you can browse all you project files, including non-Adobe files, in one place without having to start the native application for each file.

Working with camera raw files

If you have Adobe Photoshop or Adobe After Effects installed, you can open or import camera raw files from Bridge, edit them, and save them in a Photoshop-compatible format. You can edit the image settings directly in the Camera Raw dialog box without starting Photoshop or After Effects, and copy settings from one image to another. If you don't have Photoshop or After Effects installed, you can still preview the camera raw files in Bridge.

Multiple artboards preview

Adobe applications such as Adobe Photoshop CS4 Extended, Adobe InDesign CS4, and Adobe Flash CS4 Professional now support multiple artboards, allowing you to select a desired artboard from an Illustrator file on import. In Adobe Bridge CS4, you can see thumbnails of the individual artboards, so you can now peek into Illustrator files without opening them. Create a single Illustrator file with designs destined for imagery, page layout, and animation, on separate artboards that can be imported by the right tool for the next step in your creative process.

Support for 3D images and more

Additional enhancements in Bridge CS4 include new Path Bar navigation and workspace selection buttons, camera import controls, PDF-based contact-sheet creation, web-gallery creation and uploading, support for 3D images and panoramas, and the intuitive new List View, with its familiar data display and sorting controls.

Workflow enhancements

Use Bridge as a central location from which you can conveniently coordinate your work in and between the other Adobe Creative Suite applications.

Color management

You can use Bridge to synchronize color settings across all color-managed Adobe Creative Suite components, ensuring that colors will look the same in any Adobe Creative Suite application.

Multi-file placement

Speed document creation by importing multiple files at once. Drag multiple files from the desktop or from Adobe Bridge CS4 directly into your document and arrange them in any order within your layout.

Powerful search tools

Quickly locate files using the powerful Filter panel, which lets you filter content by metadata properties such as file type, file modification date, keywords, aspect ratio, and orientation. Sort results by criteria ranging from filename and creation date to label and rating. Sort and search by new types of metadata criteria, including Illustrator swatches and the DICOM medical imaging format. The enhanced Find command now lets you search images using even more types of metadata criteria, including EXIF camera settings such as exposure, focal length, and aperture.

Customizable workspace

Use the Workspace menu to switch between predefined workspaces, or create your very own preferred user interface layout.

Adobe Bridge Home

Visit Adobe Bridge Home—an online channel accessible from within Adobe Bridge CS4—to keep up with what's new from Adobe and from the design, web development, and video and audio production communities at large. Watch the latest video tutorials for your Adobe Creative Suite software, listen to a podcast interview with a leading designer, or learn about the next training event in your community. Discover tips and resources that can help you work smarter and faster, making the most of the various new applications at your disposal. (Internet connection required.)

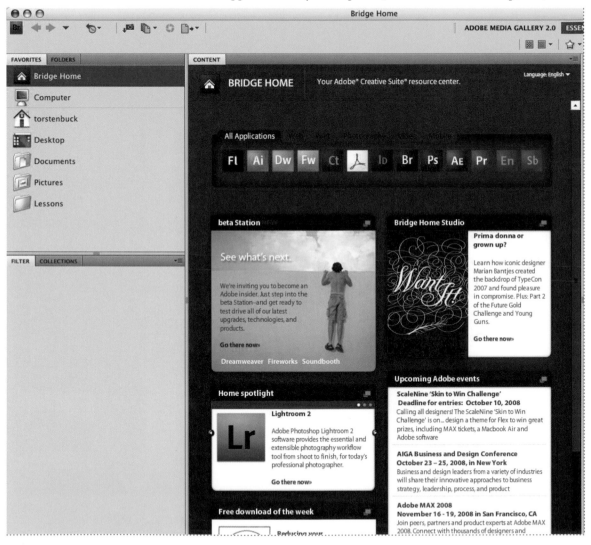

1 SETTING UP BASIC ASSETS

Lesson Overview

The way you set up your documents and create your assets will affect how easily and efficiently you can design your work. This lesson will introduce you to some important skills and concepts:

- Organizing your work in Adobe Bridge

- Refining a vector graphic in Illustrator with the Blob Brush tool

- Understanding the advantages of Live Trace

- Setting up multiple artboards for design variations

- Applying a pattern from the Illustrator library

- Getting to know Adobe kuler

- Working with the 3D tools in Photoshop Extended

- Showing your work remotely using Share My Screen

You'll probably need between one and two hours to complete this lesson.

In this lesson, you'll be working on exciting projects: painting with a pattern to add pizzazz to a graphic, creating design variations on their own artboards, and manipulating a 3D comp. You'll be preparing assets that you'll use in an interactive brochure and Flash animation in lessons to come.

● **Note:** Before you start working on this lesson, make sure that you've installed the Creative Suite 4 Design Premium software on your computer, and that you have correctly copied the Lessons folder from the CD in the back of this book onto your computer's hard disk (see "Copying the Classroom in a Book files" on page 2).

Organizing your work with Bridge

In this lesson, you'll set up some of the basic assets that you'll use for the projects in this book, which are all related to the promotion of an imaginary film noir called Double Identity. You'll be working in Adobe Bridge, Adobe Illustrator, Adobe Photoshop Extended, and Adobe Acrobat.

Adobe Bridge CS4 provides integrated, centralized access to your project files and enables you to quickly browse through your creative assets visually—regardless of what format they're in—making it easy for you to locate, organize, and view your files.

Adding folders to your Favorites

To help you access your files easily, Adobe Bridge adds your Pictures and Documents folders to the Favorites panel by default. You can add as many of your frequently used applications, folders, and documents as you like. In Bridge Preferences you can even specify which of the default favorites you wish to keep in the Favorites panel.

It would make good sense to add your Lessons folder to the Favorites panel, below your Pictures folder, where all the files you'll use for the lessons in this book will be only one click away. You could add your Lesson01 folder right below that and keep it there while you work through this chapter.

1 Launch Adobe Bridge CS4.

2 Navigate to your CS4CIB folder, and then select the Lessons folder in the Content palette. Drag it into the Favorites palette in the left panel group and drop it under the Pictures folder.

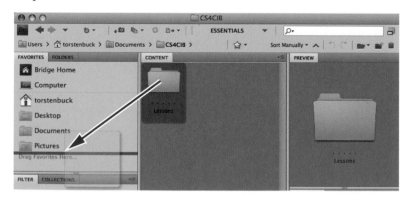

▶ **Tip:** You can also quickly add a folder to your Favorites by right-clicking / Control-clicking the folder in the Content panel and choosing Add To Favorites from the context menu.

Now your Lessons files are easily accessible. While working through the lessons in this book you'll save so much time that it'll be unimaginable to work any other way!

Adding metadata

All your documents contain some metadata, such as information about the device with which they were created. You can use Bridge to add your own metadata to a single file or to multiple files at the same time—without having to open the application specific to those files.

In this first exercise you'll see how easy it is to add metadata to a file and learn some different ways to mark it, which will make it easier to find and sort.

1 In Bridge Home navigate to your Lesson 01 folder to see the two enclosures, one Illustrator file and one Photoshop file.

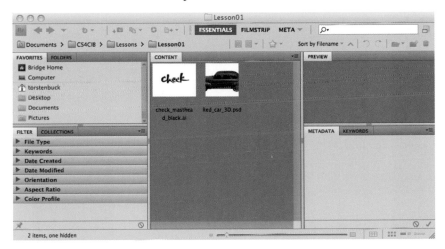

2 Click the file Red_car_3D.psd and note the metadata panel in the left panel group.

3 In the Metadata panel, open the IPTC Core panel, and type **red, oldtimer** in the Keywords text field.

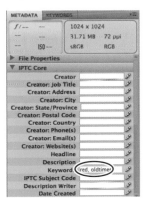

▶ **Tip:** If you can't read all your filenames or the thumbnail images are not big enough, you can enlarge them by using the Zoom slider at the lower right corner.

4 When the Adobe Bridge dialog box appears, click Apply. For future searches, the information you just added will help you to find this specific file.

Marking your files with ratings and color labels

When you're working with a large number of files and folders, assigning ratings and labels is a good way to mark a large number of files quickly, making it easier to sort and find them later.

1 In the Content menu, note the five dots above the filename Red_car_3D.psd, indicating that this file has not yet been rated. Click on the first three dots, which will change into three stars—it's that easy to assign a rating.

You can also mark a file visually by assigning a color label.

2 Right-click / Control-click the file and choose Label > Approved from the context menu. Your file is marked with a green color label, which you can also notice in the right panel group.

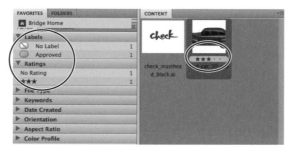

This color labeling system is not only useful to help you quickly spot the images you're looking for, but is also an effective way to sort your images by category, production status, or any other meanings you assign to the labels. This can be a useful organizational tool—especially when different people are working on the same project.

3 Right-click / Control-click the image of the car again, and this time choose Sort > By Label from the context menu. If you had multiple files with the same label they would now be grouped in the Content panel. You can change the sort order by toggling View > Sort > Ascending Order.

Synchronizing color management

Using Bridge as your central hub enables you to synchronize the color management settings across all your Creative Suite applications. It's highly recommended to use this feature so that the colors in your images will look the same regardless of which Creative Suite component application you're working with.

There are a range of options for synchronizing color management: you can specify your own color settings in the Color Settings dialog box in the relevant Adobe application, and then apply it to all the other Adobe Creative Suite applications in Bridge, or you can choose one of the Bridge presets.

1 In Bridge, choose Edit > Creative Suite Color Settings.

2 The Suite Color Settings dialog box appears. A message at the top of the dialog box tells you whether or not the settings are already synchronized. If they are not, choose North America General Purpose 2 from the color settings menu, and then click Apply.

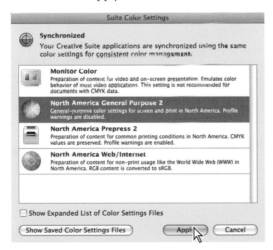

The message at the top of the Suite Color Settings dialog box should now indicate that all your CS4 applications use the same color management settings.

Creating a logo in Illustrator

When you're designing graphics such as logos and corporate identities, it's an absolute must that your design be scalable, as the graphic will be used in a wide range of applications, from web pages at screen resolution to high resolution printed matter or even monumental signage. For designing graphics that need to be resolution independent, Adobe Illustrator is the world's leading vector based application. Nowadays other applications in the Creative Suite such as InDesign and Photoshop also let you create vector graphics using the Pen tool (amongst others); however, your best choice is still Illustrator, as it includes the most comprehensive suite of drawing tools.

Bitmap versus vector graphics

Pixel- or raster-based applications such as Photoshop, are unbeatable when it comes to producing photographic (or photo-like) images. However, these images are composed of a fixed number of pixels, resulting in a jagged—or pixelated—look when they are enlarged. The illustration below shows clearly the difference between a resolution-independent vector graphic (left) and a pixel-based graphic (right).

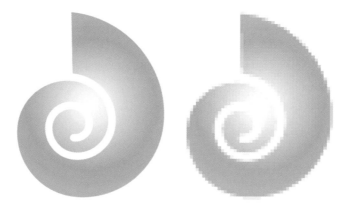

With Illustrator, you create vector graphics—artwork that is made up of points, lines, and curves that are expressed as mathematical vectors. Vector-based graphics are resolution independent—they can be scaled to any size without losing quality or crispness.

About Live Trace

A lot of great design ideas start out as a great pencil sketch on paper. To keep the precious spontaneity of such hand-drawn scribbles it's best to bring the graphics straight into Illustrator and trace them. Placing a scanned file into Illustrator and automatically tracing the artwork with the Live Trace command is the easiest way to do so. The illustrations below show masthead logo studies for a magazine called Check. You'll be working on this magazine in this and later lessons.

Live Trace automatically turns placed images into detailed vector graphics that are easy to edit, resize, and manipulate without distortion. And, as Illustrator fans know already, Live Trace enables you to produce stunning looking illustrations by changing rasterized images into vector-based drawings. You'll appreciate how quickly you can recreate a scanned drawing on-screen, maintaining its quality and authentic feel.

Refining a vector graphic with the Blob Brush tool

If you have been working with the brushes in Flash and Photoshop, you'll find similarities in Illustrator's new Blob Brush, which enables you to generate a clean vector shape as you paint. Used in combination with the Eraser tool, the Blob Brush provides a truly painterly, intuitive way to create vector shapes—merging your brush strokes into a single, fluid outline that can then be filled with solid color or painted with a gradient or even a pattern.

In this exercise you'll design a variation on an existing graphic by refining the outline of a masthead logo that was traced from handwritten artwork using Live Trace in Illustrator.

1 Click your Lessons folder in the Favorites panel, double-click the Lesson01 folder in the Content panel, and then double-click the file called check_masthead_black.ai.

● **Note:** To make sure to open your files with the right application, you can always right-click / Control-click and choose Open with in the contextual menu.

2 In Illustrator, select the Zoom tool (🔍) in the Toolbox, or press the Z key, and then zoom in close enough to scrutinize the outline of the logo in detail. Some of the unevenness you see could be smoothed out with the Blob Brush tool.

3 Before using the brush, let's first make sure it's loaded with the correct color for the check logo, which is filled with black and has no stroke. Select the Eyedropper tool (🖊) in the Toolbar and click on the logo. The Color palette will display a black fill and no stroke.

4 In the Toolbar, double-click the Blob Brush tool (🖌). When the Blob Brush Tool Options dialog box appears, choose Selection Limits Merge, drag the Fidelity slider to 3 pixels, and change the brush Size to 3 pt in the Default Brush Options. Then click OK.

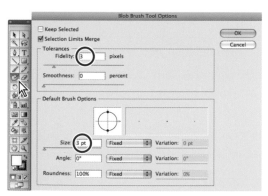

5 To demonstrate the refinements possible with the Blob Brush, let's have a closer look at the letter "e" in the check logo. Notice the dent in the lower left side. With the Blob Brush still selected, add a few strokes to smooth the outline.

6 If you are not happy with the strokes you just painted with the Blob Brush tool, use the Eraser tool from the Toolbox to correct them—you can erase your strokes without ever breaking the outline.

7 Once you're happy with your refinements to the logo, select the Zoom tool (🔍), press the Alt / Option key for the Zoom Out mode, and then click on the logo to zoom out until you can see the entire document.

You'll continue to experiment with the Blob Brush in a moment, but first you'll take advantage of another great feature of Illustrator CS4: multiple artboards, which are like separate pages within one file. You'll create another artboard for a copy of the logo.

Setting up multiple artboards

Adobe Illustrator CS4 gives you the option of working with up to 99 different artboards in a single file. You have control of the size of the artboards as well as the spacing in between them. Multiple artboards are numbered and can be printed separately.

Being able to have several artboards within one file suits very much the way most designers work: usually numerous iterations of a design concept are necessary in order to arrive at the polished finalist.

In the next exercises you'll create a design theme with variations in this way: working on different versions of a logo—naturally on separate artboards.

1 In Illustrator, select the Artboard tool (▥), or press Shift+O on your keyboard. This tool enables you to manipulate the position of an artboard or change its size, and also create new artboards. *(See illustration on next page.)*

● **Note:** During the process of opening a new Illustrator document you can specify the number of artboards you want and their size, position, and spacing in the New Document dialog box.

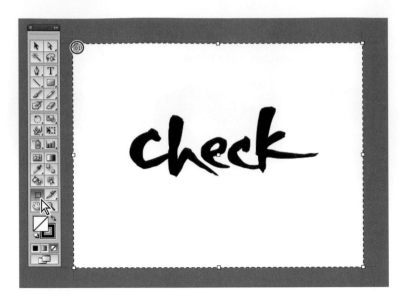

As soon as the Artboard tool is selected, the drawing area around the artboard, called the canvas, becomes grey. You can use the Zoom tool and zoom out to see the entire canvas, which is quite large. Notice also the handles on the bounding box around the artboard, which enable you to resize it whenever you choose.

2   Click the Move / Copy button (🖦) in the Artboard toolbar, where you'll also find values for the size and exact positioning of the selected artboard.

3   Press the Alt / Option key and drag the artboard with the logo to the right to create a copy. Don't release the mouse button yet. Press the Shift key to align the copy horizontally with the original artboard as shown in the illustration below. Release the mouse button before releasing the Alt / Option and Shift keys.

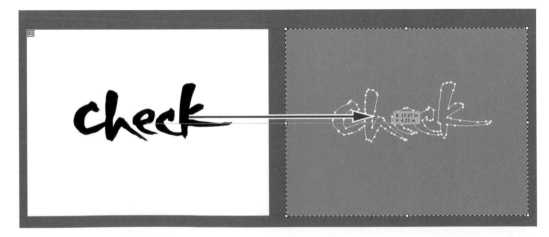

Now your Illustrator document contains two artboards, each of which is numbered in the upper left corner. Next you'll add some color to the logo on the second artboard.

Painting with a pattern

In this exercise you'll create a design variation by coloring the logo with a pattern and adding an underline using the Blob Brush tool.

1 In the Toolbox, click the Selection tool (▶) and select the check logo on the second artboard, which is marked with 02 in the upper left corner.

2 Choose Window > Swatch Libraries > Patterns > Decorative > Decorative_ Classic. The Decorative_Classic swatch palette will open up.

The Illustrator Libraries

If you have a moment, a trip to Illustrator's libraries is very worth your while. At the bottom of the Window menu you'll find access to four large libraries: The Brush Libraries, the Graphic Style Libraries, the Swatch Libraries, and the Symbol Libraries. Here you'll find a lot of little gems, which are very useful for your illustrations, whether you want a special arrow or symbol, need to customize a button for a website, are looking for a particular texture, or wish to imitate a calligraphic brushstroke or other effect—it's all in there; but wait, there's more!

Just taking a closer look at the different patterns in the Swatch Libraries, which you'll be using in the next steps, you can see that you have a wide choice of basic graphic patterns, from dots and lines, to more decorative designs and patterns derived from nature, like animal skin and foliage.

3 To adjust the size of the swatches, click the Palette Options button at the upper right of the palette and choose Large Thumbnail View from the menu.

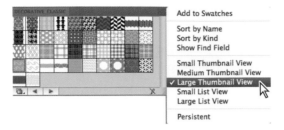

4 In the Decorative_Classic palette, select the swatch called Waves Color.

5 In the Toolbar, select the Blob Brush tool (), and paint an upwards moving line under the logo, stopping at the end of the stroke of the letter "k." Don't worry if your stroke doesn't line up completely, this can easily be fixed.

6 Using the Blob Brush, smooth out the connection of the line and logo. You might want to use the Zoom tool to have a closer look. It's quite amazing what is possible with the Blob Brush.

Generating color themes with Adobe kuler

Adobe kuler is a web-hosted application from Adobe Labs for generating color themes that can inspire any project. Whether you're creating websites, interior designs, scrapbooks, fabric patterns, graphic identities, or any other visual, you can experiment quickly with color variations and browse thousands of themes from the kuler community. Kuler themes can be accessed through any browser, via the kuler desktop, or from within Adobe Illustrator CS4.

Kuler is especially interesting when you are working with Illustrator's Live Paint, where you can choose color sets which are then alternated on a multicolored design. However, for this lesson we'll just have a quick glance at how you can find the perfect color theme for a project, and then add the colors to your Illustrator swatches.

1 In Illustrator, choose Window > Extensions > Kuler. After the Internet connection is established, the Kuler panel will appear.

2 Click to open the menu on the left at the top of the
Kuler panel. You can choose to browse through kuler's
color themes by category, or to view them in random
order. The kuler community is updated with each
new uploaded theme, so your kuler palette probably
features different themes than the ones you see in the
illustration below.

3 For now, just pick your favorite theme. We stayed
within the highest rated category and chose the theme
called Firenze. Click the second button from the right
at the bottom of the Kuler panel to add the selected
theme to your swatches.

4 When you're done, you can close the Kuler panel
by clicking the circle in the upper left corner, and
then open the Swatches palette from the menu
on the right side of your screen. The Firenze color
swatches have been added at the bottom.

This new set of colors could be used together for multicolored designs, or applied
individually, as in the illustration below. Whichever way you use it, Adobe kuler is a
great way to get inspired by color.

Verifying your document's quality settings

1   Before saving your logo variations, it's a good idea to verify the quality of your document by choosing Effect > Document Raster Effects Settings. When the Document Raster Effects Settings dialog box appears, change the default Screen Resolution (72 ppi) to High (300 ppi), and then click OK.

▶ **Tip:** When you apply an effect from Illustrator's Stylize menu such as a drop shadow or inner glow it's crucial to check the Raster Effects settings, as the wrong setting might result in ugly, fuzzy renderings of those effects.

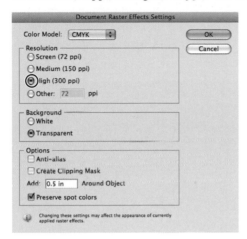

2   Choose File > Save As and save your logo variations into your Lesson01 folder, naming the file **check_masthead_variations.ai**. In the Illustrator Options dialog box, make sure the options Create PDF Compatible File, Embed ICC Profiles, and Use Compression are all activated, and then click OK.

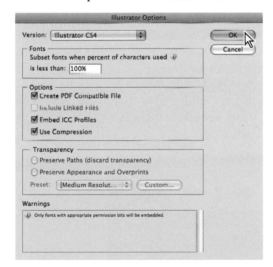

3   Close the file.

Bravo! You've finished your work on the logo, which you'll use again in the next lesson. Next you'll experiment with the 3D features in Photoshop to create an asset you'll need for a Flash animation later on. Have fun!

Working with a 3D image in Photoshop

Whether you are a professional working with 3D programs in combination with Photoshop or a traditional 2D Photoshop user—Adobe Photoshop CS4 Extended makes it easy to enhance your designs by adding 3D objects.

In the following lessons, you'll create a Flash document and website for an imaginary film noir called Double Identity. One asset for those projects is yet to be created—the three cars in the foreground. You'll use a single 3D modeled car and simply rotate it to vary the perspective.

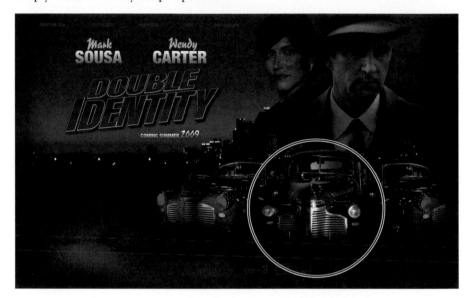

1 Switch back to Adobe Bridge and select your Lessons folder in the Favorites panel. Navigate to the Lesson01 folder and double-click the file Red_car_3d.psd—or right-click/Control-click the file and choose Open With > Adobe Photoshop CS4—to open it in Adobe Photoshop CS4.

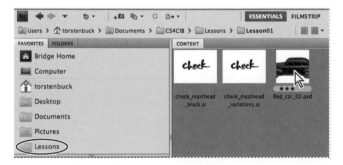

2 Once the file has opened in Photoshop CS4, you'll notice the two 3D tools in the Toolbar: The 3D Rotate tool (🔄), for rotating 3D objects, and the 3D Orbit

tool(⟳), for setting the position of the camera. In the Layers palette, make sure Layer 1 is active (selected).

3   In the Toolbar, select the 3D Rotate tool (🖐). The pointer changes to an orbit icon. Notice also that an orientation indicator with three colored axes appears in the upper left corner of the main window. The indicator's axes will help you stay oriented in the file's 3D space and correctly visualize the way you wish to manipulate the 3D object.

● **Note:** Both the 3D Rotate tool and the 3D Orbit tool have variants which can be accessed from the Toolbox and are also displayed in the Tool Options bar. You can also access the different tool variants and switch between them using keyboard shortcuts.

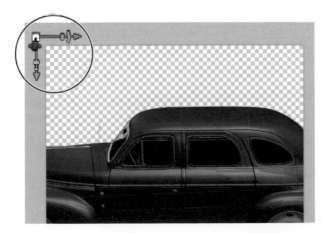

4   Position the cursor on the engine hood and drag it horizontally to the right, until you see the car almost directly from the front. Refer to the vehicle in the center

in the movie poster on page 136. You can also use the various controls on the orientation indicator to adjust the orientation of the car.

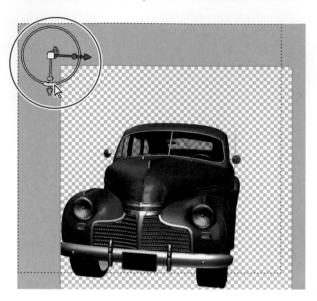

Fantastic, isn't it? You'd probably like to play around with this feature some more; go ahead—enjoy!

5 In the Tool Options bar above the document window, you can fine-tune the positioning of the car by changing the values in the Orientation settings. Type new X, Y, and Z values of **100**, **0**, and **73** respectively.

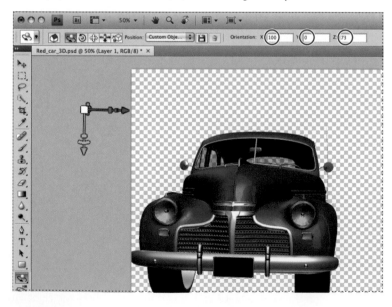

6 Save the file in your Lesson01 folder, as **Red_car_frontal.psd**, and then close it.

Painting directly onto 3D objects and applying 2D graphics

In Photoshop CS4 Extended you can paint directly onto 3D models. Textures contained in a 3D file are editable with the painting and adjustment tools.

Additionally, the new 3D engine not only speeds up the time for 3D renderings, but also offers a much richer editor for materials. Just looking at the different textures for the red car listed in the Layers palette you might get the idea of the complexity of such modeling. To display or hide an individual texture on a 3D model, click the Eye icon next to the Texture layer.

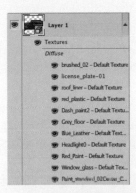

You could pick the Brush tool, choose a color, and change the color of the car—all the different materials and textures you paint on are preserved. This is what had to be done with this model for the movie poster. Choose 3D > 3D Paint Mode to see the different options for applying paint. To change the color of the car for the movie poster, which could be another little project, you'd probably start out with the Diffuse option.

You can also merge 2D image data or gradient maps onto 3D objects, and convert layers into volumes. Wrap a flat design onto a 3D object by merging the 2D layer directly onto your 3D layer. Merge two different 3D layers into a single scene. Basic presets will speed the process of turning two-dimensional designs into common 3D shapes such as spheres and cylinders. To learn more about the 3D capabilities in Photoshop, please refer to Photoshop Help.

Showing your design explorations via Share My Screen

Whether you want to review documents, provide software training, demonstrate an action within an application, or collaborate on other types of projects, using Adobe applications makes the process easy.

Lesson 6 goes into more depth about the different ways to share your work. For this lesson, let's just take a quick glance at a CS4 feature called Share My Screen, which allows you to show your work remotely—without worrying about version control or platform compatibility, or even having the same programs installed.

A picture is worth a thousand words—having the same view during a conference call with people interacting live on-screen can be of tremendous help in a meeting. You could use Share My Screen to show your logo variations to a colleague or client. Not only could you show the different artboards, but you could leave the Swatches palette and the Kuler panel open to get more input.

The big advantage of presenting your work this way is that you can control what your client or colleagues are looking at as you walk them through your project. Your input is immediate and spontaneous—all happening in real time.

1 Switch back to Adobe Bridge and select your Lessons folder in the Favorites panel. Navigate to the Lesson01 folder and double-click the file check_masthead_variations.ai to open it in Adobe Illustrator CS4.

2 In Illustrator, arrange the logo variations and palettes on your screen as you would like the other attendees at a teleconference to see them. Choosing Window > Arrange > Float In Window may help you to adjust the size of the main window.

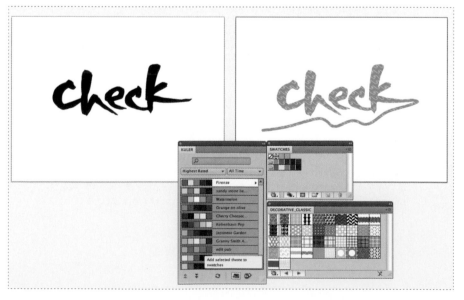

3 Choose File > Share My Screen, which will bring up the Connect Now dialog box. If you don't yet have an Adobe ID, you need to first click Create A Free Adobe ID and fill out a form before you can sign in to share you screen. You can also create an account by visiting Adobe.com.

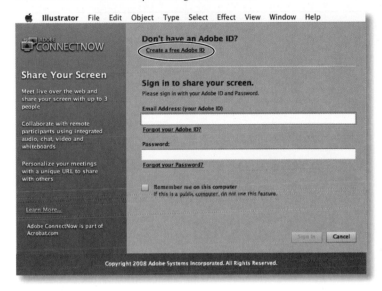

4 Once you created your Adobe ID, you need to fill in your e-mail address and password, and then click the Sign In button.

It might take a moment while Illustrator connects to the Adobe Server to sign you in. Once that happens, you'll receive a URL which you need to send to the other attendees. The other participants are then able to join your conference by logging into the web-based space from their own computers.

● **Note:** You need an active Internet connection to be able to work with Share My Screen.

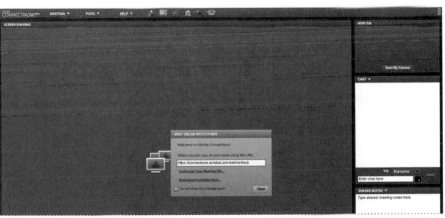

What your remote viewers will see will look something like the following screen-shot, regardless of which web browser they're using.

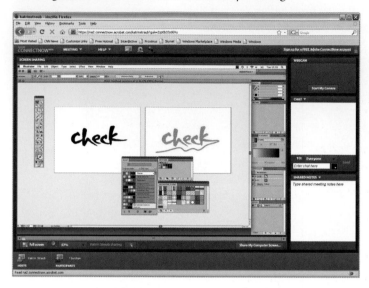

Taking a closer look at the screenshot, you'll notice that the right panel group offers more options than just sharing your desktop: use a Webcam or Live Chat, publish your notes online and more collaborative features. You'll find out more about using Share My Screen in Lesson 6.

Bravo, you've finished your first lesson! You should now feel more comfortable navigating between the different applications in the CS4 Suite using Bridge as a hub. Some of the features you used in this Lesson are rather exciting, such as the Blob Brush and the new possibilities for working in 3D—hopefully they will inspire your creative work!

Review questions

1 How can you speed up the process of finding files and folders in Adobe Bridge?

2 Why would you use Adobe Bridge to synchronize your color settings when working within Adobe Creative Suite 4 applications?

3 What is so special about the Blob Brush tool in Adobe Illustrator CS4?

4 Photoshop CS4 Extended offers two new tools to address 3D modeling. What are their names and what's the difference between them?

5 What's so cool about Adobe kuler?

Review answers

1 Select a file or folder and choose File > Add to Favorites. The file or folder will appear in the Favorites palette in the left panel group of the Bridge window, where you have easy access to it. Alternatively, you can drag the file or folder—or even an application—directly into the Favorites palette.

2 Adobe Bridge provides centralized access to your project files and enables you to synchronize color settings across all color-managed Creative Suite 4 applications. This synchronization ensures that colors look the same in all Adobe Creative Suite 4 components. If color settings are not synchronized, a warning message appears at the top of the Color Settings dialog box in each application. It is highly recommended that you synchronize color settings before starting to work with new or existing documents.

3 While sketching with the Blob Brush tool you can create a filled vector shape with a single outline, even when your strokes overlap. All the separate paths merge into a single object, which can easily be edited. You can customize the Blob Brush by specifying the stroke character and pressure sensitivity. Using the Blob Brush tool in combination with the Eraser tool enables you to make your shapes perfect—still keeping a single, smooth outline.

4 In the Toolbox, Photoshop CS4 Extended offers the 3D Rotate tool ( ) and the 3D Orbit tool ( ). Both tools enable you to work with 3D models without navigating dialog boxes or special layer contents. The 3D Rotate tool, as the name suggests, allows you turn the 3D object itself, while the 3D Orbit tool lets you define the view of a 3D object by moving the camera directed at it.

5 Finding harmonious color combinations is a challenge for a lot of creative projects. Adobe kuler, an online application, offers not only powerful tools to create such color harmonies and the ability to save them to your projects, but also the chance to share them with others, contributing to an immense on-line swatch library.

2 CREATING A BROCHURE

Lesson Overview

In this lesson, you'll learn all the skills and techniques you need to put together a sophisticated multi-media brochure:

- Using Bridge to preview and select files

- Creating a document in InDesign

- Working with multiple artboards in Illustrator files and layer comps in Photoshop files

- Adjusting Raw images

- Importing and styling text

- Working with transparency

- Adding hyperlinks and page transitions

- Editing movie files in Photoshop

- Exporting to PDF and Flash format

 You'll probably need between one and two hours to complete this lesson.

Learn how to use templates in InDesign to speed
up your design process. Add text and graphics in a
variety of file formats. Then prepare your documents
for high quality print or add interactive elements for
on-screen viewing.

Note: Before you start working on this lesson, make sure that you've installed the Creative Suite 4 Design Premium software on your computer, and that you have correctly copied the Lessons folder from the CD in the back of this book onto your computer's hard disk (see "Copying the Classroom in a Book files" on page 2).

Using Bridge to select an InDesign template

InDesign enables you to create stylish documents for a wide range of publications such as brochures, stationary, business cards, postcards, CD covers, and posters— to name just a few. For each type of document you can specify appropriate page sizes, formatting options, page layouts, type styles, and various other settings. Using a template as a starting point helps you to create professional-looking results quickly. Templates contain formatting options and settings appropriate for the type of document you want to create.

InDesign comes with a large selection of templates preinstalled. You can preview the templates in Bridge before opening them in InDesign.

1 Launch Adobe InDesign CS4.

2 In the Welcome screen, click the From Template button to create a new document from a template. If you don't see the Welcome screen, choose File > New > Document From Template.

Tip: There are many more templates available online. Go to the Adobe Exchange web site (www.adobe.com/go/exchange) and search for "templates" in the InDesign section.

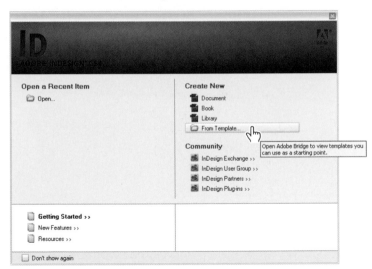

3 Wait for Adobe Bridge CS4 to open, showing the folder containing the templates that come preinstalled with your copy of InDesign. The templates are grouped in subfolders named for document categories such as Books, Brochures, and Newsletters.

Note: The location of the template files on your hard disk depends on your operating system as well as the language and version of your InDesign application. On Windows, you'll find the US English templates for InDesign CS4 in C:\Program Files\Common Files\Adobe\Templates\en_US\InDesign\6.0. On Macintosh, they are located in the folder [startup disk]:/Library/Application Support/Adobe/Templates/en_US/InDesign/6.0.

4 In Bridge, double-click to open the Miscellaneous folder and select the file Magazine.indt. In the Preview panel you can see a larger preview of the

document. If the template contains multiple pages you can use the navigation controls at the bottom of the Preview panel to inspect the additional pages.

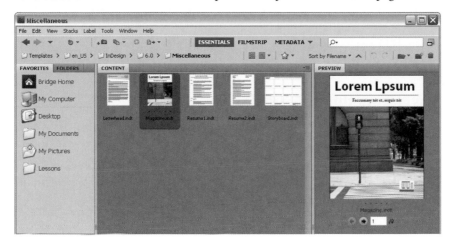

The Lesson02 folder contains an InDesign template that you will use for this lesson, which is very similar in many ways to the Magazine.indt template you've just previewed in step 4.

5   In Bridge, navigate to the Lesson02 folder on your hard disk. Within that folder, select the file Brochure_Start.indt. Then, choose File > Open With > Adobe InDesign CS4.

InDesign will create a new, untitled document, based on the selected template. You'll save this document under a new name; the template file will remain unchanged.

6   In InDesign, choose File > Save. In the Save As dialog box, navigate to the Lesson02 folder, name the document **Brochure.indd**, choose InDesign CS4 document from the Save As Type / Format menu, and then click Save.

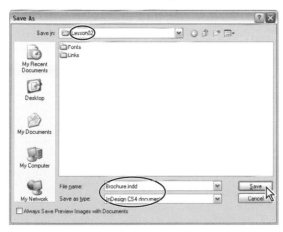

Modifying an InDesign document

Now that you have created a document from the InDesign template, you can adjust it just as you can any other InDesign document. You can replace illustrations and photos, add and stylize text, and even change the document layout settings you've acquired from the template.

Navigating through the document

Before making any changes to the document, navigate through its pages so you can plan which elements you'd like to customize.

▶ **Tip:** The visibility of menu items can be customized in InDesign. Selecting a predefined workspace may result in some menu items being hidden. If you can't find the menu item you're looking for, choose Show All Menu Items at the bottom of the menu, when available.

1 Choose Window > Workspace > [Advanced]. This will lay out all the panels you'll need for this lesson and make all menu commands visible.

2 Use the navigation buttons in the lower left corner of your document window to navigate through the pages of the brochure. Then, use the menu next to the current page number to return to the first page.

3 Click the Pages button in the right panel bin to open the Pages panel. If necessary, enlarge the Pages panel by dragging its lower right corner downwards so you can see preview images of all six pages. Double-clicking a page in the Pages panel will open that page in the main document window. Double-clicking the page number under the preview image will center the page spread in the main document window.

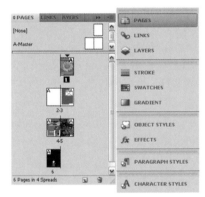

4 Click the Pages button in the right panel bin again to close the Pages panel.

Viewing the reference document

In the Lesson02 folder you'll find a PDF version of the completed brochure that you can use as a reference as you work through this lesson.

1 Switch to Bridge by choosing File > Browse In Bridge.

2 In Bridge, select the file Brochure_Final.pdf in the Lesson02 folder and choose File > Open With > Adobe Acrobat Pro 9.0.

3 In Acrobat, select View > Page Display > Two-Up and View > Zoom > Fit Width. Then, use the arrow keys on your keyboard to navigate through the spreads.

4 When you're done, return to InDesign.

Placing an Illustrator file with multiple artboards

You will start by replacing the masthead on the cover page.

1 In InDesign, navigate to the cover page. Choose View > Screen Mode > Normal and, if it's not already activated, View > Show Frame Edges.

2 Select the Type tool in the Toolbox and click anywhere inside the masthead text frame. You'll see a blinking text cursor.

3 Choose Edit > Select All, and then type **check** as the name of the brochure. Select the Selection tool ( ) from the Toolbox. Note how the title picks up the paragraph style defined in the template for the masthead, including the Inner Shadow object style assigned to the text frame.

If you're pleased with the appearance of the title as it is now, you could go on to fine-tune the type size or style or reposition the text frame on the page. For this exercise however, you'll replace the masthead text frame from the template with artwork in an Illustrator file.

4 With the masthead text frame still selected, press the Delete key or choose Edit > Clear.

5 Choose File > Place. Navigate to the Links folder inside the Lesson02 folder. Select the file Masthead.ai, activate Show Import Options, and then click Open.

The file Masthead.ai contains two artboards, each one containing a variation of the masthead design. In the Place PDF (Masthead.ai) dialog box, which appeared because you activated Show Import Options in step 5, you can preview the designs and decide which one you wish to place in the InDesign document.

6   In the Place PDF (Masthead.ai) dialog box, activate the Show Preview option in the lower left corner. In the General tab, select Previewed Page under Pages to select only the artwork visible in the Preview pane. Use the navigation controls below the preview image to navigate to page 2, containing a white version of the masthead with a drop shadow. From the Crop To menu under Options, choose Bounding Box, and then click OK.

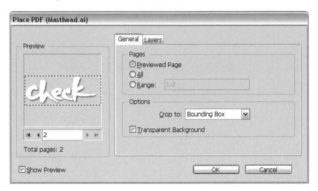

7   Position the loaded graphic cursor, which displays a preview of the illustration, near the top left corner of the cover page. Drag downwards and to the right to create a graphic frame that is about as wide as the page, and then release the mouse button.

8   Use the Selection tool to resize and reposition the text frame as shown in the illustration on the next page. Click inside the frame and wait for a moment before starting to drag—that way you'll see a preview image while you're dragging, which helps when you're positioning the frame. While resizing the graphic by dragging any handle of the frame's bounding box, hold down the

Ctrl / Command key to scale the content with the frame and hold down the Shift key to scale the graphic proportionally.

● **Note:** If your placed graphic does not look as smooth as shown in the illustration on the left, choose View > Display Performance > High Quality Display.

Selecting and repositioning frames that are stacked behind other frames

The text frame with the tagline and date is now partly hidden behind the masthead image and needs to be repositioned.

1 To select the frame with the tagline and date—which is stacked behind the frame with the masthead graphic—hold down the Ctrl / Command key, and then click inside the frame with the tagline and date.

2 Once the frame is selected, you can drag it by the anchor point at its center. Drag the frame to the left, holding down the Shift key to constrain the movement horizontally. Release the mouse button when you see the smart guide appear to indicate that the frame is centered horizontally on the page.

● **Note:** With multiple overlapping frames you may need to click repeatedly until the correct frame is selected.

3 Save your changes.

That's all there is to do for the masthead design. Next, you'll replace the main image used as the background for the front cover.

Placing a Photoshop file with Layer Comps

The Links folder contains the Photoshop file—a photo of the actor Mark Sousa—that you'll use as the background image for the front cover. You will first place the photo, replacing the sunflower image from the template, and then make adjustments to the image in Photoshop.

1 Use the Selection tool to select the frame with the sunflower image.

2 Choose File > Place. Navigate to the Links folder inside the Lesson02 folder. Select the file Cover_Image.psd, activate both Show Import Options and Replace Selected Items, and then click Open.

3 In the Image Import Options (Cover_Image.psd) dialog box, activate the Show Preview option. In the Layers tab, choose Original from the Layers Comp menu, and then click OK.

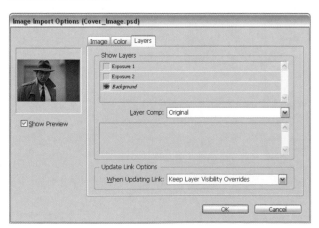

4 Choose Object > Fitting > Fill Frame Proportionally.

5 Select the image using the Direct Selection tool (🔃) and scale it proportionally to 150% using the controls in the Tools Option bar; then, drag to reposition the image as shown in the illustration below.

6 To view the cover without page frames and guide lines, click the Screen Mode button towards the right end of the menu bar and choose Preview from the menu. When you're done previewing, choose Normal from the same menu.

You will now darken some areas of the photo in Photoshop.

7 Use the Selection tool (🔃) to select the frame with the cover image and choose Edit > Edit With > Adobe Photoshop CS4.

The Quick Selection tool (🔃) in Photoshop, which is grouped with the Magic Wand tool (🔃) in the Toolbox, enables you to quickly select the silhouette of the man. By using the Refine Edge dialog box (Select > Refine Edge) you can then feather the selection to avoid harsh contrasts. Inverting the selection (Select > Inverse) creates a mask that can be used for an adjustment layer. An adjustment layer can be used to lighten or darken an image, or adjust it in many other ways. With an active selection in place only the selected image area is adjusted; the unselected areas are masked.

The file Cover_Image.psd has been prepared with one adjustment layer to darken the background (adjustment layer *Exposure 1* in the Layers palette) and another to darken the hat and clothes of the man in the foreground (adjustment layer *Exposure 2* in the Layers palette).

8 In the Layers panel, make the adjustment layer *Exposure 1* visible by clicking the eye icon and notice the effect it has on the image background. Make the adjustment layer *Exposure 2* visible and notice the effect it has on the man's hat and clothes.

You could now save the changes you've made and close the image file. When you returned to InDesign the linked file would automatically reflect the changes. But instead of doing that now, you'll learn how to use layer comps to manage multiple versions of a Photoshop image.

9 Open the Layer Comps panel (Window > Layer Comps). Two layer comps have already been defined, named *Original* and *Adjusted*. Select the layer comp *Original* and notice the effect it has on the visibility of the layers in the Layers panel. A layer comp is simply a snapshot of the visibility settings for the various layers in the Layers panel.

When placing a Photoshop file containing layer comps in InDesign you can choose which version—or layer comp—you want to use in your publication without having to reopen and adjust the file in Photoshop.

10 Close the file without saving any changes and then switch back to InDesign.

11 With the cover image still selected in InDesign, choose Object > Object Layer Options. From the Layer Comp menu in the Object Layer Options dialog box, choose Adjusted, and then click OK.

▶ **Tip:** You can hide or show each layer independently. Layer Comps are just a convenient way to hide or show preselected groups of layers.

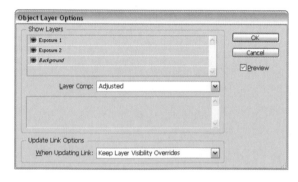

Applying paragraph styles

The brochure template offers three different sets of paragraph styles for the sell lines—the short list of contents in the text box on the left hand side of the cover. You'll select one style and apply it for all of the sell lines.

1 Open the Paragraph Styles panel (Window > Type & Tables > Paragraph Styles).

2 Select the Text tool from the Toolbar and click to place the flashing cursor inside the text frame near the left edge of the front cover.

3 Use the up and down arrow keys on your keyboard to move the text cursor from one sell line (and its description line) to the next. In the Paragraph Styles panel, notice the paragraph style specified for each of these sell lines.

To change the paragraph style for a given sell line or its description line, simply choose a different paragraph style from the Paragraph Styles panel. The style is applied to the entire paragraph in which the text cursor is currently located; it is not necessary to select the entire paragraph.

4 Place the text cursor inside the text of the first sell line "It's you… only better." In the Paragraph Styles panel select the *sell line title 2* paragraph style. Notice the change in the text in the document window.

5 Position the text cursor inside the text of the first description line "Today's Self Improvement." In the Paragraph Styles panel select the *sell line description 2* paragraph style. Notice the change in the text in the document window.

6 Change the paragraph styles for the third sell line title and description accordingly. Move the text frame with the three sell lines down on the page to complete the cover design.

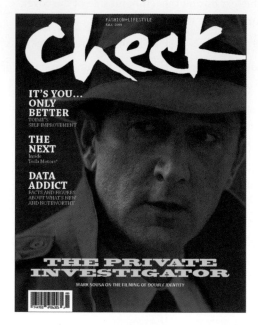

7 Save your changes.

Next you'll work on page 2 of the brochure where you'll place an image you've created from a Raw format photo. Please refer to page 2 in the Brochure_Final.pdf.

Working with Raw format images

The Raw format is becoming more and more popular for high quality digital photographs. Photoshop's Camera Raw plug-in enables you to adjust the Raw image and to then save it in a file format that can be placed in InDesign.

1 In InDesign, navigate to page 2 which is blank for now. If not already selected, choose View > Screen Mode > Normal. If you don't see guidelines on the page, choose View > Grids & Guides > Show Guides.

The red line you see around the black page border indicates the bleed area. When you want to print up to the edges of a page you generally let the image or artwork overlap into the bleed area to allow for slight inaccuracy when the page is printed and trimmed.

2 Choose File > Document Setup. In the Document Setup dialog box click the More Options button to see the Bleed and Slug section. You'll be creating an image large enough to cover the page and bleed area. The image aspect ratio should be 8,625 inch (page width plus bleed on left side) by 11,25 inch (page height plus bleed on top and bottom). Click Cancel to close the Document Setup dialog box.

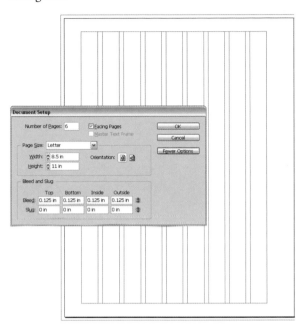

3 Choose File > Browse In Bridge to switch to Bridge. Navigate to the Lesson02 folder. Select the Raw image file named DC-3053.dng, and then choose File > Open With > Adobe Photoshop CS4. The image will open in the Camera Raw dialog box.

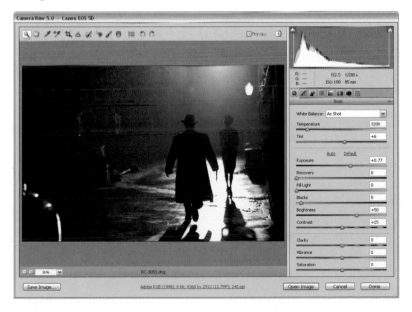

▶ **Tip:** For detailed information about digital camera raw file support in Photoshop please refer to www.adobe.com/products/photoshop/cameraraw.html.

4 To adjust the white balance in a Raw format image you can choose from a predefined setting or pick a reference area within the image. Explore the different settings in the White Balance menu in the Basic panel and note the effect on the image colors. To adjust the color relative to an area in the image that should be a neutral mid-gray, select the White Balance tool from the Toolbar and then click inside the reference area—as shown in the illustration.

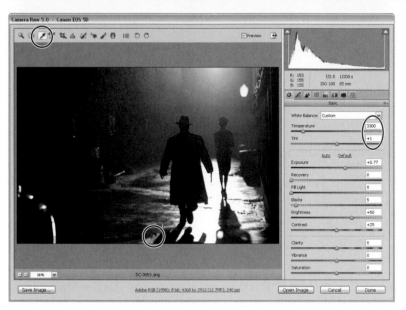

5 To specify a fixed aspect ration for the Crop tool, click and hold the Crop tool button in the Toolbar, and then select Custom from the menu. In the Custom Crop dialog box, select Inches from the Crop menu, enter **8.625** by **11.25** as crop ratio, and click OK.

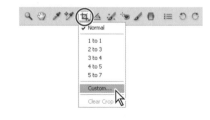

6 Using the Crop tool, drag right across the image to create a crop rectangle. Drag the crop rectangle to the top right corner of the image, and then drag the lower left handle of its bounding box towards the center of the bottom of the image—as shown in the illustration.

7 In the Lens Correction panel, create a post crop vignette effect by entering the values **80** as Amount and **10** as Midpoint.

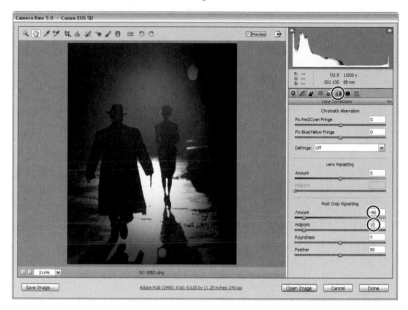

You could now click Open Image to open the image in Photoshop and make further adjustments if necessary. For this exercise, you'll just save the file in a format that can be used to be placed in InDesign.

8 Click the Save Image button in the lower left corner of the Camera Raw dialog box. In the Save Options dialog box, select the Links folder inside the Lesson02 folder as the destination for the saved file, type **_cropped** to be added to the document name, select Photoshop for the file format, and then click Save.

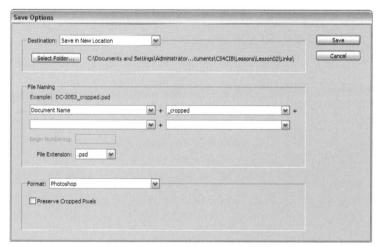

9 Click Done to close the Camera Raw dialog box and return to InDesign.

10 In InDesign, choose File > Place. In the Place dialog box, navigate to the Links folder inside the Lesson02 folder, select the file DC-3053_cropped.psd, deactivate both the Show Import Options and the Replace Selected Item options, and then click Open. Position the loaded graphic cursor, which displays a preview of the photo, at the top left corner of the slug area—that's above and to the left of the top left page corner and click—but don't drag—to place the image. The photo fits onto the page, overlapping into the slug area.

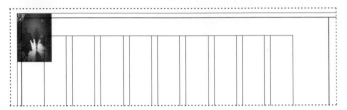

This is all there is to be done for page 2 at the moment. Additional text, such as the Double Identity logo and information about the movie and the actors, could be placed over the background image. In a more interactive version of the brochure—specifically designed for on-screen viewing—a movie trailer could be incorporated on this page. But for now, let's move on to page 3 where you'll load text from a Word document.

Importing and styling text

You can enter text directly into an InDesign document by typing into the text frames. For longer text passages, however, it is more common to import text from an external text document. You can style the text as part of the import process or manually change the text appearance later.

1 In InDesign, navigate to page 3 of the brochure document.

The three text columns of the main story are filled with placeholder text. You'll replace the placeholder text with text from a Word document.

2 Select the Type tool in the Toolbar and place the cursor anywhere in the text in the three main text columns on page 3. Choose Edit > Select All. The text in all three columns is selected because the text columns are linked.

3 Choose File > Place. In the Place dialog box, navigate to the Lesson02 folder, select the file Main_Story.doc, activate both the options Show Import Options and Replace Selected Item, and click Open.

4 Under Formatting in the Microsoft Word Import Options (Main_Story.doc) dialog box, activate the options Preserve Styles And Formatting From Text And Tables, and Customize Style Import. Click the Style Mapping button.

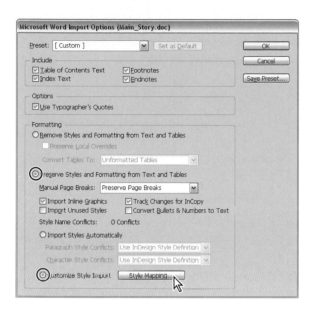

The Style Mapping dialog box enables you to match type styles defined in the Word document to type styles defined in the InDesign document. If you set up the styles with identical names, InDesign can perform the mapping automatically.

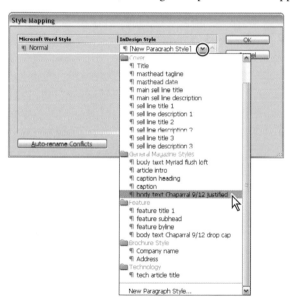

In this case the text in the Word document is not preformatted. You'll import the text without formatting information and then apply text styles in InDesign.

5 Click Cancel to close the Style Mapping dialog box.

6 Under Formatting in the Microsoft Word Import Options (Main_Story.doc) dialog box, select Remove Styles And Formatting From Text And Tables, and then click OK. If a Missing Fonts dialog box appears, click OK.

The imported text replaces the text in the three text frames. You can now apply text styles to design the page layout.

7 With the Type tool still selected and the text cursor located anywhere inside the text you just imported, choose Edit > Select All. In the Paragraph Styles panel, select the paragraph style *body text Chaparral 9/12 justified* located in the General Magazine Styles subfolder.

The text now fits easily into the allocated space.

8 Place the text cursor in the first paragraph of the story, and then select the paragraph style *body text Chaparral 9/12 drop cap* from the Feature subfolder in the Paragraph Styles panel. This paragraph style uses a drop cap; especially designed to draw attention to the beginning of a story. To visually structure the text story, you can apply a different character style to the beginnings of a few paragraphs, as shown in the illustration below. Select the text portion you want to stylize, and then choose the character style *feature section start bold* from the Feature subfolder in the Character Styles palette.

Wrapping text around frames

To finish the design of this page, you'll place an image in the frame set aside for this purpose and place a pull-quote over the main text. The main text—wrapping around the pull-quote—will then fit perfectly into the three text columns.

1   Use the Selection tool to select the frame positioned across the top of the two text columns on the right. To select this frame, either click carefully between the two text columns, or hold down the Ctrl / Command key and click inside the frame.

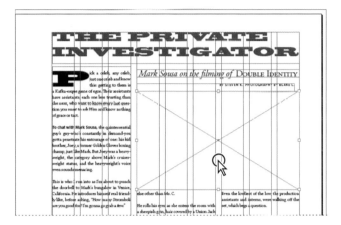

2   Choose File > Place. In the Place dialog box, navigate to the Links folder inside the Lesson02 folder. Select the file Feature_Image.tif, deactivate Show Import Options, activate the Replace Selected Item option, and then click Open.

3   Choose Object > Fitting > Frame Fitting Options. Under Alignment in the Frame Fitting Options dialog box, select the center reference point, and then choose None from the Fitting menu under Fitting On Empty Frame. Then click OK.

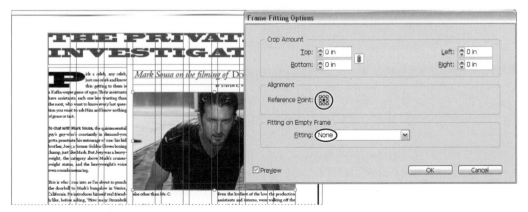

4   In the Tools Options bar, select the Wrap Around Object Shape option. If necessary, you can adjust the amount of space around the image in the Text Wrap panel (Window > Text Wrap).

5   Using the Direct Selection tool, select the image inside the frame by carefully clicking between the two text columns. Use the controls in the Tools Options bar to scale the image proportionally to 150%; then, drag to reposition it inside its frame as shown in the illustration below.

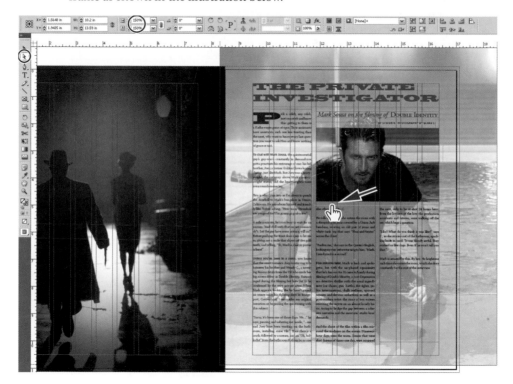

6   Select the Type tool from the Toolbox. Drag in the slug area to the right of the page to create an empty text frame about 5 inch wide and 2 inch high; you'll adjust the dimensions later. Enter a short quote from the main text into that text frame. We used: "**It was bloody awful. They worked us like dogs.**"

7   Select the entire quote and choose the paragraph style *feature subhead* from the Feature folder in the Paragraph Styles panel. Use the controls in the Tools Options bar to set the type size to 31 pt, the leading to 36 pt, and the alignment to Align Left.

8   With the Selection tool, drag the new text frame from the slug area onto the page. Referring to the smart guides, release the mouse button when the center

of the new text frame is aligned with the vertical center line of the middle text column and the top is aligned with the horizontal center line of the main text frame.

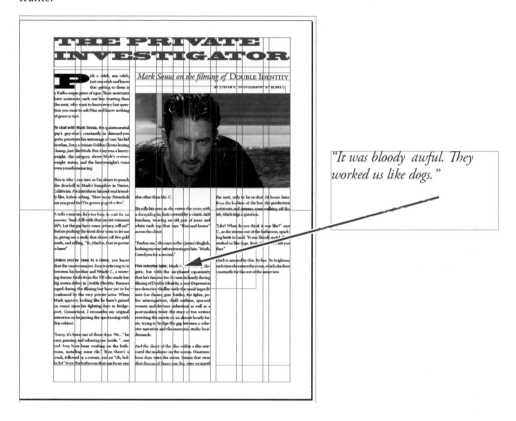

9   In the Tools Options bar, select the Wrap Around Object Shape option. Select the center reference point at the left end of the Tools Options bar, and then set the Width of the text frame to 4.7 inches and the Height to 1 inch.

10 Click the text frame and wait a short moment before you start dragging it downwards. Hold down the Shift key as you drag to constrain the movement. Notice how the main story text reflows as you drag, giving you a live preview of your change. Release the mouse button when the Y position value is between 7.15 inch and 7.17 inch. The main story text should now fit perfectly into the three text columns. Refer to the file Brochure_Final.pdf as reference.

11 Select the text of the pull-quote with the Text tool, and then click the Eyedropper tool in the Toolbox. Hold down the Shift key and sample the text color from the main headline to be used for the pull-quote; then save your work.

Preparing for printing

You've completed the design of the brochure. Since the document contains transparency effects there are a few more adjustments necessary to get the best print results.

Working with transparency

1 In InDesign, navigate to page 4 of the brochure document.

The two text frames in the lower part of the page contain a partially transparent background color—white with an opacity value of 65% (see Window > Effects). This is noticeable as a faded or dimmed effect where the two text frames are overlaid on the background image in the upper part of the page. Transparent areas in a document need to be flattened—or rasterized—when printed. For best results, flattening should be done as the last possible step in your print workflow—normally performed by your print service provider. To keep transparency effects live up until they need to be flattened, preserve

the layers by saving your InDesign documents (or placed Illustrator or Photoshop files) in native format.

● **Note:** If the backgrounds of the text frames display as solid white on your screen, choose View > Display Performance > High Quality Display. If you still don't see the transparency, check your view settings preferences (Edit > Preferences > Display Performance); set transparency to be rendered at high quality for your display performance mode. Your preferences for the display performance have no effect on how transparency is rendered when exported or printed.

2 To see which areas of your document are affected by transparency effects, open the Flattener Preview panel (Window > Output > Flattener Preview), select Transparent Objects from the Highlight menu and choose [High Resolution] from the Preset menu. Then choose in turn in the Highlight menu: All Affected Objects, Affected Graphics, and All Rasterized Regions.

One thing to watch out for is text placed behind objects with transparency effects. Transparency affects all objects placed lower—or further back—in the display stacking order. Printed text might not look as crisp as it should if it was converted to outlines and rasterized behind an object with a transparency effect.

3 Choose Outlined Text from the Highlight menu. There is no problem area visible on this page.

4 Switch to the cover page of the brochure—page 1—and choose Transparent Objects from the Highlight menu in the Flattener Preview panel. Notice that the placed Illustrator artwork for the masthead contains a transparency effect: the drop shadow.

5 Choose Outlined Text from the Highlight menu. Notice the highlighted text in the text frame containing the masthead tagline and date.

You can fix the problem by moving that text frame above the Illustrator artwork in the stacking order.

6 To select the frame with the tagline and date, which is stacked behind the masthead graphic, hold down the Ctrl / Command key, and then click inside the frame with the tagline and date. Choose Object > Arrange > Bring To Front. The text frame is now placed above the Illustrator artwork and no longer affected by the transparency effect.

7 Close the Flattener Preview panel.

To preserve transparency effects rather than flattening them when exporting a document as a PDF intended for printing, save your file in a format compatible with Adobe PDF 1.5 (Acrobat 5.0) or later—by selecting the PDF/X-4 PDF export preset, for example. The Adobe PDF Print Engine (APPE)—widely embraced by OEM partners and print service providers since first released in 2006 and updated to version 2 in 2008—uses native rasterizing for PDF documents, ensuring file integrity from start to finish in a PDF-based design workflow. To learn more about the Adobe PDF Print Engine, please refer to www.adobe.com/products/pdfprintengine.

If you need to flatten your document as part of the export or print process, set the transparency blend space (Edit > Transparency Blend Space) to the color space (CMYK or RGB) of the target output device. For more information about working with transparency see "Best practices when creating transparency" in InDesign Help.

Checking the effective resolution of linked images

You can use the Links palette to verify that the linked images have a high enough resolution for your intended mode of output. The effective resolution of a placed image is defined by the resolution of the original image and the scale factor at which it is placed in InDesign. For example, an image with a 300 ppi (pixels per inch) resolution only has an effective resolution of 150 ppi when it's scaled to 200%.

For images to be viewed at screen resolution—published on a website or in a low resolution PDF document, for example—an effective resolution of 72 ppi is sufficient. For desktop printing, the effective resolution should be between 72 ppi and 150 ppi. For commercial printing your images should have an effective resolution between 150 ppi and 300 ppi (or higher), depending on the requirements of your prepress service provider.

1   In InDesign, open the Links panel. Choose Panel Options from the panel options menu. In the Panel Options dialog box, activate the Actual PPI, Effective PPI, and Scale options in the Show column. Click OK to close the Panel Options dialog box. If necessary, resize the Links panel so that you can see the additional columns.

2   For each image placed in your document, check the actual resolution, the effective resolution, and the scale factor. The cover image on page 1, for example, has an actual resolution of 240 ppi but only an effective resolution of 160 ppi because a scale factor of 150% was applied to the image. If a higher effective resolution is required for your print job, you could reduce the scale factor, which would show more of the image background,

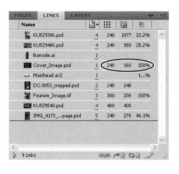

reduce the dimensions of the placed image—not really an option for the cover photo, which needs to cover the entire page—or select an image with a higher actual resolution: perhaps a close-up photo of the face rather than the wider shot that we used.

3   Close the Links panel.

Performing a preflight check

Rather than painstakingly checking through a list of possible problem areas each time you want to print or export a document; you can rely on InDesign to do all the work for you.

1   Choose Window > Output > Preflight. In the Preflight panel, click the On checkbox to activate Preflight checking, so that InDesign will continuously check for possible problems while you're working on your document.

You can set up a preflight profile to specify which potential problems you want InDesign to look out for.

2   To define a preflight profile, choose Define Profiles from the Preflight panel options menu or from the Preflight menu located near the lower left corner of the document window.

3   In the Preflight Profiles dialog box, click the Add button (➕) below the list of profiles to create a new profile. Name the new profile **My Preflight Profile**. Activate the Image Resolution option inside the IMAGES And OBJECTS folder. Leave the Image Color Minimal Resolution set at 250 ppi, and then click OK.

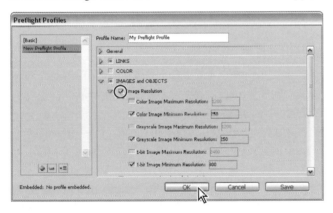

4   From the Profile menu in the Preflight panel, choose My Preflight Profile. InDesign finds several placed images which don't meet the set requirements. To review an error found by the Preflight check, click the page link in the Preflight panel. InDesign selects and jumps to the object causing the error. A description of the error and suggestions on how to fix the problem are given in the Info section of the Preflight panel. *(See illustration on next page.)*

5 Switch back to the previous preflight profile by choosing [Basic] from the Profile menu in the Preflight panel, and then close the Preflight panel.

6 Save your document.

Exporting to PDF

Exporting your document as a PDF file enables you to preserve the look and feel of your InDesign document in a device independent format that can be viewed on-screen or printed on any printer. This can be particularly useful when you want to print a quick draft of your document on the inkjet printer at home or in your office. You can tweak the export settings, balancing quality and file size to create a PDF that is optimized to suit its intended purpose.

1 Choose File > Export. In the Export dialog box, navigate to the Lesson02 folder. From the Save As Type / Format menu, choose Adobe PDF; then, name the file **Brochure_Print.pdf** and click Save.

2 In the Export Adobe PDF dialog box, choose [High Quality Print] from the Adobe PDF Preset menu. Review—but don't change—the settings for this export preset in the various panels of the dialog box, and then click Export.

3 Open the Lesson02 folder in Windows Explorer / the Finder. Right-click / Control-click the file Brochure_Print.pdf and choose Open With > Adobe Acrobat Pro from the context menu.

4 In Acrobat, choose View > Page Display > Two-Up and then choose View > Page Display > Show Cover Page During Two-Up.

5 Use the page navigation controls in Acrobat to review the pages of the brochure. Pay special attention to the position and quality of the images you placed, the text styles you've adjusted, and the areas containing transparency effects.

6 When you're done reviewing, close the document in Acrobat and switch back to InDesign.

Adding interactive elements

When you publish a brochure (or a newsletter, or flyer—you name it) for on-screen viewing rather than for print, you can include dynamic and interactive content in the document. Add animated page transitions, hyperlinks between pages, links to web pages on the Internet, embedded or streamed video files, and more.

Creating hyperlinks

Web surfers and readers of interactive PDF or Flash documents are so accustomed to using hyperlinks that their absence would be more surprising than their presence. Readers expect that when they click an entry in a table of contents they will jump to the respective page in the document. Luckily, hyperlinks are easily created in InDesign and are fully functional when exported to PDF or Flash format.

1 In InDesign, navigate to the cover page of the brochure.

2 Choose View > Screen Mode > Normal. With the Selection tool, click the text frame near the bottom of the page containing the headline "The Private Investigator." Once the document is exported, clicking anywhere on that text should take the reader to the main story on page 3.

3 Right-click / Control-click the text frame and choose Interactive > New Hyperlink from the context menu.

4 From the Link To menu in the New Hyperlink dialog box, choose Page. Under Destination, select Brochure.indd from the Document menu and type **3** as the destination Page number. To maintain the same level of magnification the reader is using when they click the hyperlink, choose Inherit Zoom from the Zoom Setting menu. Under Appearance, choose Invisible Rectangle from the Type menu and Invert from the Highlight menu. Make sure your settings are exactly as shown on the illustration on the next page, and then click OK.

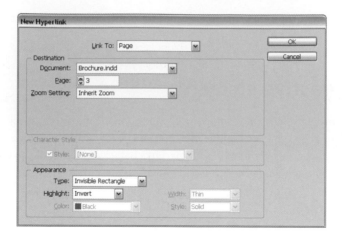

You've just created a hyperlink that uses a text frame as the source and a page inside the document as the destination. You can create a hyperlink that uses a graphic frame as the source in the same way. In the next step you'll define a text selection—instead of an entire text frame—as a hyperlink source.

5   Use the Type tool to select the second sell line title and description inside the text frame on the left side of the cover page. Right-click / Control-click the text selection and choose Interactive > New Hyperlink from the context menu, or, with the text selected in the text frame, click the Create New Hyperlink button in the Hyperlinks panel (Window > Interactive > Hyperlinks).

6   In the New Hyperlink dialog box, use the same settings you used in step 4, but type **4** instead of 3 for the destination Page number. Click OK to close the New Hyperlink dialog box.

▶ **Tip:** The destination of a hyperlink can be a page in the same document—as in this case—or a page in another document. It can be a specific location within a page which you've previously defined as a hyperlink destination, or a URL address on the Internet. You can set up a hyperlink to open another document or open a new e-mail message in a mail application with a predefined recipient and subject line. See InDesign Help for more information on hyperlinks.

Creating page transitions

One way you can make your document more dynamic is by adding page transitions. Choose the transition you want in InDesign—then export your document in PDF or Flash format and see the effect in action in Adobe Reader, Acrobat, the Flash player, or even a web browser.

1   In InDesign, open the Pages panel (Window > Pages). From the panel options menu, choose Page Transitions > Choose. In the Page Transitions dialog box, hold the pointer over each of the transition thumbnails to see animated previews of the various page transition effects.

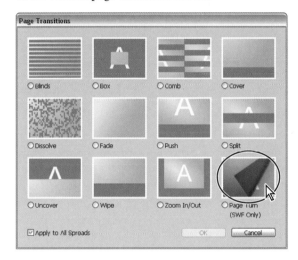

2   The first eleven page transitions correspond to the page transitions with the same names available for a PDF document in Adobe Acrobat. For this exercise, select the Page Turn (SWF Only) page transition, activate the Apply To All Spreads options, and then click OK.

Exporting in SWF (Shockwave Flash) format

InDesign enables you to export your documents directly in SWF (Shockwave Flash) format, a file format especially designed for multimedia presentation containing animations and interactive elements.

1   SWF files use an RGB color space. To avoid color changes when flattening the areas with transparency in the document during export, choose Edit > Transparency Blend Space > Document RGB.

2   Choose File > Export.

Tip: Choose Adobe
Flash CS4 Pro (XFL) as
file format to process
your document further
in Adobe Flash CS4.
Each page spread is
converted to a keyframe
in the main scene. The
graphic and text objects
on each page will
remain editable.

3   In the Export dialog box, navigate to the Lesson02 folder, choose SWF from the
Save As Type / Format menu, name the file **Brochure_Screen.swf**, and then
click Save.

Tip: When designing
specifically for the web
you should consider
using a horizontal page
layout.

4   In the Export SWF dialog box, activate the Fit To option and select 800 x 600
(Full Screen) from menu beside it. This will scale the document down slightly to
fit better on a standard computer screen. Choose to export All Pages, activate
the Spreads and Generate HTML File options, and disable the options Rasterize
Pages and View SWF After Exporting. Choose InDesign Text To Flash Text from
the Text menu. This option will make it more convenient if you plan to edit your
document further: you'll be able to edit the text while the document is open in
Flash. Activate all four Interactivity options, leave the image compression and
quality settings unchanged, and then click OK.

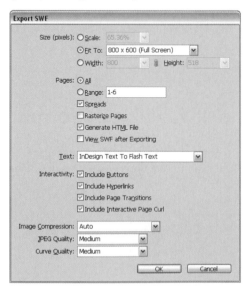

5 If an alert appears, warning that interactive elements may not work correctly when overlapping objects with transparency, click OK.

6 Wait until the export is complete, then switch to Windows Explorer / the Finder. Right-click / Control-click the file Brochure_Screen.swf in the Lesson02 folder and choose Open With > Adobe Flash Player 10 from the context menu.

7 In Adobe Flash Player, hold the pointer over either the upper right or lower right corner of the cover page and notice that the page starts peeling back as if it were a paper version of the brochure. Drag all the way to the left to turn the page *(see illustration below)*, or click to have the Flash Player turn the page for you.

8 Return to the cover page. Hold the pointer over the two hyperlinks you created earlier on in this lesson. When you hold the pointer over a hyperlink, the hand cursor appears. Click the hyperlink to jump directly to the hyperlink destination.

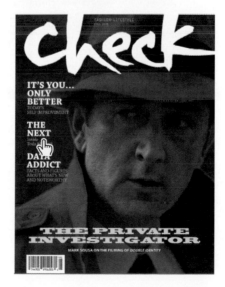

9 When you're done reviewing the brochure and playing with the page turn effect, close the Adobe Flash Player and return to Windows Explorer / the Finder.

10 Double-click the file Brochure_Screen.html in the Lesson02 folder to open it in your default web browser. Depending on your security settings, you may have to allow blocked content.

▶ **Tip:** You can upload the files to your web server and have your client preview the page design in a standard web browser.

In a standard web browser, flipping through the pages of the brochure works the same way as it did in the Adobe Flash Player. You can drag to turn pages or click on hyperlinks to jump directly to the articles you're interested in.

11 When you're done, close your web browser and return to InDesign.

Placing movies

You can place movies in an InDesign document in the same way as you would place static images. Although you can't preview the movie within the InDesign document you can specify a variety of options on how the movie will behave in the exported document.

1   In InDesign, navigate to page 2 of the brochure document.

2   Choose File > Place. In the Place dialog box, navigate to the Links folder inside the Lesson02 folder. Select the file Trailer.mov, disable the options Show Import Options and Replace Selected Item, and then click Open. Click on the page to place the movie in the document and then position the frame near the lower right corner of the page, as shown in the illustration below.

● **Note:** You'll need QuickTime 6.0 or later to work with movies in InDesign. You can add QuickTime, AVI, MPEG, and SWF movies, and WAV, AIF, and AU sound files. InDesign supports only uncompressed 8- or 16-bit WAV files.

3   Using the Selection tool, double-click the frame containing the placed movie to open the Movie Options dialog box.

4 Under Options in the Movie Options dialog box, select Choose Image As Poster from the Poster menu. Click the Browse / Choose button, navigate to the Links folder inside the Lesson02 folder and select the file TrailerAlt.psd; then, click Open. This image is shown on the page when the movie is not playing. Choose Play Once Then Stop from the Mode menu and activate the option Show Controller During Play. Under Source, activate the Embed Movie In PDF option, and then click OK.

Tip: To keep the file size of the resulting PDF file small you can choose to stream the video from a file server on the Internet rather than embedding the movie file. This also enables you to change the content of the streamed movie even after the PDF document has been distributed. You could stream a different trailer each day or change the text shown across the movie.

When exported to either PDF or SWF format, you can play the trailer within the document by clicking on the movie poster. But before you do that let's review how the trailer was prepared using Photoshop Extended CS4.

Editing movies in Photoshop

When you import video in Photoshop Extended, the image frames are placed in a video layer. You can add layers above that video layer to apply image adjustments or to overlay text and graphics. You can even add keyframes to have your adjustments change over time.

1 Switch to Photoshop Extended CS4. Choose File > Open. In the Open dialog box, navigate to the Lesson02 folder. Select the file Trailer_Double_Identity.psd and click Open.

2 Choose Window > Workspace > Video. Notice the Animation panel across the bottom of the work area. Drag the current-time indicator to navigate through the individual image frames of the movie. *(See illustration on next page.)*

3 In the Layers panel, notice the text layer placed above the video layer. The text FOR REVIEW PURPOSES ONLY is overlaid for the duration of the trailer. You can change the text, draw or place other graphics, add adjustment layers, and create timeline-based animation. For more information see the Video And Animation section in Photoshop Help. For now, just leave everything as it is.

4 Choose File > Export > Render Video. The Render dialog box offers a variety of file formats and compression options. Rendering may take some time depending on the performance of your computer. Click Cancel to close the Render Video dialog box; the movie file you've just placed in the InDesign document is a rendered version of this file.

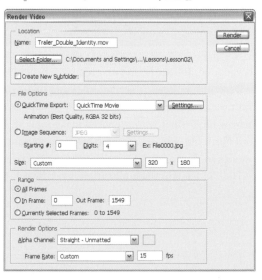

● **Note:** You must have
Acrobat 6.x or later to
play MPEG and SWF
movies in a PDF file—or
Acrobat 5.0 or later to
play QuickTime and AVI
movies.

5 Switch to Windows Explorer / the Finder. Right-click / Control-click the file
Brochure_Movie.pdf inside the Lesson02 folder and choose Open With > Adobe
Acrobat 9 from the context menu.

6 Navigate to page 2 of the document and click the poster image to start the
playback of the trailer inside your PDF document.

7 Sit back and enjoy the show!

This concludes the lesson on creating a brochure. You've learned how to use
InDesign templates, place graphics and text, work with Illustrator files containing
multiple artboards and Photoshop files with layers comps. You've adjusted photos
in Raw file format, and prepared files for print. You learned about exporting to PDF
and Flash file format, adding hyperlinks and interactive elements, and adjusting
movies in Photoshop. For a more in-depth coverage of all these subjects please refer
to Help in each of the applications and the other books in the Classroom in a Book
series.

Review questions

1 How can you select a frame that is stacked behind another in an InDesign document?

2 When placing an Illustrator file with multiple artboards in InDesign how do you specify the artboard from which to import?

3 What is a layer comp?

4 What is the effective resolution of an image placed in InDesign?

5 How do you place a movie file in an InDesign document?

Review answers

1 To select a frame that is stacked behind another frame, hold down the Ctrl / Command key, and then click inside the frame you want to select. With multiple overlapping frames you may need to click repeatedly until the correct frame is selected. You can also select the top-most frame, and then choose Object > Select > Next Object Below.

2 In the Place dialog box, activate Show Import Options. In the Place PDF dialog box, select which pages to import. You can select the content of more than one artboard and InDesign will let you place one illustration after the other into the document without invoking the Place command repeatedly.

3 A layer comp is a snapshot of the visibility settings of layers in a Photoshop document that can be used to organize multiple versions of a design in a single document. When placed in InDesign, you can quickly switch between the layer comps using the Object Layer Options dialog box.

4 The effective resolution of a placed image is defined by the actual resolution of the original image and the scale factor when placed in InDesign. For example, an image with a 300 ppi (pixels per inch) resolution only has an effective resolution of 150 ppi when scaled to 200%. Documents intended for print require images with a higher effective resolution than documents to be viewed only on screen.

5 You can place movies in an InDesign document in the same way as you would place static images. Choose File > Place and select a movie file in QuickTime, AVI, MPEG, or SWF format. Set playback options in the Movie Options dialog box.

3 PROTOTYPING AND BUILDING A WEBSITE

Lesson Overview

In this lesson, you'll learn these skills and techniques:

- Prototyping a website in Fireworks
- Placing, scaling, and adjusting images
- Working with layers
- Adding a navigation bar
- Using master pages
- Adding dummy text and rollover behaviors
- Presenting the prototype
- Developing a website in Dreamweaver
- Setting up a page framework with CSS
- Incorporating pages from Fireworks
- Round-trip editing between Fireworks and Dreamweaver

 This lesson will take about two hours to complete.

Learn how to use Fireworks to rapidly prototype a website design—complete with interactive links and rollover behaviors. Preview the pages in a standard web browser and get client approval before you start the website development in Dreamweaver. Incorporate the assets created in Fireworks and replace placeholder items.

Note: Before you start working on this lesson, make sure that you've installed the Creative Suite 4 Design Premium software on your computer, and that you have correctly copied the Lessons folder from the CD in the back of this book onto your computer's hard disk (see "Copying the Classroom in a Book files" on page 2).

Planning for a website

Creating a website requires careful planning and preparation. Before spending a considerable amount of time coding the actual pages, you'll need to ensure that what you're developing is what your client expects. But since the client usually wants to see how the project will look like when it's finished before approving the design you have a dilemma.

You need to present the client a visual representation of the website design—ideally with fully functional rollover buttons and page links—without actually coding the pages in Dreamweaver.

The solution is to use Fireworks as a rapid prototyping tool. Fireworks enables you to quickly create a mock-up of a few pages of a website—including interactive elements—that can then be previewed in a standard web browser. Once the client approves the design you can reuse the work you've done in Fireworks for the development of the website in Dreamweaver.

In fact, as you will see in Lesson 4, "Creating interactive Flash and PDF documents," you can use the same design prototype for more that just building a website.

A typical workflow

Designing a website from start to finish follows these basic steps:

- Together with the client, define the scope of the project, including the objectives of the website, the target audience, schedule, and available resources.

- Develop a design strategy and establish the look and feel of the web pages.

- Create a prototype of the website in Fireworks.

- Present the design to the client and refine it as necessary to obtain approval.

- Assemble the required assets and create the website in Dreamweaver.

This lesson will focus on designing the website prototype in Fireworks, and then incorporating that work into a Dreamweaver project.

The website you'll develop consists of a main page and three other pages, connected by hyperlinks as show in the illustration below.

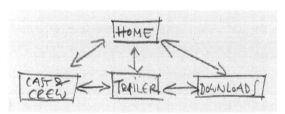

The design sketch for the home page shown in the illustration below was the result of a meeting with the client to establish the overall look and feel of the website.

Based on the design sketches some images have been specially prepared incorporating the common assets created in Lessons 1 and 2.

Previewing the assets in Bridge

To get a first impression of the images that will be used in this lesson you can preview the files in your Lesson03 folder using Bridge.

1 Start Adobe Bridge CS4.

2 In Bridge, navigate to the Lesson03 folder on your hard disk. Within that folder, select the file CityBackground.psd. This image will serve as the background for the website pages.

3 In the Metadata panel, note the pixel dimensions for this image: 1280 x 787 pixels. This will be the page size—the size of the stage or canvas, if you prefer to using these terms—for the design in Fireworks.

4 Select the file Cars.psd. Only the car in the middle comes from a photo taken during the shooting of the film. The image of the car on the left was created from a 3D model as shown in Lesson 1. The car on the right is a flipped copy of the image on the left.

5 Select the file WendyAndMark.psd. The photos of the two main actors were placed on separate layers in the Photoshop file. The silhouettes were masked using the Quick Selection tool and the image background removed—a technique similar to that used for the brochure cover in Lesson 2.

6 Select the file LogoLockup.psd. The Double Identity logotype was designed in Illustrator, and then placed in a Photoshop file. The other text was created in Photoshop by applying a gradient overlay to a type layer. For the purposes of this exercise the type layers have been rasterized, in case you don't have the appropriate fonts installed.

You won't use the rest of the images in the Lesson03 folder until later in this lesson.

Creating a prototype website in Fireworks

In the following exercises you'll work on two pages of a prototype website in Fireworks. In the process you'll place images, use layers to arrange and organize the page elements, create master pages for items that are shared across pages, add hyperlinks and rollover behaviors, and finally preview the design in a web browser.

Setting the stage

You'll begin by creating a new document in Fireworks.

1 Launch Adobe Fireworks CS4.

2 Click the Create New Fireworks Document (PNG) button in the Welcome screen, or choose File > New.

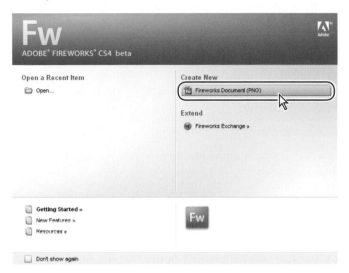

3 In the New Document dialog box, type **1280** in the Width text box and choose Pixels from the units menu beside it. Type **787** in the Height text box and choose Pixels from the units menu. Type **72** in the Resolution text box and choose Pixels/Inch from the resolution menu beside it. This is the default resolution for web pages. You can ignore the background color options under Canvas Color; for this prototype website you will use an image as a background. Click OK.

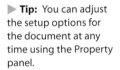

Tip: You can adjust the setup options for the document at any time using the Property panel.

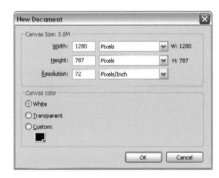

4 Choose File > Save As. In the Save As dialog box, navigate to your Lesson03 folder, select Fireworks PNG (*.png) from the Save As Type/Format menu, name the file **Mockup.png**, and then click Save.

Placing images

You can insert images into a Fireworks document in many different ways. You'll discover just a few of the options in the following exercises.

Using copy and paste

Copy an object or text in a variety of file formats from another application to the clipboard, and then use the Place command in Fireworks to insert the clipboard content into the Fireworks document.

1 Choose File > Browse In Bridge to switch to Bridge.

2 In Bridge, select the file CityBackground.psd, and then choose File > Open With > Adobe Photoshop CS4.

3 In Photoshop, choose Select > All, and then choose Edit > Copy.

4 Switch back to Fireworks, and then choose Edit > Paste. The background image is inserted into the document Mockup.png.

5 Ensure that the background image is selected. In the Properties panel, set the X and Y offset values to **0**. The image covers the entire document size.

▶ **Tip:** If necessary, you can choose a lower magnification level from the Zoom menu in the lower right corner of the document panel in order to see the entire document on your screen.

Using drag and drop

You can drag vector objects, bitmap images, or text directly into a Fireworks document from any application that supports drag-and-drop—including Photoshop, Illustrator, Flash, and others. You can also drag a file from Bridge or from Windows Explorer / the Finder into the Fireworks document.

● **Note:** In Windows, if the document window is maximized you need to click the Restore Down button, located beside the Close button in the top right corner of the document window, before you can reposition the window.

1 Choose File > Browse to switch to Bridge.

2 Position the Bridge window so that you can see both the Bridge window and the Fireworks document in the background at the same time.

3 From Bridge, drag the file WendyAndMark.psd onto the Fireworks document.

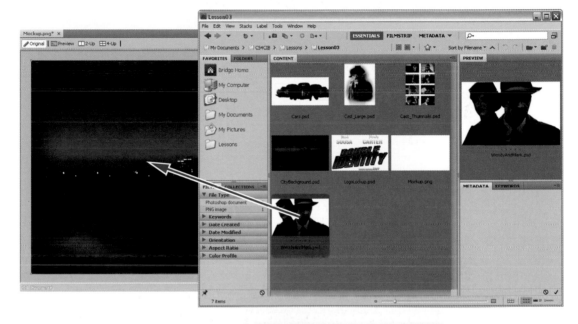

4 In Fireworks, the Photoshop File Import Options dialog box appears. Click OK without making any changes to the default options.

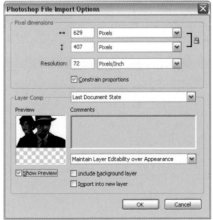

5 Drag the placed image towards the top right corner of the document window. Align the top of the image with the top of the document window and the left edge with the center of the document. Use the smart guides and the X and Y offset values in the Properties panel to guide you.

Tip: Set the magnification level to 100% from the Zoom menu in the lower right corner of the document panel so you can position objects more accurately.

Applying a gradient mask to a placed image

Tip: The Photoshop File Import Options dialog box gives you the option to flatten a layered Photoshop file to a single-layer image.

As you might have noticed, you've just imported not one but two images, each placed on a separate layer. To have these images blend in better with the background you'll apply a gradient mask to each of them.

1 Choose Select > Deselect. Click to select the image of the man.

2 Choose Commands > Creative > Auto Vector Mask. In the Auto Vector Mask dialog box, select the downward-fading gradient from the Linear options, and then click Apply.

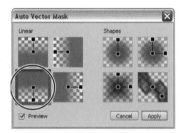

3 Reposition the two handles of the gradient mask so that the fade starts near the man's collar line and ends just below the horizon in the background image.

4 Add a gradient mask for the image of the woman in the same way.

Using the Import command

If you prefer to use a menu command to import images, use the Import command.

1 Choose File > Import.

2 In the Import dialog box, navigate to your Lesson03 folder, select the file Cars.psd, and then click Open.

3 In Fireworks, the Photoshop File Import Options dialog box appears. Click OK without making any changes to the default options. Your pointer changes to a graphics placement cursor (⌐).

4 Click near the center of the background image to place the image of the cars. Drag to position the cars as shown in the illustration below. We set a top left position of X: 380 and Y: 394 for the group of images.

> ▶ **Tip:** You can also position objects by entering X and Y values in the Properties panel.

Organizing objects in the Layers panel

The images you've placed so far have been added one above the other and each in its own layer to the Layers panel. Before things get too unwieldy, you should organize your image components into folders in the Layers panel.

1 Choose Select > Deselect.

2 Undock the Layers panel by dragging it out of its panel group, and then resize the panel by dragging its lower right corner. This will make it easier to work with your layers in the next exercise.

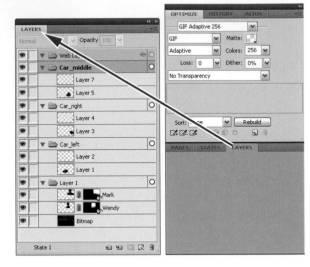

Creating new folders

● **Note:** The stacking order of the layers also defines the visibility of objects if they overlap.

Try to organize the components in your document by logical groups—the background, the actors, the cars, and so on—and then put each group into its own folder. You'll start by creating a new folder for the images of the actors, which are currently on the same folder as the background image.

1 Select the folder *Layer 1* at the bottom of the Layers panel.

2 From the Layers panel Options menu (▤), located at the right side of the panel header, choose New Layer.

3 In the New Layer dialog box, type **Actors** in the Name text box, disable the Share Across States option, and then click OK.

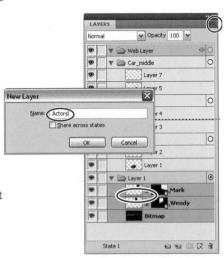

A new folder, named *Actors*, is created just above the folder *Layer 1*.

● **Note:** You can rearrange layers and folders in the Layers panel by dragging them. Release the pointer when you see the horizontal insertion bar at the desired new location.

Moving objects between and within folders

You can move an object from one folder to another either by simply dragging it or by first selecting the object, and then clicking the selection indicator in the destination folder.

1   Choose Select > Deselect.

2   Drag the layer *Mark* onto the folder *Actors*. Release the pointer when you see a black insertion line just below the *Actors* folder. The layer *Mark* has been moved inside the *Actors* folder.

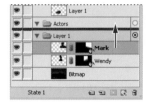

▶ **Tip:** If you drop a layer or folder into the wrong location, choose Edit > Undo and try again.

3   Select just the layer *Wendy* and click the selection indicator in the *Actors* folder. *(See first illustration below.)* The layer *Wendy* has been moved inside the *Actors* folder and placed above the layer *Mark*. To reestablish the previous stacking order drag the layer *Wendy* below the layer *Mark* inside the *Actors* folder. *(See second illustration below.)*

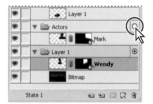  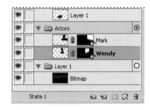

Move *Wendy* into *Actors* folder   Change order in *Actors* folder   Final arrangement

▶ **Tip:** In the Layers panel, you can move multiple selected objects at the same time. Ctrl-click / Command-click one or more objects, and then move them to a new folder by one of the two methods described above. The original stacking order of the objects will be preserved.

Nesting folders

Folders can be nested. You'll now create a new folder to hold the three folders for the cars, as shown in the illustration.

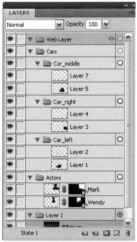

1   In the Layers panel, select the folder *Car_middle*, just below the folder named *Web Layer*.

2   From the Layers panel Options menu, choose New Layer. In the New Layer dialog box, type **Cars** in the Name text box, disable the Share Across States option, and then click OK.

3   First, drag the folder *Car_left* onto the new *Cars* folder, followed by the folder *Car_right*, and finally the folder *Car_middle*. Don't click the selection indicator in the folder *Cars*—this would only move the selected layers but without their parent folder.

Renaming folders

Giving your folders descriptive names is good organizational practice and helps you keep an overview.

1. Double-click the name of the folder *Layer 1* near the bottom of the list in the Layers panel, type **Background** as the new name, and then press Enter / Return.

Collapsing and expanding folders, locking and unlocking folders and layers

You can collapse and expand folders to show only the level of detail that currently interests you. Folders and layers you're not currently working with can be locked to avoid unintentional changes.

1. Click the triangles next to the folder names *Cars*, *Actors*, and *Background* to collapse those folders.

2. Click a triangle again to expand a folder.

3. To avoid changing objects unintentionally, click the box in the column immediately to the left of the folder or layer name. A padlock icon (🔒) appears in the box, indicating that the objects in that folder or on that layer are locked.

4. Click the padlock icon to unlock the folder or layer.

5. You can leave the Layers panel undocked for the remainder of this lesson. Alternatively, return the Layers panel to its original location by dragging it by its tab into the same group as the Pages and States panels. To dock the panel in that group, release the mouse button when you see a blue line surrounding the panel group.

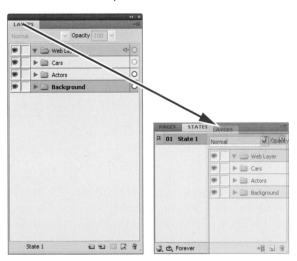

Working with layer comps and flattening images during import

You'll now import a logo lockup into the document from a Photoshop file. A lockup is a set arrangement of a logo together with one or more text elements as defined by the designer. This logo lockup consists of several objects, in multiple layers. The file also contains layer comps; during import you can choose which layer comp to import. As you won't need access to the individual objects in the logo lockup for this exercise you can flatten the imported layer comp into a single layer in Fireworks.

1 Choose File > Import. In the Import dialog box, navigate to your Lesson03 folder, select the file LogoLockup.psd, and then click Open.

2 In the Photoshop File Import Options dialog box in Fireworks, activate the Show Preview option. Preview each of the available layer comps in the Layer Comps menu in turn; then, select the layer comp *Complete_Lockup*. From the menu below the Comments pane, choose Flatten Photoshop Layers To Single Image. Activate the option Import Into New Layer. Make sure your settings are exactly as shown in the illustration, and then click OK.

3 The pointer changes to a graphics placement cursor (⌐). Click near the top left corner of the background image to place the logo image. Drag to reposition the image as shown in the illustration below. We set a top left position of X: 100 and Y: 80 for the image, leaving some space above for the menu bar.

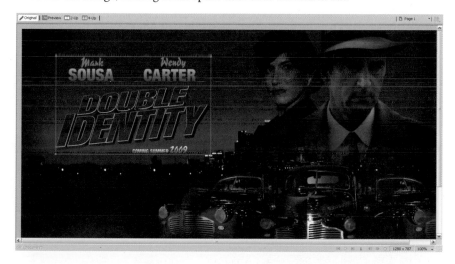

4 Create a new folder above the *Cars* folder in the Layers panel, name the new folder **Logo**, and then drag the layer with the newly placed logo image into that folder.

Adding a navigation bar

Note: Rich symbols are editable design and interface components that can be used and reused for website designs, interface prototypes, or any other graphic composition.

Your first page is almost complete. All that's missing is a navigation bar. Fireworks comes with a library of ready-to-use *rich symbols*, such as interactive buttons and navigation bars.

1 In the Common Library panel (Window > Common Library), scroll down if necessary to see the Menu Bars folder. Double-click the folder name to expand the folder. Select Menu_Bar_04. You can see a preview of the menu bar design in the area at the top of the Common Library panel.

2 Create a new folder in the Layers panel and name the folder **Menu_Bar**. Position the new folder just below the folder *Web Layer*. Click to select the new folder, and then drag Menu_Bar_04 from the Common Library panel onto the Fireworks canvas. In the Layers panel, the menu bar symbol is placed in the folder *Menu_Bar*.

3 Double-click the new navigation bar on the canvas to enter symbol-editing mode. The other objects on the canvas are dimmed. Note the path to the symbol currently being edited—the symbol Menu_Bar_04 located inside the Page 1—in the tray at the top of the document.

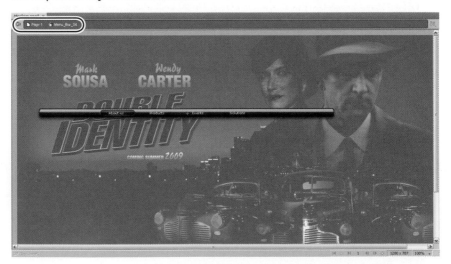

4 In the Layers panel, you can see that this menu bar is composed of six objects—four text layers for the button names, a small rectangle to indicate the currently selected button, and a large background rectangle. Select the large background rectangle in the Layers panel; blue selection handles appear at the corners of the menu bar on the canvas.

5 In the Properties panel, enter **500** in the W (Width) text box.

6 Drag the large rectangle to the right on the canvas, holding the Shift key as you drag. Center the rectangle again relative to the four buttons.

7 In the Toolbar, select the Type tool (**T**). Click inside the text on the *About us* button to place an insertion cursor. Delete the current text and type **Home**. Rename the remaining buttons in the same way to **Actors**, **Trailer**, and **Downloads**.

8 In the Toolbox, select the Pointer tool ( ). Exit the symbol-editing mode by double-clicking outside the navigation bar.

9 Drag the navigation bar to position it near the top of the document, above the logo. Release the pointer when you see the smart guide, indicating that the navigation bar is centered above the logo image as shown in the illustration below. Save your work.

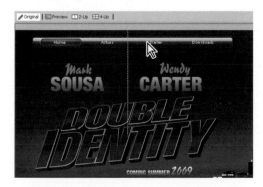

Using a master page

For elements such as a navigation bar that you want to share across all pages, you can create a master page. Elements placed on the master page appear on all the other pages and subsequent edits made to the master page are reflected on every other page.

Creating a master page

You will now create a new page for the navigation bar and designate it as the master page.

1. In the Pages panel, choose New Page from the panel Options menu to add a new, empty page, named *Page 2*, to the Pages panel right below *Page 1*.

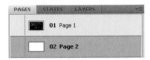

2. Select *Page 1* in the Pages panel.

3. Click to select the navigation bar on the canvas, and then choose Edit > Cut.

4. Select *Page 2* in the Pages panel, and then choose Edit > Paste. The navigation bar is now the only element on page 2.

5. With *Page 2* selected in the Pages panel, choose Set As Master Page from the panel Options menu. *Page 2* moves to the top of the list in the Pages panel and *[Master Page]* is added to its name.

6. Select *Page 1* in the Pages panel. Note that the navigation bar is not (yet) visible on the canvas. That's because by default the master page elements are added to each page inside a folder called *Master Page Layer* that is placed right at the bottom of the layer hierarchy. In our case this layer is hidden behind the background image so you need to move the folder *Master Page Layer* up in the layer hierarchy to make its elements visible on page 1.

7. In the Layers panel, drag the folder *Master Page Layer* from the bottom of the list to just below the now empty *Menu_Bar* folder. If you see an alert warning that a shared layer can not be made a sublayer, try to reposition the *Master Page Layer* again, taking special care to release the folder when its located between the other two folders and not over one of them (which is indicated by the folder icon beside the name turning yellow).

8. Note the padlock icon (🔒) in the column immediately to the left of the *Master Page Layer* name. You can't unlock this layer from a normal page by clicking the padlock icon; master page objects can only be edited on the master page itself.

Editing objects on a master page

The navigation bar contains a gradient overlay to give the impression of a depressed button, now indicating the Home page as the current page. Since this gradient overlay needs to be over a different button on each page you will now delete it from the master page and reposition it on page 1.

1 In the Pages panel, select *Page 2 [Master Page]*.

2 Double-click the navigation bar on the canvas to enter symbol-editing mode.

3 Click to select the gradient overlay rectangle over the Home button, being careful not to select the Home button itself. You should see the blue selection handles at the four corners of the gradient overlay rectangle as well as the two black handles for the gradient. You can also select the gradient overlay rectangle in the Layers panel (the second layer from the bottom).

4 Choose Edit > Cut, and then exit symbol-editing mode by double-clicking outside the navigation bar.

5 Switch to Page 1 by choosing its name from the Page menu in the top right corner of the document pane.

6 Note that there is no longer a gradient overlay rectangle visible over the Home button. The change to the master page is reflected this page.

7 In the Layers panel, select the empty *Menu_Bar* folder, and then choose Edit > Paste. The gradient overlay rectangle is placed on a new layer inside the Menu_Bar folder in the Layers panel, but off the page in the document window. To move it to where you can see it, enter **200** as X position and **20** as Y position in the Properties panel.

8 Drag the gradient overlay rectangle to center it over the *Home* text button. We set X: 110 and Y: 22 as the position of the top left corner.

Creating new pages based on the master page

Any pages you add to your document after you have created a master page will inherit the master page settings. You will now create three more pages that will all automatically contain the navigation bar from the master page.

1 In the Pages panel, choose New Page from the panel Options menu three times to create three additional pages. As you add pages note that the navigation bar is automatically placed on each page.

2 Before continuing, it's a good idea to give the pages descriptive names. In the Pages panel, select each page in turn, double-click the page name, and then enter a new name and press Enter. Rename *Page 2* to **navbar**—*[Master Page]* is added automatically—, *Page 1* to **home**, *Page 3* to **actors**, *Page 4* to **trailer**, and *Page 5* to **downloads**.

To complete the mockup for the navigation bar and before moving on to make the buttons interactive, you'll place the gradient overlay rectangle over the correct button for each page.

3 In the Pages panel, select the page *home*. On the canvas, select the gradient overlay rectangle over the Home button, and then choose Edit > Copy.

4 Switch to the page *actors*. In the Layers panel, select the folder just above the *Master Page Layer* folder, and then choose Edit > Paste.

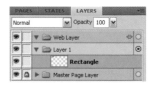

5 Drag to center the gradient overlay rectangle over the Actors text button. Hold down the Shift key while dragging to restrict the movement to one direction. We set X: 229 and Y: 22 as the position of the top left corner.

6 Change the *trailer* and *downloads* pages accordingly—we set the X positions 348 and 467 respectively, for the two rectangles. When you're done, save your work.

Defining hotspots and linking pages

Hotspots are areas of an image that link to other pages when clicked. To make the navigation bar functional, you'll create hotspots for the four menu buttons and have them link to the appropriate pages.

▶ **Tip:** If you want to add rollover effects, use slices rather than hotspots . You'll work with slices later in this lesson.

1 In the Pages panel, click each of the four main pages and note how the appearance of the menu bar changes. The visual mock-up of the navigation bar is complete; you'll now add functionality.

2 Select the master page *navbar [Master Page]*.

3 In the Toolbox, select the Rectangle Hotspot tool (), which is grouped with the Circle Hotspot tool () and the Polygon Hotspot tool ().

4 Using the Rectangle Hotspot tool, drag over the Home button to draw a hotspot area. To reposition the rectangle while dragging, hold down the spacebar.

When you release the mouse button the hotspot area is highlighted over the Home button.

5 With the hotspot rectangle still selected, choose the page home.htm from the Link menu in the Properties panel.

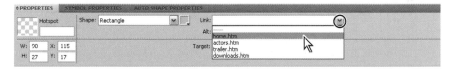

6 Create hotspot areas for the Actors, Trailer, and Downloads buttons in the same way, linking them to the pages actors.htm, trailer.htm, and downloads.htm, respectively.

7 In the Layers panel, note that the four hotspot areas have been created inside the *Web Layer* folder on the master page. The Web Layer folder appears as the top layer in each document and contains web objects used for adding interactivity to documents exported from Fireworks.

8 Save your work.

Previewing web pages in a web browser

1 In the Pages panel, select the page *home*. Notice the hotspot areas overlaid over the navigation bar menu buttons. To hide or show hotspots and slice areas while working on your page layout press 2 on your keyboard or click the Hide Slices And Hotspots button or the Show Slices And Hotspots button in the Toolbox.

A. Hide Slices and Hotspots button
B. Show Slices and Hotspots button

▶ Tip: You can set up both a primary and a secondary web browser to be accessible from the Preview In Browser menu by choosing File > Preview In Browser > Set Primary Browser and File > Preview In Browser > Set Secondary Browser.

2 To test the functionality of your hotspots, choose File > Preview In Browser > Preview All Pages In *[Web Browser Name]*.

3 In your web browser, move your pointer over the menu buttons. Notice how the pointer changes to the Hand cursor when it's over a hotspot area. Click a menu button to jump to that page.

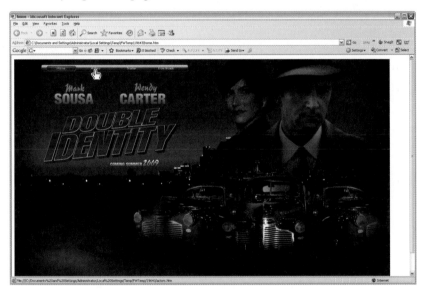

4 You can see which page you're on by the position of the gradient overlay over the menu buttons and by the file name in the address bar.

5 If your links don't work as expected, close the browser window, switch back to Fireworks, and check that the correct links are specified for the hotspot areas on the master page. Correct any errors, save your changes, and again preview all pages in your web browser.

6 When you've finished testing your navigation bar, close the web browser window and return to Fireworks.

You've completed the mock-up design of the Home page and the navigation bar. Next, you'll work on the Actors page, creating slices and disjoint rollover behaviors.

Sharing layers to pages

You can share a layer across multiple pages in a document. You'll share the background image from the Home page to the Actors page. Unlike elements on a master page, elements on a shared layer can be modified from any page.

1 In the Pages panel, select the page *home*.

2 In the Layers panel, select the folder *Background*. From the Layers panel Options menu, choose Share Layer To Pages. In the Share Layer To Pages dialog box, select the page *actors* in the left column, the Exclude Layer From Page(s) column, and then click Add to add it to the right column, the Include Layer To Page(s) column.

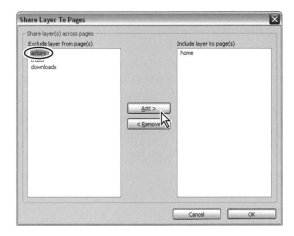

3 Click OK to close the Share Layer To Pages dialog box.

4 Switch to the page *actors* and in the Layers panel move the shared *Background* folder to the bottom of the layer list.

Detaching shared layers

The logo from the *home* page should also be placed on the *actors* page but should be scaled down slightly to make more room for other items. To do this, you'll first share the folder *Logo* to the page actors, and then disable the sharing of this layer, allowing you to modify the object on each page individually.

1 In the Pages panel, select the page *home*.

2 In the Layers panel, select the folder *Logo*. From the Layers panel Options menu, choose Share Layer To Pages. In the Share Layer To Pages dialog box, select the page *actors* in the left column and click Add to add it to the right column.

3 Click OK to close the Share Layer To Pages dialog box.

4 Switch to the page *actors* and in the Layers panel drag the shared folder *Logo* between the folders *Master Page Layer* and *Background*.

5 With the shared folder *Logo* selected in the Layers panel, choose Detach Shared Layer from the panel Options menu.

6 Click the Pointer tool in the Toolbox and select the logo artwork on the page *actors*. Position the pointer over the lower right bounding box handle. When the pointer icon changes from filled (▶) to hollow (▷), drag the handle upwards and to the left to reduce the size of the logo image. While dragging, hold down the Shift key to scale the artwork proportionally. Release the mouse button when the width (W) reads 380 in the Properties panel, and then release the Shift key.

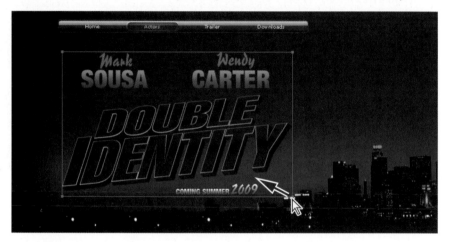

7 Switch to the *home* page to confirm that the logo placed there didn't change in size, and then switch back to the *actors* page.

Creating disjoint rollover behaviors

In the lower left corner of the actors page you'll place thumbnail images of the main actors. Moving the pointer over one of the thumbnail images should bring up some text and a large image of the actor in the space to the right of the thumbnails. This is called a disjoint rollover behavior.

Placing the elements

1 In the Layers panel, select the folder *Background*. Choose New Layer from the panel Options menu. In the New Layer dialog box, type **Actors Thumbnails** in the Name text box, and then click OK.

2 Choose File > Import. In the Import dialog box, navigate to your Lesson03 folder, select the file Cast_Thumbnails.psd, and then click Open.

3 In the Photoshop File Import Options dialog box, choose Maintain Layer Editability Over Appearance, and then click OK.

4 Your cursor changes to a graphics placement cursor (⌐). Click near the left edge of the background image to place the thumbnail images. Drag to reposition the thumbnail images as shown in the illustration below. We set a top left position of X: 100 and Y: 444 for the group of images.

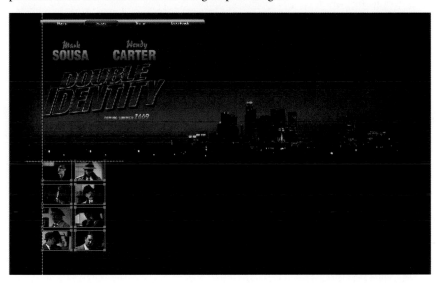

5 Select New Layer from the panel Options menu. In the New Layer dialog box, type **Actors Large Images** in the Name text box, and then click OK.

6 Choose File > Import. In the Import dialog box, select the Photoshop file Cast_Large.psd, and then click Open. In the Photoshop File Import Options dialog box, choose Last Document State from the Layer Comp menu, choose Maintain Layer Editability Over Appearance from the menu below, activate the option Include Background Layer, disable the option Import Into New Layer, and then click OK. Your cursor changes to a graphics placement cursor (⌐).

7 Click near the center of the background image to place the large images. Drag, use the arrow keys, or enter X and Y values directly in the Properties panel to reposition the large images. We set a top left position of X: 550 and Y: 400 for the group of images.

8 Select New Layer from the panel Options menu. In the New Layer dialog box, type **Actors Names** in the Name text box, and then click OK.

9 Choose File > Import. In the Import dialog box, select the file Cast_Names.psd, and then click Open. In the Photoshop File Import Options dialog box, choose Last Document State from the Layer Comp menu, choose Maintain Layer Editability Over Appearance from the menu below, activate the option Include Background Layer, disable the option Import Into New Layer, and then click OK. Your cursor changes to a graphics placement cursor (⌐).

10 Place the name graphics between the thumbnails images and the large images. We set a top left position of X: 340 and Y: 420 for the group of images. Your page should now look like the illustration below.

11 Save your work.

Using dummy text

For the purpose of a website mock-up you'll normally use dummy text to show how text will look on the page.

1 Select New Layer from the Layers panel Options menu. In the New Layer dialog box, type **Actors Text** as the folder name, and then click OK.

2 Choose Commands > Text > Lorem Ipsum. A text frame filled with dummy text appears on the page. With the text frame still selected, set the text color to white using the color picker for Fill Color in the Toolbox or the Properties panel.

3 To reposition the text box, enter the following values in the Properties panel: X: **340** and Y: **520**.

▶ **Tip:** You can format and style the dummy text using the controls in the Properties panel.

4 Position your pointer over the lower right bounding box handle. When the pointer changes from filled (▲) to hollow (▷), drag the handle downwards and to the left. Release the pointer when the width (W) reads 206 and the height (H) reads 192 in the Properties panel.

Creating slices

The disjoint rollover effect works by swapping images inside defined slice areas on the page. You'll create slices for the actors names, the large images, and the dummy text.

1 Right-click / Control-click the text frame containing the dummy text, and then choose Insert Slice from the context menu.

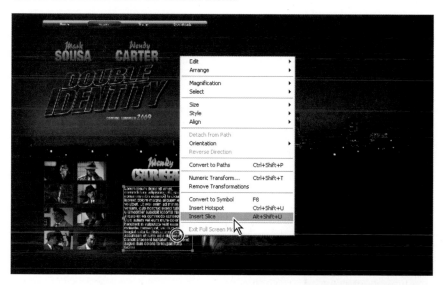

2 In the Layers panel, turn on the visibility of the layer *Background* inside the folder *Actors Names*. A gray rectangle will appear behind the actors names in the document window. Right-click / Control-click near the edge of that gray rectangle, being careful not to click too close to the actors names. You should see a blue selection rectangle around the gray rectangle. Choose Insert Rectangular Slice from the context menu.

3 In the Layers panel, turn on the visibility of the layer Layer 5 inside the layer *Actors Large Images*. A gray rectangle will appear behind the actors images in the document. Right-click / Control-click near the edge of that gray rectangle— being careful not to click to close to the actors images; you should see a blue selection rectangle the size of the gray rectangle—, and then choose Insert Rectangular Slice from the context menu.

▶ **Tip:** You can now delete the two gray rectangles to avoid clutter in the Layers panel; the gray rectangles were only added to the Photoshop file to make it easier to define the dimensions of the slices in Fireworks.

4   You've created three slices that have all added to the *Web Layer* in the Layers panel.

Adding states

Pages can have multiple states. For example: the normal state, the state when the pointer moves over the first hotspot with a rollover behavior, the state when the pointer moves over the second hotspot with a rollover behavior, and so on. States can also be used to implement frame animations. For this exercise, you'll design just two extra states for the page; doing more is possible but doesn't add anything essential to the website mock-up.

1   In the States panel, confirm that there is currently only one state, *State 1*, which is selected by default.

2   With *State 1* selected in the States panel, turn off the visibility of the folders *Actors Text*, *Actors Names*, and *Actors Large Images*. Click the Hide Slices And Hotspots button in the Toolbox to see the page as it would appear in the normal state.

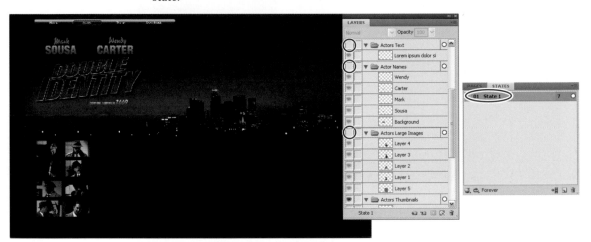

3   In the States panel, choose Duplicate State from the panel Options menu. In the Duplicate State dialog box, type **2** in the Number text box, select the After Current State option, and then click OK.

4   If it's not already selected, select *State 2* in the States panel. For this state you'll design how the page will look when the pointer moves over the first actor's thumbnail image.

5   In the Layers panel, turn on the visibility of the folders *Actors Text*, *Actors Names*, and *Actors Large Images*. Within the folder *Actors Names* turn off the visibility of all but the two layers *Wendy* and *Carter*. Within the folder *Actors Large Images* turn off the visibility for all but *Layer 1*, as shown in the illustration below.

6   Select *State 3* in the States panel. For this state you'll design how the page will look when the pointer moves over the second actor's thumbnail image.

7   In the Layers panel, turn on the visibility of the folders *Actors Text*, *Actors Names*, and *Actors Large Images*. Within the folder *Actors Names* turn off the visibility of all but the two layers *Mark* and *Sousa*. Within the folder *Actors Large Images* turn off the visibility for all but the one layer *Layer 2*, as show in the illustration below.

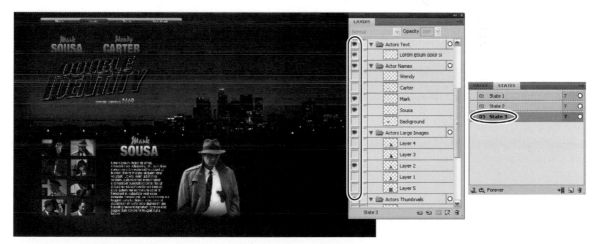

8   Save your work.

You've completed the design for the three states of your *actors* page. In the next steps you'll define the hotspot areas and attach disjoint rollover behaviors.

Creating hotspot areas and attaching disjoint rollover behaviors

Moving the pointer over the first thumbnail image should trigger the images you've placed in *State 2* to appear in the three slices. You'll place a hotspot area over the thirst thumbnail image and then attach a disjoint rollover behavior, which will swap an image in a slice area. You can swap images in more than one slice at the same time by attaching additional disjoint rollover behaviors.

1 Select *State 1* in the States panel.

2 Right-click / Control-click the top left thumbnail image, and then choose Insert Hotspot from the context menu.

3 Drag the behavior handle (⊛) from the hotspot area onto the first target slice, as show in the illustration below.

4 In the Swap Image dialog box that appears when you release the mouse button, choose State 2 from the Swap Image From menu, and then click OK.

5 Repeat steps 3 and 4 twice to create two more disjoint rollover behaviors for the hotspot area over the top left thumbnail image—one for the slice containing the large image and one for the slice containing the dummy text. Both times, choose State 2 from the Swap Image From menu in the Swap Image dialog box, and then click OK.

6 Create a hotspot area over the top right thumbnail image and attach a disjoint rollover behavior for each of the three slice areas, each time choosing State 3 from the Swap Image From menu in the Swap Image dialog box. When a hotspot is selected, blue behavior lines indicate the connection between the hotspot and the controlled slice areas.

7 Save your work.

8 Choose File > Preview In Browser > Preview In *[Web Browser Name]*.

9 In your web browser, position your pointer over each of the thumbnail images to test the disjoint rollover behaviors.

10 Close your web browser window and return to Fireworks.

Presenting the prototype website to the client

There a many ways in which you can demonstrate the prototype website to your client—many more than we can explore here. You may settle for only one of the methods described here or use several methods in combination.

Exporting the website as a PDF document

Fireworks enables you to export your website prototype as a high-fidelity, interactive, secure PDF document that you can use in an e-mail based or online review process.

1 Choose File > Export.

2 In the Export dialog box, navigate to your Lesson03 folder, choose Adobe PDF from the Export menu, choose All Pages from the Pages menu, and activate the option View PDF After Export.

3 (Optional) Click Options to specify compatibility and image quality settings or to set up password protection for the PDF.

4 Click Save.

Fireworks will generate a PDF version of your website and then open the document in your default PDF viewer.

5 Navigate through the pages using any of the regular page navigation controls. Alternatively, click the menu buttons of the navigation bar inside the document to jump directly to the corresponding pages. Note that in a PDF document you will not be able to preview rollover effects such as those you created on the actors page.

6 Close the PDF document and return to Fireworks.

Creating an auto-run slideshow

To present the pages of your website as a slideshow without the need for user inter-action, use the Demo Current Document command.

1 Choose Commands > Demo Current Document.

2 In the Demo Current Document dialog box, Ctrl-click / Command-click to deselect the master page *navbar*, set the background color to black by typing **#000000** in the color text box or by using the color picker beside it, and then click Create Demo. In the Folder For Export dialog box, navigate to your Lesson03 folder—optionally, you could create a subfolder inside the Lesson03 folder—and then click Select "*[Folder name]*" / Choose.

▶ **Tip:** To create a subfolder while you're in the Folder For Export dialog box, do one of the following: On Windows, right-click the file list pane and choose New > Folder from the context menu. On Mac OS, click the New Folder button.

3 After the export is complete, your default web browser will open and automatically begin displaying the pages of your website as a slideshow. Move the pointer towards the lower edge of the browser window to see the navigation controls. You can stop the playback or switch to full screen mode. Note that once again you can't preview the rollover effects.

4 When you're done reviewing the slideshow, close the web browser window and return to Fireworks.

Exporting states of a page as individual images

When demonstrating complex rollover behaviors you might want to take snapshots of the various states of a page as individual images.

1 Switch to the page *actors*.

2 Choose File > Export.

Tip: To create a subfolder while you're in the Export dialog box, do one of the following: On Windows, right-click the file list pane and choose New > Folder from the context menu. On Mac OS, click the New Folder button.

3 In the Export dialog box, navigate to your Lesson03 folder—optionally, you could create a subfolder inside the Lesson03 folder—choose States To Files from the Export menu, and then click Save / Export.

Fireworks will generate one image for each state of the current page. You can review the images in Windows Explorer / the Finder or in any image processing application.

Exporting HTML pages

Probably the best way to demonstrate a website mock-up is to actually export a working website prototype. Fireworks can generate HTML pages and images directly from the Fireworks document—complete with functional navigation bar and rollover behaviors.

1 Choose File > Export.

2 In the Export dialog box, navigate to your Lesson03 folder.

3 Create a subfolder inside the Lesson03 folder: On Windows, right-click the file list pane and choose New > Folder from the context menu. On Mac OS, click the New Folder button. Name the new folder **html_export**.

4 Navigate to the newly created subfolder inside the Lesson03 folder. Choose HTML And Images from the Export menu. Choose Export HTML File from the HTML menu and Export Slices from the Slices menu. Activate the option Include Areas Without Slices and disable both the options Current State Only and Current Page Only.

5 Activate the option Put Images In Subfolder. By default, this will place all images in a folder named *images* inside the selected folder, which is suitable for our purposes.

6 Confirm that everything looks exactly as shown in the illustration below, and then click Save / Export.

7 When the export is complete, switch to Windows Explorer / the Finder. Navigate to the html_export subfolder inside the Lesson03 folder and double-click the file home.htm. The page will open in your default web browser.

8 Test the functionality of the navigation bar by clicking on its menu buttons. You should be able to jump from each page directly to any other page. Navigate to the Actors page and move the pointer over the two top thumbnail images. You should be able to see the disjoint rollover behaviors you created in Fireworks.

Your website mock-up is ready for review by your client or colleagues. You can upload the content of the html_export folder onto a web server and point your client to it. Or, you could demonstrate the functionality of the website in an online meeting. See Lesson 6, "Submitting Work for Review," for more information about collaborating in online meetings using Share My Screen and Connect Now. Once you've obtained your client's approval on the design it's time to build the website in Dreamweaver, reusing the work you've done in Fireworks.

Building a website in Dreamweaver

The tight integration between Fireworks and Dreamweaver makes it very easy to create a Dreamweaver website from assets created in Fireworks. Simply export the elements you want to use from your Fireworks document, and then insert them into your Dreamweaver document. From the assets exported from the Fireworks document, you can pick and choose the elements you want to use: images, entire tables containing sliced graphics, individual rollover buttons or ready-to-use navigation bars, complete web pages with all elements already positioned, or any combination thereof.

Creating a new site

You'll begin by creating a new site in Dreamweaver. Part of the site creation process is to define a location on your hard disk where all the pages and images for your new website will be stored. This location is referred to as the *local root folder* for your Dreamweaver site.

1 Launch Adobe Dreamweaver CS4.

2 Click the Dreamweaver Site button under Create New in the Welcome screen, or choose Site > New Site.

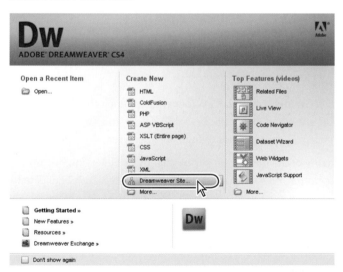

3 In the Site Definition dialog box, type Double Identity Site in the site name text box. Leave the address in the HTTP address text box incomplete, and then click Next. *(See illustration on next page.)*

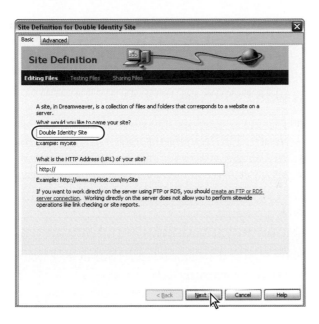

4 In the next pane of the Site Definition dialog box, activate the option No, I Do Not Want To Use A Server Technology, and then click Next.

5 In the next pane of the Site Definition dialog box, activate the option Edit Local Copies On My Machine, Then Upload To Server When Ready (Recommended). Click the folder icon next to the menu under Where On Your Computer Do You Want To Store Your Files.

6 In the Choose Local Root Folder For Site dialog box, navigate to your Lesson03 folder. Create a new folder called **website** inside the Lesson03 folder. Open the new website folder, and then click Select / Choose.

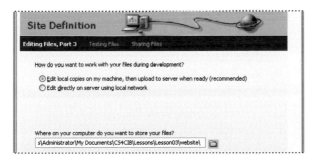

7 Click Next in the Site Definition dialog box.

8 In the next pane, choose None from the How Do You Connect To Your Remote Server menu, and then click Next.

9 In the final pane of the Site Definition dialog box, click Done.

10 Your new site is added to the Files panel, where you can easily access and organize all the files that make up your website.

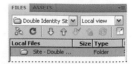

Creating new pages with CSS styles

You will now add blank html pages to your website into which you will place the html pages exported from Fireworks. The Dreamweaver pages will serve as containers for the Fireworks pages. The CSS style attached to the Dreamweaver pages will keep the placed images horizontally centered in the web browser window when the window is enlarged.

1 Choose File > New.

2 In the New Document dialog box, select the Blank Page category, if necessary, from the first column. In the Page Type column, select HTML. In the Layout column, select 1 Column Elastic, Centered; then click Create.

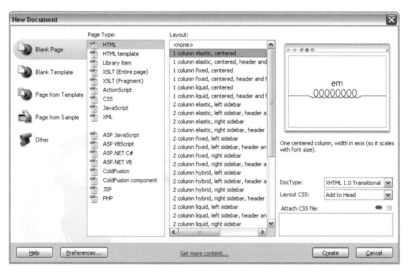

3 Choose File > Save As. In the Save As dialog box, click the Site Root button, type **home.htm** in the File Name / Save As text box, and then click Save.

This simple web page layout has a CSS (Cascading Style Sheets) class named *oneColElsCtr* (1 Column Elastic, Centered) assigned to the body of the page, containing a single DIV (page division) with the ID *container*. If this is starting to sound confusing, don't worry. We won't dive deep into the topic of CSS. For now it's only important to understand that using CSS separates page content from page layout. For example, the style definition of the class *oneColElsCtr* establishes that the content of the page (inside the container) remains horizontally centered on the page. You could easily change the content to be left aligned, for example, by editing the style definition. No change is necessary to the content of the page.

Inserting Fireworks HTML pages

You'll replace the entire content of the DIV container with the html page exported from Fireworks. You'll begin by setting the width of the container to the width of the html page it should contain.

1 Click anywhere in the dummy text of the home.htm page in Dreamweaver.

2 At the bottom of the document view, click the tag *<div#container>*, then click the Edit CSS button in the Properties panel.

3 In the CSS Styles panel, double-click the property *width* to open the CSS Rule Definition dialog box. Type **1280** in the Width text box and choose px (pixels) from the units menu beside it. Click OK to close the dialog box.

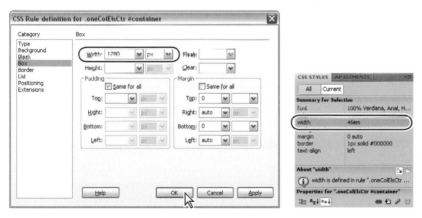

4 In the Code view, select everything between the two tags *<body class="oneColElsCtr">* and *</body>*, as shown in the illustration on the next page, and then choose Insert > Image Objects > Fireworks HTML.

5 In the Insert Fireworks HTML dialog box, click the Browse button to locate the Fireworks HTML file you want to insert. In the Select The Fireworks HTML File dialog box, navigate to the html_export folder inside your Lesson03 folder, select the file home.htm, and then click Open. Disable the option Delete File After Insertion, and then click OK to close the Insert Fireworks HTML dialog box.

6 In the warning dialog box, click OK to copy referenced files into the site folder. It is recommended that you move all files related to the website inside the local root folder. You could also have created the website in Dreamweaver first, and then exported the HTML pages from Fireworks into the local root folder.

7 In the Copy Image Files To dialog box, navigate to the local root folder *website*, create a new folder inside that folder and name it **images**, open the new *images* folder, and then click Select / Choose.

8 In the CSS Styles panel, click the Refresh button to view your updated content in the document pane.

9 Choose File > Save and then choose File > Preview In Browser > *[Web Browser Name]*. The page will open in your default web browser. If your computer screen is large enough, enlarge the width of the browser window and note that the image stays centered within the browser window. Later in this lesson you will

change the background color of the page to black so the image blends perfectly into the background.

10 Close the browser window and return to Dreamweaver.

Roundtrip editing between Dreamweaver and Fireworks

The web page consists of a single large GIF image and an image map for the hot spot areas of the navigation bar. To edit the image, if necessary, you can take advantage of the tight cross-product integration between Fireworks and Dreamweaver: In Fireworks, edit the original file in PNG format, which was used to generate the Fireworks HTML pages and have the changes incorporated automatically when you return to Dreamweaver.

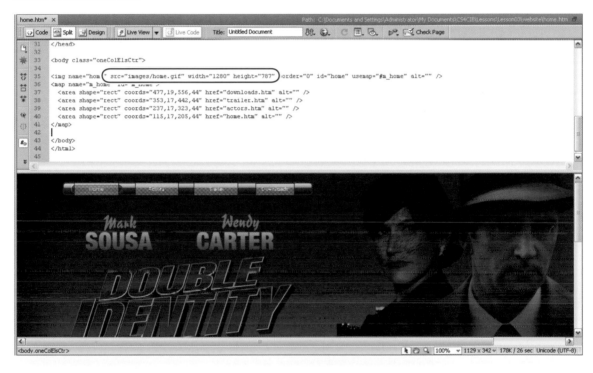

To enable round-trip editing for the main image in GIF file format on our home page, Fireworks needs to be set as the primary external editor for GIF images in Dreamweaver. This can be done in Dreamweaver preferences.

Setting Fireworks as primary editor for GIF images

1 Choose Edit > Preferences / Dreamweaver > Preferences.

2 Select File Types / Editors from the Category list.

3 Select .gif from the Extensions list.

4 Select Fireworks from the Editors list, and then click the Make Primary button.

5 With Fireworks set as primary editor for .gif images, click OK to close the Preferences dialog box.

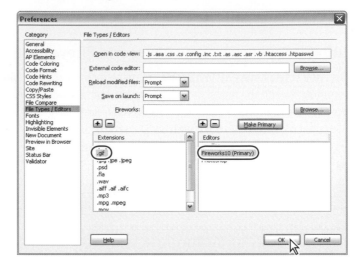

Edit the original PNG file of a GIF image placed in Dreamweaver

1 Right-click / Control-click anywhere in the main image in the Dreamweaver document window and choose Edit With > Adobe Fireworks CS4 from the context menu.

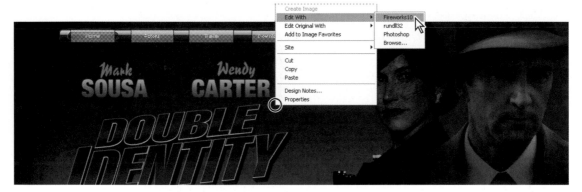

2 In the Find Source dialog box, click the Use A PNG button.

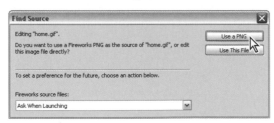

3 In the Open / Open File dialog box, navigate to the Lesson03 folder, select the file Mockup.png, and then click Open.

4 Fireworks opens the PNG file in a special editing window, indicated by an additional bar across the top of the window.

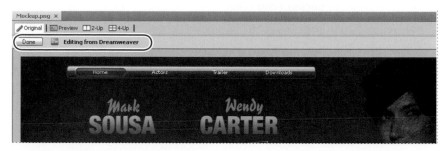

5 In the Layers panel, expand the folder *Cars*, if necessary. Turn off the visibility of *Layer 2* inside the subfolder *Car_left* and *Layer 4* inside the subfolder *Car_right*. Select *Layer 6* inside the subfolder *Car_middle* and change the layer opacity to about 80%. These changes will turn on the headlights of the three cars.

6 Click Done in the bar across the top of the editing window to save your edits to the image, close the file, and return to Dreamweaver.

The GIF image used for the home page in Dreamweaver is automatically updated to reflect the edits you made to the PNG document.

Wrapping up

To complete this lesson, you'll change the background color of the home page to black and then use that page as a starting point for your work on the actors page.

Changing the page background color

1 In Dreamweaver, click the tag *<body.oneColElsCtr>* at the bottom of the document view.

2 In the CSS Styles panel, double-click the property *color* to open the CSS Rule Definition dialog box. Type **#000000** in the Color text box or click the color swatch beside it and use the Color picker to set the background color to black. Click OK to close the dialog box.

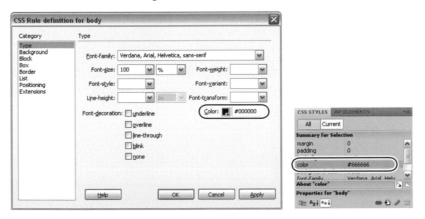

Creating new pages using the current page settings

To create the *actors* page you can use a copy of the *home* page and then replace the content of the container.

1 Choose File > Save As. In the Save As dialog box, click the Site Root button, type **actors.htm** in the File Name / Save As text box, and then click Save.

2 The new page is added to the list of files in the Files panel.

3 In the Code view, select everything between the two tags *<body class="oneColElsCtr">* and *</body>*, as shown in the illustration below, and then choose Insert > Image Objects > Fireworks HTML.

4 In the Insert Fireworks HTML dialog box, click the Browse button. In the Select The Fireworks HTML File dialog box, navigate to the html_export folder inside your Lesson03 folder, select the file actors.htm, and then click Open. Disable the option Delete File After Insertion, and then click OK to close the Insert Fireworks HTML dialog box.

5 In the warning dialog box, click OK to copy referenced files into the site folder. In the Copy Image Files To dialog box, navigate to the *images* folder inside the local root folder *website*, and then click Select.

6 In the CSS Styles panel, click the Refresh button to view your updated content in the document pane.

7 Save your document.

Reviewing the disjoint rollover behavior

The *actors* page contains hotspot areas with disjoint rollover behaviors. You can use the Tag Inspector in Dreamweaver to review—or, if necessary, add, delete, or modify—the behaviors for the hot spot areas on the page.

1 In the Design view, click to select the hotspot area over the top left thumbnail image.

2 Choose Window > Behaviors to open the Behaviors tab of the Tag Inspector. Double-click the *onMouseOver* behavior to open the Swap Image dialog box.

3 In the Images list, start from the top and slowly scroll down. One at a time, select each entry with an asterisk (*) behind its name, such as the entry for *image "actors_r2_c6"* * in the illustration below. The individual images are the slices that make up the entire page. With the *"actors_r2_c6"* * entry selected, the currently defined replacement image (or slice) is listed as *images/actors_r2_c6_f2.jpg* in the Set Source To text box.

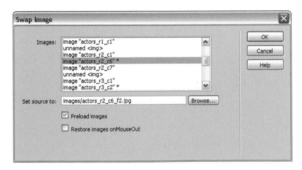

4 Click OK to close the Swap Image dialog box.

5 You can verify the name of a slice and the name of the image that will be displayed in that slice in the page's normal state by clicking to select the slice in the Design view.

The _f2 at the end of the name of the replacement image *images/actors_r2_c6_ f2.jpg* indicates that this is the image you placed inside that slice with *state 2* of the page selected in Fireworks. The *f* is a relic of the fact that states were formally called *frames* in Fireworks.

Previewing the pages in a web browser

1 Choose File > Save and then choose File > Preview In Browser > *[Web Browser Name]*. Depending on the security settings on your computer you may first need to allow blocked content before you can display the page.

2 The page will open in your default web browser.

3 Click the Home and Actors buttons in the navigation bar to switch between the two pages you've created so far.

4 If your computer screen is large enough, enlarge the width of the browser window and note that the background color of the page is now black so the image blends perfectly into the background.

5 On the Actors page, move the pointer over the top two thumbnail images to test the disjoint rollover behavior.

6 When you're done reviewing, close the browser window and return to Dreamweaver.

This completes our brief introduction to Fireworks and Dreamweaver.

To complete the website you would remove the dummy text on the actors page in Fireworks and create an absolute positioned text frame at the same location in Dreamweaver. Enter the final version of the text provided by the client and add a show/hide behavior to the hotspots over the thumbnail images. The text can then be styled and formatted to your liking—or your client's—using CSS style sheets, including attributes such as type style, size, color, alignment, and margins.

Needless to say you'd have to add more images and hotspots and you would also need to complete the two remaining pages.

Finally, you'd upload the pages directly from Dreamweaver to a remote web server.

Since the creation of an entire website is quite labor intensive—you just got a first-hand glimpse of the amount of work necessary as you worked through this lesson—it's essential that you agree with your client on the design direction very early on in the project using the rapid prototyping capabilities of Fireworks. Best of all, as you have seen, all the work that goes into the development of the website mock-up can later be reused for the actual implementation of the website.

Review questions

1 Describe the typical workflow for development of a website using Fireworks and Dreamweaver.

2 What is the reasoning behind building a rapid prototype of the website as the first stage of website development?

3 Name three methods for placing images in a Fireworks document.

4 What is a master page used for in Fireworks?

5 How do you use slices and states to implement a rollover behavior?

6 Explain round-trip editing between Dreamweaver and Fireworks.

Review answers

1 Designing a website from start to finish follows this basic workflow:

   • Together with the client, define the scope of the project, including the objectives of the website, the target audience, schedule, and available resources.

   • Develop a design strategy and establish the look and feel of the web pages.

   • Create a prototype of the website in Fireworks.

   • Present the design to the client and refine it as necessary to obtain approval.

   • Assemble the required assets and create the website in Dreamweaver, based on the work done in Fireworks.

2 Since the creation of an entire website is quite labor intensive it is essential that you agree with your client on the design direction very early on in the project using the rapid prototyping capabilities of Fireworks. Best of all, all the work that goes into the development of the website mock-up can later be reused for the actual implementation of the website.

3 You can place images in a Fireworks document using drag and drop, copy and paste, or the Import command.

4 For elements that you want to share across all pages, such as a common background image or a navigation bar, you can create a master page. Elements placed on the master page and any edits made to the master page subsequently are reflected on all other pages.

5 Create a slice the size of the area where you want the image to change for the rollover behavior. Place the rollover state image inside the slice area but on a different state of the page. Attach a rollover behavior from another slice or a hotspot to the new slice and select the swap image from the appropriate state of the page.

6 An image that was exported from Fireworks and then placed in Dreamweaver can be edited by opening the PNG file from which the image was created in Fireworks, making the adjustments, and then re-exporting and placing the image in Dreamweaver. This process is automated if you follow these steps: to Set Fireworks as the primary image editor for the relevant image format, choose Edit With > Adobe Fireworks CS4 from within Dreamweaver, select the original PNG image when prompted, edit the image in Fireworks, click Done in the top left corner of the special editing window, and return to Dreamweaver. The pages in Dreamweaver are updated automatically to reflect your changes.

4 CREATING INTERACTIVE FLASH DOCUMENTS

Lesson Overview

In this lesson, you'll learn the following:

- Creating a Flash document
- Importing artwork created in Fireworks
- Adding simple animations
- Defining rollover behaviors
- Using ActionScript
- Publishing for web browser and Flashplayer
- Creating an Air application

 This lesson will take about two hours to complete.

Import the website prototype created in Fireworks
into a Flash document. Add animation and special
effects. Use Actionscript to control media elements
behaviors. Test and publish your document.

About Adobe Flash

Adobe Flash is the tool of choice to add animation and interactivity to your documents. The Flash Platform delivers the most effective experiences for rich content, applications, and communications cross browsers, operating systems, and devices of all kinds.

A typical workflow

To create an interactive document in Flash you typically perform the following steps:

- Plan the animations and how the user should interact with your document.

- Create assets and import them to your Flash document.

- Arrange the elements on the Stage and the Timeline to define when and how they appear in your document.

- Add special effects and interactivity.

- Test and publish your document.

Since Flash is such a powerful tool it can be intimidating to work with at first. To give you an indication of the degree of interactivitity you can achieve by using some advanced Flash development features we've provided a relatively complex version of a website design in the Lesson04 folder. Throughout this lesson you will be working on a simpler version of the home page teaching the concepts of working with Flash without adding too much of complexity. Where appropriate, implementation differences between the simple and the complex design will be pointed out.

Viewing the complex sample document

You will start by opening a Flash document provided in the Lesson04 folder with a website design. You can keep this document open as reference while working on a simpler version of the home page.

1 In Windows Explorer / the Finder, navigate to your Lesson04 folder. Within that folder open the Complex folder. Right-click / Control-click the file index.swf and choose Open With > Adobe Flash Player from the context menu.

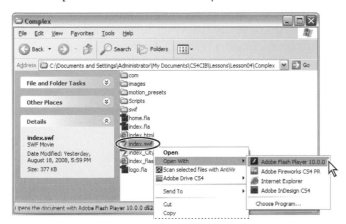

► **Tip:** To show the file name extensions in Windows Explorer, do the following: Choose Tools > Folder Options, click the View tab and under Advanced Settings, deselect the Hide Extensions For Known File Types option.

2 In Adobe Flash Player, watch the intro animation of the home page: The images fade in and slide into position. When the animation stops, move your pointer over one of the cars. The car bounces slightly up and down and the headlights go on. Move the pointer away and the car animation stops.

3 Feel free to explore the other pages of this Flash movie. Click the CAST & CREW button in the navigation bar to open a page you might recognize as the actors page from Lesson03. Click the VIDEO button in the navigation bar to open a page showing the movie trailer you worked on in Lesson02. Use the playback controls below the movie trailer to stop playback. Click the logo image to return to the home page and watch the intro animation play again.

4 When you're done, choose File > Exit / Flash Player > Quit Flash Player to close the Flash movie and quit the Flash Player.

Next you'll open the Flash document that was used to create this Flash movie.

5 Start Adobe Flash CS4 Professional.

6 Click the Open button in the Welcome screen, or choose File > Open.

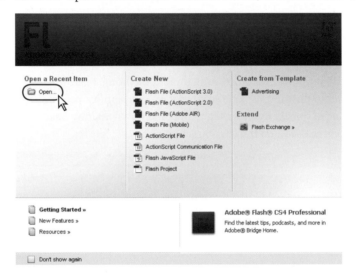

7 In the Open dialog box, navigate to your Lesson04 folder. Open the folder Complex. Within that folder select the file index.fla, and then click Open.

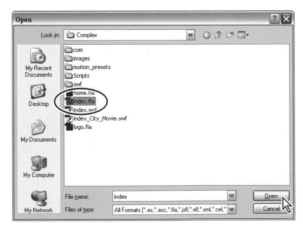

8 If a Font Mapping dialog box appears because you might not have all fonts used in the document installed on your system, click Cancel. For the purpose of this exercise you will not need to worry about font mappings.

The Flash document will open in the Flash application. However, you will only see a black page on the Stage area and the Timeline contains of only one frame with two layers. Later in this lesson you'll discover where all the content is hidden. For now, just leave the document open while you're creating a new document from scratch.

Creating a Flash document

You will be creating a simple version of the home page, using the Fireworks mockup document from Lesson03 as starting point and then adding some animation and interactivity to the document.

1 In Flash, choose File > New.

2 In the New Document dialog box, click the General tab. Under Type, select Flash File (ActionScript 3.0) and then click OK.

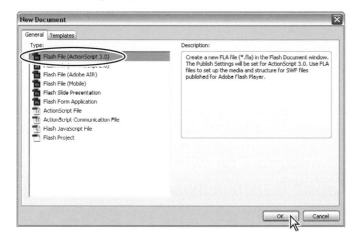

▶ **Tip:** When you are new to Flash you might prefer working with ActionScript 2.0 until you are more familiar with the application. ActionScript 3.0 adds advanced functionality but some handy features—such as behaviors—are available only in ActionScript 2.0. You can implement the same functionality in ActionScript 3.0 but you'll need to know more about writing scripts.

3 In the Properties panel (Window > Properties), expand the Properties pane, if necessary, and click the Edit button in that pane—not to be confused with the Edit button in the Publish pane—to open the Document Properties dialog box.

4 In the Document Properties dialog box, type **1280 px** in the Width text box and **787 px** in the Height text box. These are the dimensions used for the prototype document created in Fireworks that you will later place onto the Stage in Fireworks. Click the color swatch next to Background Color and set the color to black in the color picker. Type **12** fps (Frames Per Second) in the Frame Rate text box, and then click OK.

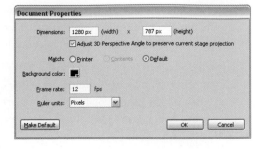

5 To see the entire content of the stage in the document window, choose View > Magnification > Fit In Window, or choose Fit In Window from the Magnification menu located in the upper right corner of the document window.

Placing images

Flash supports importing of vector and bitmap images in a variety of file formats. You can import artwork directly onto the stage or only to the library to position it later on stage. In this exercise you'll import the website prototype you've created in Fireworks in Lesson03, preserving all layers and the image composition.

1 Choose File > Import > Import To Stage.

2 In the Import dialog box, navigate to your Lesson04 folder, select the file Mockup.png, and then click Open / Import.

3 In the Import Fireworks Document dialog box, deactivate the Import As A Single Flattened Bitmap option. From the Import menu, choose the page *home*. From the Into menu, choose Current Frame As Movie Clip. For both Objects and Text, activate the options to maintain appearance when importing, and then click OK.

The image is placed on the stage. Frame 1 of Layer 1 in the Timeline contains one element: the entire home page converted into a single movie clip.

4 Double-click the image on stage to enter symbol-editing mode. Note the path to the symbol currently being edited—the movie clip home in Scene 1—in the Edit bar at the top of the document.

Note: A *symbol* is a graphic, button, or movie clip organized in the Library panel. You can place multiple *instances* of a symbol on stage. Each symbol has its own Timeline, where you can add layers, frames and action scripts to create animations and behaviors for the symbol.

The Timeline shows all layers and objects included in this movie clip. You may need to scroll down in the Timeline panel to see all layers. For now, the movie clip consists of only one frame.

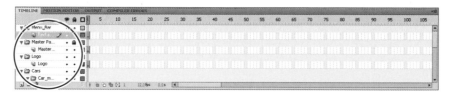

5 Click the Back button (⇦) at the left of the Edit bar to exit symbol-editing mode.

6 Choose File > Save As. In the Save As dialog box, navigate to your Lesson04 folder, choose Flash CS4 Document (*.fla) from the Save As Type / Format menu, type **Simple.fla** in the File Name / Save As text box, and then click Save.

Nesting movie clips inside movie clips

As you have seen, our entire home page is contained inside a single movie clip placed on the stage in Scene 1, Layer 1, frame 1. You'll now explore what's placed inside the first frame of the more complex document index.fla.

1 To view the document index.fla, click the index.fla tab at the top of the Document window or choose Window > 1 index.fla.

2 In the Timeline, note the two layers. The layer *MAIN AS3* contains an Action-Script (indicated by the 'a' in the upper half of the frame) but no other content (indicated by the hollow circle in the lower half of the frame). The layer *content* contains content (indicated by the filled circle in the lower half of the frame).

Tip: A Flash document can have multiple independent scenes (Insert > Scene) which are played is sequence when exported as movie. You can select which scene you're working on from the Edit Scene menu button located near the right end of the Edit bar.

We will be looking at the ActionScript in the top layer later. For now we're only interested in the content placed in the second layer.

Tip: ActionScripts, or *actions*, can be attached to any frame. It is considered best practice to place actions in their own layer at the top of the Timeline.

3 Click to select the first frame in the layer *content*. Choose Edit > Select All and View > Magnification > Show All. You'll see three cars placed off stage to the left but the stage itself is black. In the Properties panel, note that the currently selected object is a movie clip named *site* (as in website).

4 Choose Edit > Edit Selected to enter symbol-editing mode. Note the path to the symbol currently being edited—the movie clip *site* in Scene 1—in the Edit bar at the top of the document. In the Timeline you'll see four layers, named nav, logo, home, and container. Only the first frame of each layer is filled with content.

● **Note:** When the movie clip *site* is played it will trigger the objects placed on these four layers to be displayed, or played, concurrently.

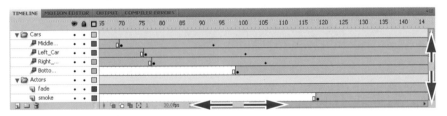

5 Click to select the first frame in the layer *home*. Choose Edit > Edit In Place. Note the path to the symbol currently being edited—the movie clip home inside the movie clip site in Scene 1—in the Edit bar at the top of the document.

6 Choose View > Magnification > Show Frame and Edit > Deselect All.

7 Use the scrollbar at the right side of the Timeline to scroll up and down and review the many layers contained in the movie clip home. Use the scrollbar at the bottom of the Timeline to scroll sidewise and review the change of content in the frames 1 through 225.

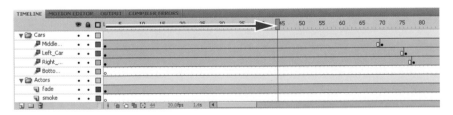

● **Note:** Dragging the current-time indicator in the Timeline to preview an animation is referred to as *scrubbing*.

8 When done, scroll all the way to the left to return to frame 1.

9 Drag the current-time indicator at the top of the Timeline towards the right and watch the animation of the objects in the main document window.

▶ **Tip:** You can create a new movie clip symbol from an animation you've created on the stage. See *Convert Animation On The Stage Into A Movie Clip Symbol* in Flash Help.

10 Stop dragging when you reach frame 190. Use the scrollbar at the right side of the Timeline to scroll all the way up, if necessary, to be able to see the layer *actions.* Click to select the frame 190 in the layer *actions.* This frame contains an action script.

11 Choose Window > Actions to open the Actions panel. The ActionScript consists of a sinlge line:

```
stop();
```

causing the playback of the movie to stop here. Playback will only continue—here or elsewhere—when triggered by an event such as a user interaction.

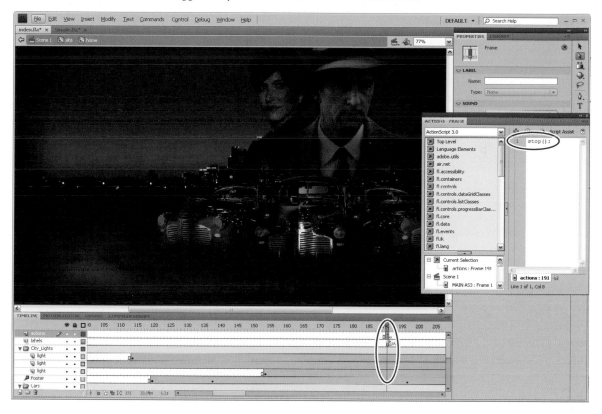

12 Close the Actions panel and choose Edit > Edit Document to exit symbol-editing mode.

In case you were wondering: You will not find the other pages of the site, such as the actors page, placed in any of the frames of the document. These pages are located as individual movie clips inside the folder *swf* inside the folder *Complex.* The movie clips are loaded dynamically into the layer *container,* triggered by a menu selection. To be precise, the buttons of the navigation bar react to mouse events (implemented as an ActionScript) and, when clicked, trigger the loading of the corresponding page.

Working with timelines

You will now create an animation of the home page similar to the one you've just seen in the complex document.

1 Click the Simple.fla tab at the top of the Document window.

2 In the Timeline, click to select the first frame in Layer 1. Right-click / Control-click the image in the document window and choose Edit > Edit In Place from the context menu. Note the path to the symbol currently being edited—the movie clip home in Scene 1—in the Edit bar at the top of the document.

3 In the Timeline, hide the content of the layer folders Menu_Bar, Master Page Layer, and Logo, by clicking for each layer folder in the column below the eye icon (👁). For this lesson you'll be animating only the images of the actors and the cars.

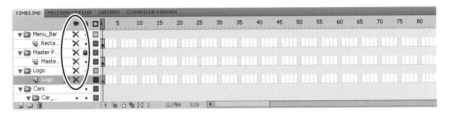

4 Try dragging the current-time indicator to the right; it will not move.

The animation, if you want to call it an animation, is currently only one frame long. You will now add frames to the timeline to extend the duration of the animation.

5 In the Timeline, scroll down, if necessary, so you can see the layer Background inside the layer folder Background. Click to select the second frame in background image layer and then choose Insert > Timeline > Frame.

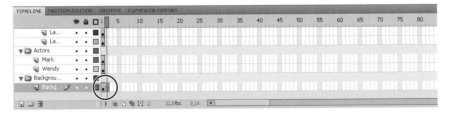

The animation is now two frames long and the current-time indicator can be moved between the two frames. Your entire animation will be about 5 seconds long. At 12 frames per second that would be 60 frames. You'll extend the length of the timeline span for the background image to 60 frames to remain visible throughout the entire animation.

6 In the Timeline, drag the second frame in the background image layer to the right. Release the pointer at frame 60.

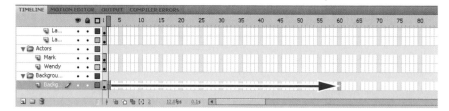

When you release the pointer the background image timeline span will extend to 60 frames.

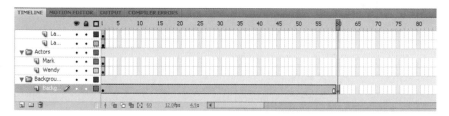

Creating motion tweens

You'll now create the animation for the image of the actor Mark. Using motion tweens enables you to define different properties of an object, such as position and opacity, in two separate frames. Flash then interpolates the property values of the frames in between to create the animation effect.

1 In the Timeline, click to select the first frame of the layer *Mark* inside the layer folder *Actors* and then choose Insert > Motion Tween. The new motion tween is indicated by a span of frames with a blue background. The default length of the span is equal to one second in duration.

2 Move the pointer over the right edge of the motion tween span. When the pointer changes to a horizontal double-arrow (↔) drag the end of the span to the right. Release the mouse button at the 60 frames mark.

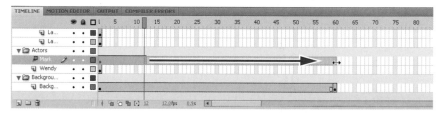

> **Tip:** If the concept of *frame animation* is new to you, review the Timelines And Animation section in Flash Help.

● **Note:** Layers containing a tween have a tween icon next to their layer name in the Timeline.

Note: if you position the pointer too far to the left it will change to a horizontal double-arrow with double-bar (◀||▶) which you would use to adjust the column width in the Timeline panel.

Note: Pixels that are partly transparent in the original image remain partly transparent even with an Alpha value of 100%.

3 To have the image appear a short moment into the animation instead of already in frame 1, you'll now adjust the position of the first key frame of the motion tween. Move the pointer over the left edge of the motion tween span. When the pointer changes to a horizontal double-arrow (◀▶) drag the beginning of the span to the right. Release the mouse button at the 9 frames mark. Drag the current-time indicator back and forth across the timeline. Note that the image of the actor Mark is not visible on stage during frames 1 through 8 and visible from frame 9 through frame 60.

To have the image fade in and slide into its final position, you'll create a property keyframe at the end of the fade and then change the parameters of the keyframe at the beginning of the fade.

4 Position the current-time indicator at the 30 frames mark. Here is where the image should be fully visible and in its final position. Click to select the image of Mark on the stage. In the Properties panel, select Alpha from the Style menu under Color Effect. The Alpha value affects the opacity of the image. Leave the Alpha value at 100%, or fully opaque. By defining a color effect and then setting a property keyframe you can later create a color effect tween by changing the corresponding value in the first keyframe.

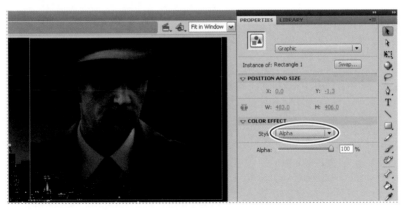

5 Choose Insert > Timeline > Keyframe. Property keyframes appear as small diamonds in the tween span.

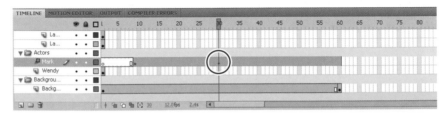

6 Position the current-time indicator at the 9 frames mark, the first keyframe of the motion tween span. Here is where the image should be transparent and in its initial position. Click to select the image of Mark on the stage.

7 In the Properties panel, set X: **-40** for the horizontal offset under Position And Size. Then set Alpha to **0**% under Color Effect to make the image fully transparent. Drag the current-time indicator in the Timeline from frame 8 to 30 to see the image fade in and slide to its final position. The animation for the image of the actor Mark is complete.

● **Note:** Beginning in Flash Professional CS4, the concepts of a *keyframe* and a *property keyframe* are different. The term *keyframe* refers to a frame in the Timeline in which a symbol instance appears on the Stage for the first time. The separate term *property keyframe*, which is new to Flash CS4, refers to a value defined for a property at a specific time or frame in a motion tween.

8 Repeat steps 1 through 7 for the image of the female actor Wendy, starting the animation two frames later and using ı50 as initial image offset.

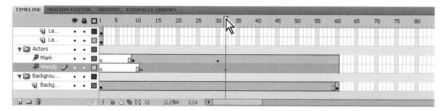

9 Save your work and then choose Control > Test Movie to review your animation in a preview window. The animation will loop giving you a chance to review your tweens a couple of times. You'll also notice that the cars are appearing briefly each time the animation starts over again. When done reviewing, close the preview window. Next, you'll add a stop command at the end of the animation to keep it from looping and then deal with the car images.

▶ **Tip:** Choose Control > Play to quickly preview the animation on stage without first exporting the movie file. However, some restrictions in playback fidelity apply.

Adding ActionScript commands

In this exercise you'll be adding a stop(); command at the end of your animation to keep it from looping. You'll create an extra layer at the top of the Timeline where you should place all your ActionScripts so you can easily find them again when you return to your Flash project at a later time.

1 In the Timeline, use the scrollbar at the right side, if necessary, to scoll up so you can see the topmost layer folder Menu_Bar.

2 Click to select the layer folder Menu_Bar and then choose Insert > Timeline > Layer. A new layer is created at the top of the Timeline.

3 Double-click the name of the new top layer and type **actions** as new name. Press Enter to commit the name change.

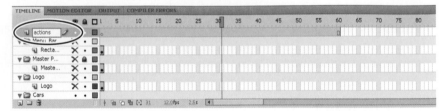

4 In the layer *actions*, click to select frame 60, the last frame of your animation.

5 Choose Insert > Timeline > Keyframe and then open the Actions panel (Window > Actions).

6 In the Actions panel type `stop();` and then close the Actions panel.

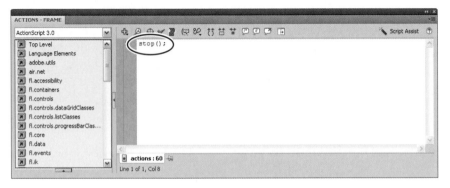

7 In the Timeline, note the small 'a' in the upper half of frame 60 in the layer actions, indicating that an ActionScript has been added to this frame.

8 Choose Control > Test Movie. In the preview window, note that your animation only plays one time and then stops. Your first ActionScript is working!

9 Close the preview window and save your work.

Creating symbols

To apply a tween to two or more objects as a group—such as the image of the car and the image of the headlights that should move in sync with the car—you need to first convert the group of objects to a symbol. The tween—such as a change in position or color effect—then applies to the symbol as single object. The individual objects grouped within the symbol can in turn be as simple or as complex as you would like them to be.

1 Drag the current-time indicator to frame 1. Using the Selection tool (➤), click one of the headlights of the car in the middle on stage. Hold down the Shift key and then click to select the body of the car as well.

2 Choose Edit > Copy.

3 Choose Insert > New Symbol. In the Create New Symbol dialog box, type **Car_middle_symbol** in the Name text box, choose Button from the Type menu, leave Library Root selected as Folder location, and then click OK.

4 Choose Edit > Paste In Center.

5 Click the Back button (⬅) at the left of the Edit bar to exit symbol-editing mode for the Car_middle_symbol. Double-click the image on stage to enter symbol-editing mode for the home symbol.

6 In the Timeline, use the scrollbar at the right side to scoll down, if necessary, so you can see the two layers inside layer folder Car_middle inside the layer folder Cars. Select the layer Layer_7, the top layer inside the Car_middle layer folder, and then choose Insert > Timeline > Layer.

7 From the Library panel (Window > Library) drag the Car_middle_symbol onto the stage, aligning it with the other image of the car in the middle.

▶ **Tip:** Use the arrow keys to nudge the placed image into position.

8 In the Timeline, select the two layers below the layer with the newly placed car symbol inside the layer folder Car_middle and then click the Delete icon (🗑) in the lower left corner of the Timeline panel to delete these two layers.

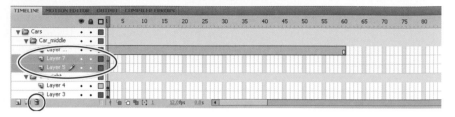

Animating symbols

You can now apply a motion tween to the Car_middle_symbol the same way you did for the images of the actors. This time you'll tween image size in addition to tweening the position and the opacity.

1 In the Timeline, click to select the first frame of the layer containing the Car_middle_symbol and then choose Insert > Motion Tween.

2 Drag the first keyframe to frame 28. This is where the animation will start.

3 Position the current-time indicator at the 38 frames mark. Here is where the image should be fully visible, full size, and in its final position. Click to select the image of the car on the stage. In the Properties panel, select Alpha from the Style menu under Color Effect. Set the Alpha value to 100%.

4 Choose Insert > Timeline > Keyframe.

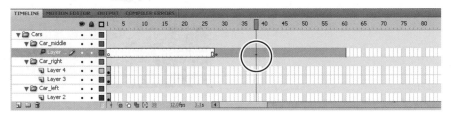

5 Position the current-time indicator at the 28 frames mark, the first keyframe of the motion tween span. Here is where the image should be fully transparent, at reduced size, and in its initial position. Click to select the image of the car on the stage.

6 In the Properties panel, set X: **800** and Y: **475** for the position under Position And Size. If you see the broken chain icon (⛓), click it to change it to the locked chain icon (🔒). This way the width and height can only change proportionally. Set W (Width) to **100**; H (Height) should change automatically to around 89 pixels. Finally, set Alpha to **0**% under Color Effect to make the image fully transparent. Drag the current-time indicator in the Timeline from frame 28 to

▶ **Tip:** You can also position objects by dragging them in the document window.

38 to see the image fade in, become larger, and slide to its final position. The animation for the image of the Car_middle_symbol is complete.

7 Convert the left and right cars to button symbols and add a tween animation in the same way. Have the left car appear on screen in frame 31 and the right car in frame 32. Use 10 frames as length for the tween. Refer to the illustrations below as guidance for the properties to use for the two cars at the start of the tween.

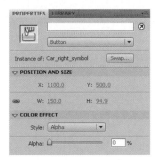

8 Choose Control > Test Movie.

9 When done previewing, close the preview window and save your work.

Defining a button behavior

Buttons are special kind of four-frame movie clips. The first frame is displayed in the normal state, the second frame on a mouse over event, the third frame if the button is clicked, and in the fourth frame you can define the area that should react to the mouse events—which could be smaller or larger than the button itself. The four frames are labeled Up, Over, Down, and Hit respectably.

1   Drag the current-time indicator to frame 42. Double-click the left car to enter symbol-editing mode for the Car_left_symbol.

2   In the Timeline, click to select the frame labeled Over in Layer 1.

3   Choose Insert > Timeline > Keyframe.

4   Choose Edit > Deselect All. Then click one of the headlights of the left car to select only the image of the two dimmed headlights. Choose Edit > Clear. The headlights of the left car are now turned on.

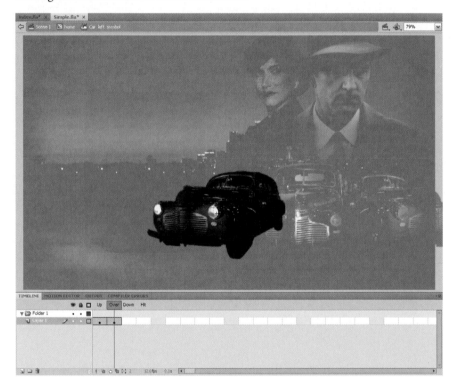

5   Drag the current-time indicator back and forth between the Up and Down frame to toggle the light.

6   Choose Edit > Edit Document to exit symbol-editing mode and then choose Control > Test Movie.

7 The the animation of the actors and the cars and then position the pointer over the left car. The headlights will turn on. Move the pointer away and the headlights will turn off again.

8 When done reviewing, close the preview window.

9 (Optional) Define a button behavior for the right car in the same manner.

10 Save your work.

For the car in the middle you will define a rollover behavior shortly. But first, let's review how the rollover behavior is implemented in the complex home page.

Defining behaviors for movie clips

When defining behaviors for buttons the event handling happens behind the scenes. All you have to do is to design the different states for your buttons. When dealing with movie clips, you'll need to write your own ActionScripts that trigger actions based on external events such as a mouse-over event.

▶ **Tip:** In ActionScript 2.0 documents you can use the Behaviors panel to choose common events and corresponding actions from a predefined list. Flash then takes care of converting your specified behaviors to proper ActionScripts that you can review in the Actions panel.

1 To view the document index.fla, click the index.fla tab at the top of the Document window or choose Window > 1 index.fla.

2 If the document is currently in symbol-editing mode, choose Edit > Edit Document.

3 In the Timeline, click the first frame in the layer *content* and then choose Edit > Edit Selected.

4 In the Timeline, click the first frame in the layer *home* and then choose Edit > Edit Selected.

5 Drag the current-time indicator to about frame 95 so you can see the middle car.

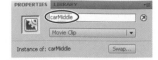

Note: You can place multiple instances of the same symbol. You need to assign a unique name to each instance before you can access it in your ActionScripts.

6 Select the middle car on stage and in the Properties panel note the name for this instance: *carMiddle*.

7 Double-click the carMiddle instance to enter symbol-editing mode.

8 In the Timeline, click the first frame in the layer actions. In the Actions panel (Window > Actions) note your old friend `stop()`;. This command keeps the movie clip from playing past the first frame, waiting for action.

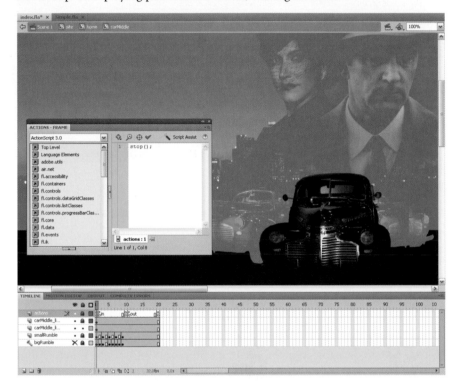

9 Scrub the current-time indicator over frames 2 through 10. This is the animation that is going to be played when the pointer is positioned over the car. Note the label in in frame 2 and the label out in frame 11 of the layer actions. Labels are used to address a specific point within an animation without relying on frame numbers. Frame numbers may change when frames are added or deleted to the timeline but labels move with the specific point on the timeline.

10 Select frame 10 in the layer actions. Note the command `gotoAndPlay ('in')`; in the Acitons panel. This causes the animation to loop between frames 1 and 10.

Triggering behaviors by events

The last piece to the puzzle is to see how the different behaviors are triggered by events. This, or course, is also done by ActionScripts.

1 Choose Edit > Edit Document to exit symbol-editing mode.

2 In the Timeline, click the first frame in the layer *MAIN AS3*.

3 In the Actions panel scroll down so you can see the lines 126 and 128. In line 126 you'll see the following command:

```
site.home.carMiddle.addEventListener(MouseEvent.ROLL_OVER, onOverCarMiddle);
```

This command installs an *event listener*, a function which is executed when a specific event occurs, for the instance carMiddle on the home page. The event to listen for is a mouse roll-over event and the function to be executed is called onOverCarMiddle. Note the similarity to defining a behavior in the Behavior panel. The command in line 128 adds another event listener for a mouse roll-out event.

● **Note:** For a complete list of available ActionScript commands and their syntax please refer to the ActionScript 3.0 (or 2.0) Language and Components Reference in Flash Help.

4 Scroll down further so you can see lines 148 through 158 where the two functions onOverCarMiddle and onOutCarMiddle are defined.

The commands in lines 149, 150, and 151 are executed when the mouse pointer is moved over the middle car. The command in line 149 positions the current-time indicator on the frame labeled in in the timeline of the instance carMiddle, triggering the rumble animation. In lines 150 and 151 the two headlights are slowly turn on using a tween command to change the alpha value of the two headlight images. (We combined the two headlight images to one image for the work on the simple page.) The function onOutCarMiddle, executed when the pointer is moved away from the middle car, stops the rumble animation and turns the headlights off again.

Copying library assets between documents

For the car in the middle you still need to design the over state. You'll do this by copying library assets from one document to the other.

1 Close the Actions panel if it's getting in your way. From the Edit Symbols menu at the right end of the Edit bar at the top of the document choose Symbols > Cars > CarMiddle.

2 In the document window, click to select the headlight to your left. In the Properties panel, confirm that you've selected the movie clip with the instance name *light2*.

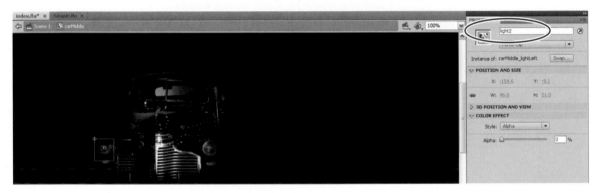

3 Choose Edit > Copy.

4 Switch to the document Simple.fla. From the Edit Symbols menu at the right end of the Edit bar choose Car_middle_symbol.

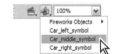

5 In the Timeline, click to select the frame Over (the second frame for a button symbol) in Layer 1.

6 Choose Edit > Paste In Place.

7 Click to select the newly placed movie clip symbol in the document window. Under Color Effect in the Properties panel, set the Alpha value to **100**%. This will be the over-state appearance for the left headlight.

8 Switch back to the complex document index.fla. Try selecting the headlight to your right by clicking it. You'll notice that you can't select it the same way as the left headlight. You will first have to unlock the layer containing the right headlight in the Timeline. Locking layers enables you to avoid unwanted modifications. You can't select and thus not copy or edit elements on locked layers.

9 In the Timeline, click the lock icon in the layer carMiddle_lightRgt.png. The lock icon disappears and the layer is unlocked.

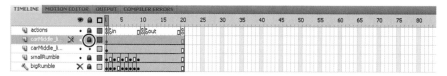

10 In the Timeline, click the lock icon in the layer carMiddle_lightRgt.png. The lock icon disappears and the layer is unlocked.

11 Copy the symbol light1 and paste it into place in the Car_middle_symbol of the Simple.fla document. Select the newly placed symbol in the document window and in the Properties panel, set the Alpha value to **100**%.

12 Choose Edit > Edit Document to exit symbol-editing mode and then choose Control > Test Movie. Move the pointer over all three cars to see the headlights go on and off.

13 When done reviewing, close the preview window and save your work.

This completes the section of this lesson about creating a Flash document. In the next section you will learn to publish your Flash document for viewing in a web browser or as an Air application.

Publishing a Flash document

Flash supports a variety of file formats to deliver your animation to an audience. For example, you can export your animation in SWF (Shockwave Flash, pronounced swif) file format for playback using the Flash Player, create a complete web page for playback in a standard web browser, or as standalone AIR application for playback on your desktops.

Exporting SWF (Shockwave Flash) files

If you intend to use your animation as content in another application, such as Dreamweaver, export the entire document as a SWF file.

1 Switch to the complex document index.fla.

2 Choose File > Export > Export Movie.

Note: You can specify publish settings for SWF files in the Flash tab of the Publish Settings dialog box (File > Publish Settings).

3   In the Export Movie dialog box, navigate to your Lesson04 folder, choose SWF Movie (*.swf) from the Save As Type / Format menu, type **Complex. fla** in the File Name / Save As text box, and then click Save.

4   In Windows Explorer / the Finder, right-click / Control-click the file Compex.fla inside the Lesson04 folder and choose Open With > Adobe Flash Player from the context menu.

5   When done reviewing the document in the Flash player, close the file.

6   Launch Adobe Dreamweaver CS4 and choose File > New. In the New Document box, select the Blank Page category, if necessary, from the first column. In the Page Type column, select HTML. In the Layout column, select <none>; then click Create.

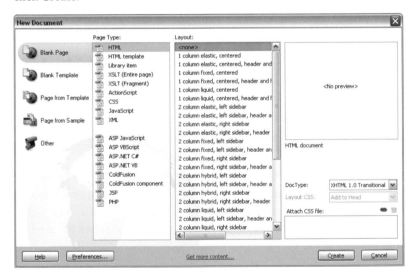

7   Choose File > Save As. In the Save As dialog box, navigate to the Lesson04 folder, type **index.htm** in the File Name / Save As text box, and then click Save.

8   Choose Insert > Media > SWF. In the Select File dialog box, navigate to the Lesson04 folder, select the file Complex.swf, and then click OK / Choose. (If you see an Object Tag Accessibility Attributes dialog box, click Cancel.)

9 Save the file and then choose File > Preview In Browser > *[Web Browser Name]*. Depending on the security settings you may need to allow blocked content before the website will open in your default web browser.

10 When done reviewing, close the web browser window and return to Dreamweaver.

Roundtrip editing between Dreamweaver and Flash

To make modifications to your website you can open the SWF file in Flash from Dreamweaver. When done editing the site in Flash the SWF is reexported and the changes are automatially reflected in Dreamweaver.

1 In Dreamweaver, select the placed SWF file in the Design view and then click the Edit button in the Properties panel.

2 In the Locate FLA File dialog box, navigate to the Complex folder inside the Lesson04 folder, select the file index.fla, and then click Open.

3 When you're done editing your document in Flash, click the Done button in the Edit bar above the Document window.

The SWF file is reexported and the content in the Dreamweaver document automatically updated.

Publishing for playback in a web browser

Playing Flash content in a web browser requires an HTML document that activates the SWF file and specifies browser settings. The Publish command automatically generates this document, from HTML parameters in a template document.

1 Choose File > Publish Settings.

2 In the Publish Settings dialog box, select the Formats tab. If necessary, activate the HTML option under Type and then click the Set Publish Destination folder icon next to the HTML Filename text box.

3 In the Set Publish Destination dialog box, navigate to your Lesson04 folder, leave the filename unchanged, and click Save.

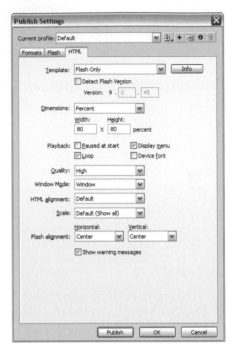
▶ **Tip:** Your publish settings are saved with the document. Use File > Publish to re-export the document with the same publish settings as last used.

4 In the Publish Settings dialog box, select the HTML tab. Choose Flash Only from the Template menu. From the Dimensions menu, choose Percent and then type **80** percent in both the Width and Height text boxes. This will proportionally reduce the dimensions of the entire website, including all images, movies, and so forth. Leave the other settings unchanged and then click Publish. A dialog box with a progress bar appears while Flash is creating the necessary files on your hard disk.

5 Wait until the publishing process has completed, and then click OK to close the Publish Settings dialog box.

6 In Windows Explorer / the finder double-click the file index.html inside your Lesson04 folder to open the exported website in your default web browser. If necessary, allow to show blocked content. Hover the pointer over the cars to confirm that your animation is still functioning—even at reduced size.

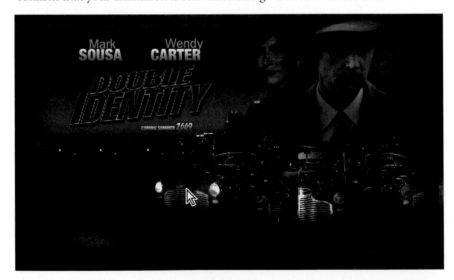

7 When done reviewing, close your web browser window and return to Flash.

Publishing for Adobe AIR

Adobe Air is a cross-platform runtime environment that enables you to run Air applications—such as Flash documents packaged as an Air application—on your computer, providing all the convenience of a desktop application without the need for a web browser. The Adobe Air runtime installer can be downloaded from the Adobe website at http://get.adobe.com/air.

To covert your to an Air application, do the following:

1   Choose File > Publish Settings.

2   In the Publish Settings dialog box, select the Formats tab. If necessary, activate the Flash option under Type and then click the Set Publish Destination folder icon next to the Flash Filename text box.

3   In the Set Publish Destination dialog box, navigate to your Lesson04 folder, leave the filename unchanged, and click Save.

4   In the Publish Settings dialog box, select the Flash tab. Choose Adobe Air 1.1 from the Player menu. Leave the other settings unchanged and then click Publish. A dialog box with a progress bar appears while Flash is creating the necessary files on your hard disk.

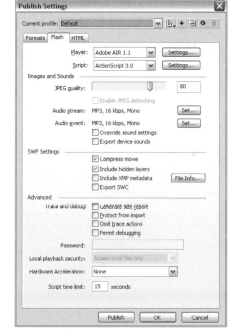

5   In the Digital Signature dialog box, activate the option Sign The AIR File With A Digital Certificate, and then click the Create button.

6   In the Create Self-Signed Digital Certificate dialog box, type names of your choice in the Publisher Name, Organization Unit, and Organization Name text boxes (all text boxes must be completed). Choose your country two-letter code from the Country menu. Type a password in the Password text box and again in the Confirm Password text box. Remember the password; you'll need it again in the next step. Choose your preferred level of encryption from the Type menu. Type a name for your certificate, click the Browse button and select your Lesson04 folder as destination folder. Finally, click OK to create your certificate and close the Create Self-Signed Digital Certificate dialog box.

7   In the Digital Signature dialog box, type the password in the Password text box.

> **Note:** You can create an AIR Intermediate (AIRI) application without a digital signature. A user is not able to install the application, however, until you add a digital signature.

8 Click OK to close the Digital Signature dialog box.

9 Click OK to close the dialog box that confirms that the AIR file has been created.

10 Click OK to close the Publish Settings dialog box.

11 In Windows Explorer / the Finder, double-click the file index.air to start the installation of the air application to your computer. Click Install when asked for your confirmation to install the application. In the next screen, activate the option Start Application After Installation, and then click Continue.

12 When the installation is complete, the website will start playing as a standalone application in its own document window.

13 When done reviewing, click the Close button to quit the AIR application.

Congratulations! You've finished this lesson about creating interactive documents using Flash. As you've seen, Flash is a very powerful application and we could barely scratch the surface of showing all its possibilities. Nevertheless, you've created a timeframe animation, added rollover behavior for buttons, actually coded in ActionScript, exported you creation as SWF file, learned about round-trip editing with Dreamweaver, and converted you animation to an Air application. You should be well prepared to answer the review questions on the next page.

Review questions

1 Describe the typical workflow for creating a Flash document.

2 What is a motion tween?

3 How do you add and ActionScript to your animation?

4 What might be the reason if you can't seem to select an object on stage?

5 What is Adobe Air?

Review answers

1 To create an interactive document in Flash you typically perform the following steps:

- Plan the animations and how the user should interact with your document.

- Create assets and import them to your Flash document.

- Arrange the elements on the Stage and the Timeline to define when and how they appear in your document.

- Add special effects and interactivity.

- Test and publish your document.

2 Motion tweens are used to quickly create an animation effect. You only need to define different properties of an object, such as position and opacity, in two separate frames. Flash interpolates the property values of the frames in between to create the animation effect.

3 ActionScripts can be attached to any frame in the Timeline. Select the frame and then open the Actions panel where you can enter the ActionScript code. It is considered best practice to place actions in their own layer at the top of the Timeline.

4 The object you're trying to select might be placed on a locked layer. You can't select and thus not copy or edit elements on locked layers. You'll first have to unlock the layer in the Timeline.

5 Adobe Air is a cross-platform runtime environment that enables you to run Air applications—such as Flash documents packaged as an Air application—on your computer, providing all the convenience of a desktop application without the need for a web browser. The Adobe Air runtime installer can be downloaded from the Adobe website at http://get.adobe.com/air.

5 COMMUNICATING THROUGH MOBILE DEVICES

Lesson Overview

In this lesson, you'll learn the following:

- Selecting a mobile device in Device Central
- Organizing mobile profiles
- Importing an image from Adobe Photoshop
- Optimizing content for mobile devices
- Previewing and testing artwork in Device Central
- Adjusting an image for mobile devices
- Creating snapshots
- Automating the testing process
- Publishing your work on Device Central
- Testing a mobile website

 You'll probably need between one and two hours to complete this lesson.

Streamline your mobile design workflow with tight integration between Device Central and other Creative Suite 4 Design Premium components. Device Central incorporates an extensive library of mobile device profiles, enabling you to quickly test the appearance and behavior of your mobile content in a simulated environment—right on your desktop!

Note: Before you start working on this lesson, make sure that you've installed the Creative Suite 4 Design Premium software on your computer, and that you have correctly copied the Lessons folder from the CD in the back of this book onto your computer's hard disk (see "Copying the Classroom in a Book files" on page 2).

Designing for mobile devices

Now that you've created print and interactive PDF versions of a document, built a website, and added animation, you might want to use your design assets for yet another significant category in the field of communication: content for mobile devices.

Mobile devices, such as cell phones, smart phones, PDAs (personal digital assistants), or gaming systems can be described as pocket-sized computers. These gadgets are becoming more and more popular, being small enough to be truly portable and yet powerful enough to readily access huge amounts of information.

Users can now call up a variety of mobile web content on these devices, many of them paying additional fees for web browsing on their mobile telephones and handheld computers. Developing successful content for delivery to these mobile devices requires that website designers work within special constraints. Text, images and navigation all need to be optimized for small screens, and file sizes minimized to reduce download times. Adobe Device Central can facilitate the process of evaluating mobile design solutions for a wide variety of mobile devices, with emulation technology designed to simulate network performance of content on mobile devices in a realistic way.

Note: To simulate real-life performance of your Flash Lite content, Device Central offers device emulation that will help you optimize your designs for the limitations of both hardware and bandwidth by giving you an idea of estimated download times and highlighting possible playback delays due to intensive interaction with a network server—enabling you to deliver a more satisfying end-user experience.

Typically, the process of assessing your mobile content with Device Central will follow a very simple workflow:

- Locate your device profile in Device Central.

- Preview and test your work in Device Central.

- Make design adjustments in the original applications, such as Photoshop.

- Publish your mobile content.

Employing Device Central

In Device Central, you can preview and test your work as if you had hundreds of portable devices at hand. In the Emulator tab, you can quickly view and assess a representation of the mobile content as it will appear on the selected device or devices. This method of testing is similar to the way you would preview website design in different target web browsers. The tight integration with other CS4 components streamlines the process: you can move smoothly between Device Central and Illustrator, Photoshop, Flash, or After Effects to adjust your designs before the final step of publishing the content to a handset.

Organizing the device library

In Device Central you can choose between profiles for hundreds of different brands and models of mobile devices, each containing the specifications and limitations for an individual handset.

1 Launch Adobe Device Central.

2 Under Device Profiles in the Welcome screen, click Browse Devices.

3 Before you begin working with device profiles, let's look briefly at some of the preference settings for Device Central. Choose Edit > Preferences / Device Central > Preferences. By default, the Preferences dialog box will open to the General preferences section. The number you see in the Default Phone ID text box *(see illustration on next page)* is the International Mobile Equipment Identity (IMEI) number of the device currently being emulated by Device Central. The IMEI is a 15-digit number that uniquely identifies a device on the mobile phone

network—containing information about the origin, model and serial number of the device. Leave the default number unchanged for now; you'll choose a device later.

4 Click Font Mapping. Here you can change the language used in the Device Central user interface (restart required) and specify the fonts that will be used on your computer to emulate the actual fonts on the device.

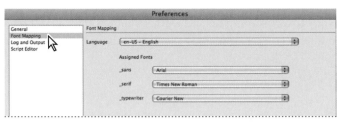

Note: Adobe Flash® Lite™ automatically tries to match the selected generic font to a font available on the device at run-time. If you know which fonts are available on a device, you can select those, or similar, fonts from the Assigned Fonts menus. On an actual mobile device, the device's native system fonts will be used to render the SWF text.

5 Click Cancel to close the Preference panel without making any changes. You'll see the main Device Central window.

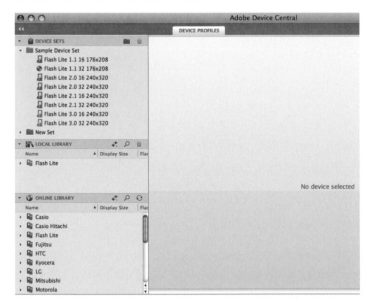

Tip: To keep up with the speed of release cycles, over 450 devices are dynamically updated in the Online Library. This way, each time you start Device Central CS4, you have access to the latest device profiles from Adobe. You can download device profiles to your local machine, and then use them offline.

Notice the three panels: Device Sets, Local Library, and Online Library, at the left of the main window. The Library panels list all the currently available device profiles. In the following steps, we'll take a closer look at the specifications of one of those handsets.

Scanning through the device specifications

● **Note:** When creating new documents, you can select device profiles only from your local library. If the profiles that you want to use aren't already in to your local library, you'll first need to locate them in the online library and add them to your local library.

1   In the Local Library panel, click the triangle beside Flash Lite to expand the list of profiles. Select the Flash Lite folder to display the different models with their specifications on the right side of the main window.

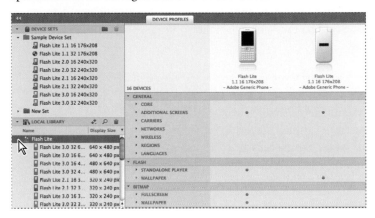

2   To take a quick look at the key specifications of a device, you might need to make the left pane wider so that you see more details of the selected device. Position the pointer over the right edge of the left pane. When the pointer changes to a double-arrow, drag to the right until you can see the specs for color depth. (You might first need to make the application window wider.)

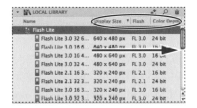

3   Click the Search button (🔍), and enter **1.1** in the search field. Select the profile with a 16 bit color depth and a display size of 176 x 208 px.

Tip: To view multiple devices simultaneously, Shift-click the device names for a consecutive selection, or Ctrl-click / Command-click for a non-consecutive selection.

In the General tab of the Device Profiles panel you will find a vast amount of detailed information for the selected device. Additional information is available in the Flash, Bitmap, Video, and Web tabs.

4 Return to the full list of devices in the Local Library panel by clicking the Clear Search button (✖) on the right side of the panel header.

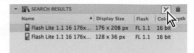

5 To facilitate your search you can group device profiles, by default sorted by Manufacturer, in the Local Library panel into various categories. Click the Grouping button (🔅) to briefly review the categories available in the context menu.

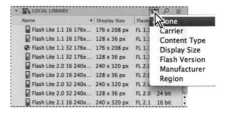

You can group devices by carrier, content type, display size, Flash version, manufacturer, or region. At one glance you are able to see the capabilities, constraints, and features of individual mobile devices. This is a very efficient way to research all the valuable pieces of information that can hugely increase your productivity in design development.

Setting up to create mobile content

You can use Device Central to select a target profile before you even begin creating your mobile content in Illustrator, Photoshop, Flash, or After Effects so that you can start with a document that is already configured correctly. Take further advantage of the close integration of CS4 applications by previewing your design in Device Central and then quickly returning to the original editing program to fine-tune it.

1 In the Local Library panel, select the profile *Flash Lite 2.0 32 240x320*, a generic device supporting Flash Lite 2.0, with a 24 bit color depth and a display size of 240 x 320 pixels.

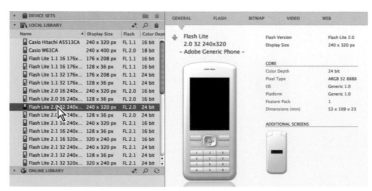

2 Choose File > New Document In > Photoshop.

3 The New Document panel appears. Select Fullscreen from the Content Type menu. Notice the document size, 240 x 320 px, which will be used as the canvas size for your mobile design project in Photoshop. Click Create.

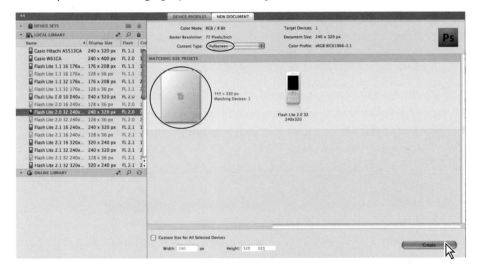

4 Device Central opens a new document in Photoshop with the correct canvas size for your target device, ready for you to start work on your design.

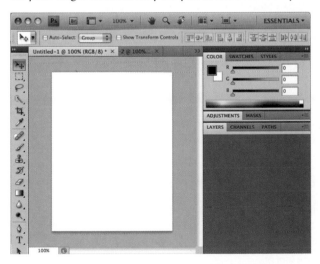

For the purpose of this exercise, we prepared two images in Photoshop and placed them in the Lesson05 folder. You have the choice between a photo of the lovely lead actress of the Double Identity movie or a photo of the fearless detective Archer's lovely car.

5   Choose File > Open, navigate to your Lesson05 folder, select either the file Wendy.psd (the actress) or the file Oldtimer.psd (the car), and then click Open. (You could have also used the Place command to import the image into the document that was created by Device Central in step 4.)

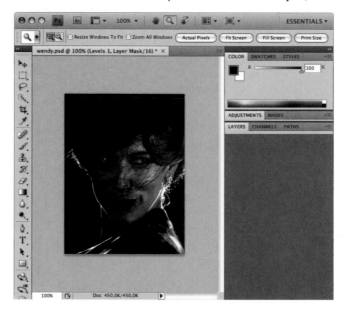

Previewing and optimizing your mobile content

In most situations you'll need to make a compromise between image quality and file size in order to fit the specifications of mobile devices. Before making any adjustments using Photoshop's Adjustments panel, let's first preview the image for the selected profile in Device Central.

1 Choose File > Save For Web & Devices.

2 In the Save For Web & Devices dialog box, choose JPEG High from the file format menu, and then click the 4-Up tab to display previews for four different optimization options.

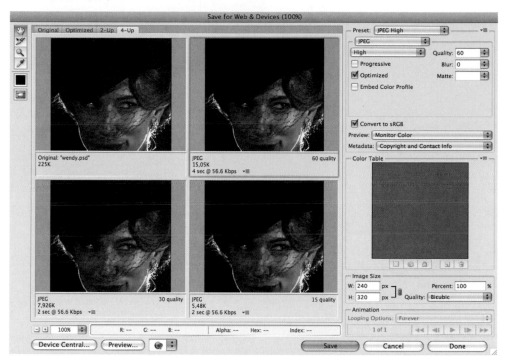

3 Select the image in the lower right corner, where the quality still seems quite acceptable despite the low file size. Then, click the Device Central button.

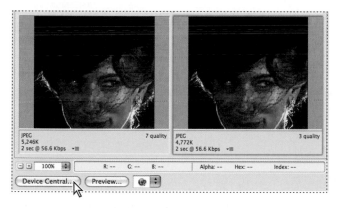

4 Device Central's Emulator tab opens automatically, displaying in the image as it would appear on the previously selected device. *(See illustration on next page).*

The Emulator tab is designed to simulate the performance of various media types—such as Flash, bitmap, and video—on mobile devices in a realistic way. In the Content Type panel in the panel group on the right you can specify your mobile content as either a full screen image, screen saver, or wallpaper. In the Display panel you can test how your image performs in different environments.

● **Note:** If you are emulating performance for Flash content, make sure that the device you've specified supports the same Flash Lite version and content type. If your Flash SWF file requires Flash Lite version 2 and the emulated device supports only Flash Lite 1.1, the file will not appear in the Emulator view. You can sort devices by supported Flash Lite version to make sure that your mobile content is compatible.

5   In the Display panel, choose Indoor from the Reflections menu. In the Emulator tab you'll see how your image might look on your mobile device under indoor lighting conditions.

6   Choose Outdoor and Sunshine from the Reflections menu in turn and review the resultant effects on the image in the Emulator tab. When you're done reviewing the simulation, select None from the Reflections menu.

It goes without saying, that an emulator can not fully substitute for testing on real devices. Once you have previewed your initial results and refined your favorite it may still be advisable to run a test on a few actual devices.

Creating images for mobile devices

Whether you create your mobile content in Illustrator, Photoshop, Flash, or After Effects, your design has to take into account constraints such as screen size and color depth. In an environment of bandwidth and hardware limitations, the goal is to keep file sizes small.

Simplify whenever possible
For Flash files, reducing the number of objects or making them less complex (fewer vector points) reduces greatly the amount of information needed to describe the artwork. For repeated objects, use symbols so that the artwork is defined only once instead of multiple times. For animations it's a good idea to limit the number of objects used and, where possible, to apply animations to groups of objects rather than to individual objects to avoid repetition of code. Additionally, compression can reduce file size dramatically. Therefore you should keep in mind that, depending on the content, using the SVGZ file format (scalable vector graphics file format compressed by gzip) could be a viable option.

For Photoshop files , like the one use in this exercise, consider the following tips to create images that will display well on your targeted mobile device:

Work within the final size of the mobile device
Creating your graphics at the correct dimensions of your target device will help you achieve the best results. Use Device Central to set up your document in Illustrator, Photoshop, Flash, or After Effects to ensure the file has the appropriate dimensions and color space for the target device. Scrolling is often impossible on mobile devices, so If content does not fit the screen, portions of it may not be accessible to viewers.

Reduce the number of colors
Consider using grayscale or reducing the number of colors as much as possible. Most of the common devices still support only 16-bit color (thousands), not 24- or 32-bit color (millions). Color effects such gradients might be rendered as bands of solid color rather than smooth blends. WBMP (Wireless Application Protocol Bitmap Format), the standard format for optimizing images on mobile devices, supports only 1-bit color (black and white pixels) to keep the image size to a minimum. Applying the Sharpen filter to your images (possibly several times) increases the contrast, which can help reduce the number of colors.

Refining your Photoshop artwork

Seeing a simulation of how the image might look like in various light conditions on the target device should give you an idea of how the image might be improved in Photoshop. It's easy to jump quickly between Central Device and Photoshop to preview and refine your work.

1 To switch back to Photoshop so you can apply your adjustments, choose File > Return To Photoshop.

2 In Photoshop, the Save For Web & Devices dialog box is still open. Click Cancel since you want to adjust the original image before exporting the final version.

▶ **Tip:** If you want to make adjustments to a portion of your image, select that portion. If you make no selection, the adjustment is applied to the entire image.

3 Open the Adjustments panel (Window > Adjustments).

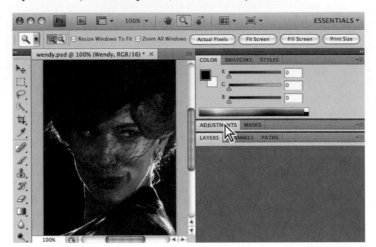

4 In the Adjustments panel, click the first button to create a new Brightness/Contrast adjustment layer, which will enable you to make adjustments to the tonal range of an image.

5 Drag the Brightness slider to the right to increase the Brightness value to about 30, or enter **30** in the text box. Set the Contrast value to 20.

6 Choose Filter > Sharpen > Sharpen Edges. You might see the changes better if you enlarge the zoom level. Increase the magnification level to 250% by typing **250** in the magnification level text box in the lower left corner of the document window.

7 Choose File > Save For Web & Devices. In the Save For Web & Devices dialog box, the 4-Up tab should still be selected from the previous exercise.

8 This time select the image in the lower left corner, and then click the Device Central button.

9 Again, the Photoshop file is displayed on the originally targeted device in the Emulator tab. Open the Online Library and select another profile with the same display size of 240 x 320 px. To make the selection easier you might want to group the devices by display size. We chose the Nokia 5610—just double-click and you the Emulator shows you how your image will look on the new device!

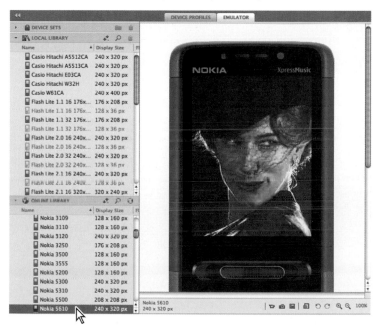

▶ **Tip:** Once you have identified the range of device profiles for which you'd like to test your mobile content, it's a good idea to create a device set, to save time and effort in the future. You can add those profiles in the Device Sets panel by selecting the device and adding it to the list. For more about using Device Sets, refer to Device Central Help.

It could be interesting to continue fine-tuning your image; trying out a monochromatic version for example. However, for this exercise we're happy with the result. The file size has been reduced from over 500k for the original image to less than 8k for the adjusted version without really compromising on quality when the image is viewed on the small screen of the mobile device.

10 Choose File > Return To Photoshop. In the Save For Web & Devices dialog box, click Save.

11 In the Save Optimized As dialog box, navigate to your Lesson05 folder, select Images Only (.jpg) from the Save As Type / Format menu, name the file **Wendy_Final.jpg**, and then click Save.

Taking snapshots

It doesn't take much effort to change devices and to test your mobile content under different light conditions in the Emulator, but you might want others to see the results as well. Device Central CS4 enables you to take snapshots of your work at any point in the testing process and quickly share those snapshots with colleagues or clients.

1 Switch back to Device Central. With the image still emulated on the Nokia 5610 device, click the Take Snapshot button (📷) in the row of controls at the bottom of the Emulator tab.

2 From the Reflections menu, choose Indoor, and then click the Take Snapshot button again.

3 Take a snapshot with each of the Outdoor and Sunshine Reflections options.

4 Click the Show Snapshots button (▦) in the row of controls at the bottom of the Emulator tab. The Log panel opens and displays the snapshots. You may need to increase the width of the panel to see all four snapshots at the same time.

5 In the Log panel, click the Export Snapshot Log As button (📲), and then choose Export As HTML from the menu.

6 In the Export Snapshot Log dialog box, navigate to your Lesson05 folder, type **Snapshots_Wendy** in the File Name / Save As text box, and then click Save.

7 Switch to Windows Explorer / the Finder and open your Lesson05 folder. Inside that folder, open the Snapshots_Wendy folder that you've just created on your hard disk. Double-click the index.html file to open it in your default web browser.

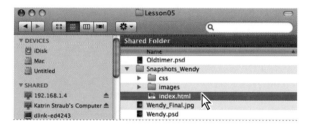

8 The exported snapshot log opens directly in your web browser showing the target device and the image under different lighting conditions. When you're done reviewing the snapshot log, close the web browser window.

9 Return to Device Central, and close the Log panel.

Those familiar with testing content for mobile devices will appreciate just how quickly you can test your mobile content on many different devices and how easily you can share the test results as snapshots with others.

About automated testing

Testing mobile content, especially games and animations, across a range of device profiles can be time consuming and complex. Device Central CS4 helps mobile developers to become more efficient by automating this task. You can record, save, edit, and share test sequences, including snapshots captured at specified frames. The Automated Testing panel enables you to record all interactions with the virtual phone as well as any changes made to the testing environment as a script, which you can modify with a JavaScript editor.

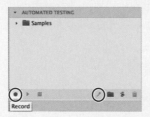

By pressing the Play button you can then run the script to batch process a selection of target handsets. Your content is loaded on the first mobile device and the test script runs automatically. After the script has ended, Device Central switches to the next mobile device in your selection. When testing is complete, the Log panel displays a detailed list of snapshots captured and errors detected, so that problems or bugs can be identified easily. Automating your testing can result in huge increases in productivity!

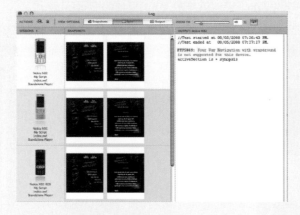

Publishing mobile content

Now that you have finalized the mobile content, you're probably eager to see Wendy's smile (or detective Archer's car) on the screen of your actual handset. Device Central offers different export options, all guided by a wizard for quick results and to avoid the need to use 3rd party tools.

To publish the image you just created, you can send it to a mobile device via Bluetooth or USB cable, upload it to a server via FTP, or copy it to your hard disk.

Provided you have a computer and mobile phone that are both Bluetooth-enabled, you can follow the instructions in the next exercise to export the image to your phone. Otherwise, reading through those steps will hopefully give you a good idea of the process.

1   In Device Central, choose File > New Project.

2   Click the Add Resource Files button ([icon]) in the Resource Files panel.

▶ **Tip:** Since Wendy_Final.jpg is the file displayed in the Emulator tab, you could also select the first button, the Add Currently Emulated File button.

3   Navigate to your Lesson05 folder, select the file **Wendy_Final.jpg** you created earlier on, and then click Open.

4   In the Local Library, select a profile that matches your phone's characteristics (in the illustration below we used the profile *Flash Lite 2.0 32 240x320*), and then drag it onto the Devices panel.

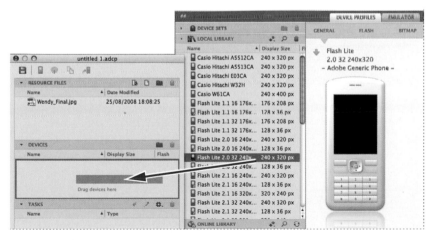

Note: Bluetooth is a standard communications protocol primarily designed for low power consumption. It functions in short range (power-class-dependent: 1 meter, 10 meters, 100 meters). Bluetooth enables devices to communicate with each other when they are within range.

5 In the Tasks panel, click the New Task button (⚙) and choose Send To Bluetooth Device from the menu.

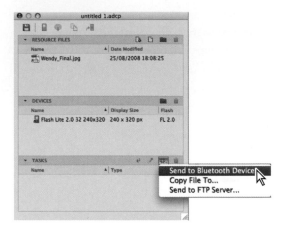

6 Switch on your Bluetooth-enabled mobile phone and make it discoverable. If necessary, refer to the instructions that came with your phone.

7 In the New Task: Send To Bluetooth Device dialog box, click Search, which will prompt Device Central to look for your mobile device.

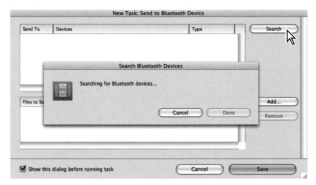

8 Once your phone has been found, click Add, select the file **Wendy_Final.jpg**, and click OK. Then click Save to close the New Task: Send To Bluetooth Device dialog box.

9 In the Tasks panel, click the Run Task button.

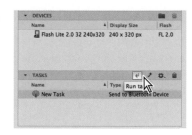

10 Under Send To in the Run Task: New Task dialog box, make sure that the check box next to your device is enabled and that the file Wendy_Final.jpg is listed under Files To Send, and then click the Save & Run button.

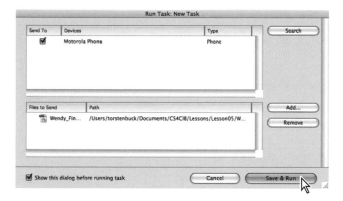

Device Central will process the file and send it to your mobile phone, where you'll receive a notification of the transfer. Once the image has arrived, refer to the instructions that came with your phone to simply view the image or to install it as your new wallpaper or background image.

Previewing a mobile Flash Lite website

In addition to testing static images such as the wallpaper image from the previous exercise, you can evaluate other mobile content as well. For the next exercise you'll work again with imagery from the movie Double Identity: a website—especially designed for mobile devices—with background information about the movie.

1 In the Local Library, double-click the profile *Flash Lite 3.0 16 240x320*.

2 In Device Central, choose File > Open.

3 Navigate to your Lesson05 folder. Open the folder *Flash content* and within that folder open the file MobileFilmSite.adcp. The content of the file will be displayed in a Project window.

4 In the Resource Files panel of the Project window, double-click the file index. swf. The Emulator tab opens and displays the intro animation of the Double Identity home page.

5 To move up and down the menu on the home page click the navigation keys displayed below the phone's screen in the Emulator tab. Alternatively, you can use the arrow keys on your keyboard or the navigation controls displayed in the Key Pad panel.

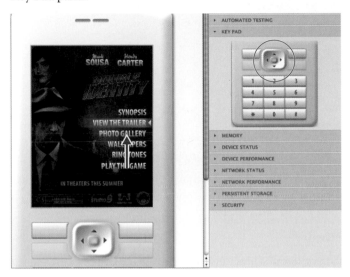

6 It's always fun to watch the trailer. Select the View The Trailer menu item, and then click the Select button or press Return on your keyboard. The trailer plays on the screen of the device in the Emulator tab. To control playback of the video, click a button on the phone below the respective option displayed near the lower edge of the phone screen.

7 Select Back to return to the home page.

As you did previously in this lesson, you could test how the movie might look under different lighting conditions by choosing a setting from the Reflections menu in the Display panel.

8 Once you feel that you played around enough with this little mobile website, you can quit Device Central.

This concludes the lesson about communicating through mobile devices. You've learned a lot about Device Central's vast library of profiles, as well as how to test different content from wallpapers to websites. Ultimately you might agree that this area of communication is not only engaging but, thanks to Device Central, much less time-consuming and therefore even enjoyable!

Review questions

1 What's the difference between Device Central's Local Library and Online Library?

2 How would you create new mobile content from within Device Central?

3 What is the Emulator tab?

4 How can you quickly share your test results with others?

Review answers

1 The Local Library offers device profiles that you've specifically added to your local computer. These profiles are available to you whether you have an Internet connection or not. With the Online Library you have access to device profiles in the Adobe database. These profiles are dynamically updated to ensure that each time you launch Device Central, you will have access to the latest, most accurate information. Double-clicking on any device profile in the online library will add that profile to your local library.

2 In Device Central, Choose File > New Document In > and choose between After Effects, Flash, Photoshop, or Illustrator. Depending of your target profile, Device Central determines which document size to propose for the file you want to create, and displays a picture and a matching size preset of the selected device(s) in the New Document tab. Double-click the preset you want, and Device Central CS4 opens a new blank document in the specified CS4 application.

3 The Emulator tab in Device Central is designed to simulate network performance of content on mobile devices in a realistic way. A number of collapsible panels for testing and performance tuning appear on the right of the Emulator tab. Each panel has options for different media types, such as Flash, bitmap, and video. and offers options apply them as different content types, such as wallpaper, or screen saver.

4 Adobe Device Central CS4 enables you to take snapshots of your content at any time throughout your testing routine. Those snapshots will be collected together with the relevant device in the Snapshots Log. You can easily share those results by exporting them from Device Central as HTML pages, which you can then conveniently send to your clients or colleagues.

6 SUBMITTING WORK FOR REVIEW

Lesson Overview

In this lesson you'll be introduced to the different types of document review and learn the techniques you'll need to take advantage of the exciting collaborative features in Acrobat and CS4:

- Attaching a PDF for e-mail based review

- Adding and replying to comments

- Customizing the appearance of your notes

- Marking up a document

- Collaborating in online meetings

- Initiating a server-based shared review

- Tracking and managing PDF reviews

- Protecting your work

 You'll probably need between one and two hours to complete this lesson.

Whether you want to get input on a spreadsheet or to collaborate on a design project, or you just need a project approved, Acrobat facilitates a range of review workflows. You can set up a review to suit your needs and have Acrobat keep track of comments, send notifications, and more. You can also collaborate live in online meetings—all in secure settings.

Note: Before you start working on this lesson, make sure that you've installed the Creative Suite 4 Design Premium software on your computer, and that you have correctly copied the Lessons folder from the CD in the back of this book onto your computer's hard disk (see "Copying the Classroom in a Book files" on page 2).

Introducing the different types of review

When it's time to present and share your work, Acrobat delivers many features to facilitate the review process. As you experienced in Lesson 1, you can also demonstrate and review your work live, directly from other CS4 applications such as Adobe Illustrator via the Share My Screen feature. You have a choice between different types of review—and for each of them there's a wizard to guide you step by step through the process.

The e-mail based review

An e-mail based review is an excellent option when reviewers do not have access to a remote server or when it's unnecessary to interact with each other directly or in real time. Reviewers in an e-mail-based review have the opportunity interact by replying to each other's comments once the initiator of the review has merged them. Later in this lesson you'll add and reply to comments in an e-mail-based review.

Note: Only users of Adobe Acrobat Pro can initiate a document review and invite users of Adobe Reader to participate.

To start this review, the initiator sends an e-mail invitation to review the PDF file by choosing Comments > Attach For E-mail Review. The e-mailed PDF file includes commenting and mark-up tools for the addressees to state their opinions. The Review Tracker enables the initiator to automatically merge those reviewers' comments into the master copy when monitoring them. You'll be guided through this process later on in this lesson.

The shared review

The highly collaborative nature of the shared review makes it the perfect solution for a group of people with common access to a centralized server. A shared review allows reviewers to read and reply to the comments of other participants rather than only being able to do so through the initiator.

When you initiate a shared review, you post a PDF file by choosing Comments > Send For Shared Review, specifying your own server location (a network folder, a Windows server running Microsoft SharePoint Services, or a web server folder). The reviewers receive an e-mail message with a setup file in Forms Data Format (FDF). When the reviewers double-click this file, the PDF opens in the default web browser with the settings for the review configured so that the comments can be uploaded to a comments repository—an online location that is accessible to all reviewers. While publishing their comments and markups—again, stored as FDF files—the reviewers are able to see other reviewers comments and follow up with the poster directly.

Acrobat's Review Tracker facilitates the entire review process: Not only will the comments be merged and collected, but you can also invite additional reviewers as well as send e-mail reminders to participants. By the way, the reviewers get an e-mail summary of review comments, even if Acrobat is not running on their machines.

The online, real-time review

There's no better way to show and tell than sharing your work online and live via your desktop. Using Adobe ConnectNow, a personal web-conference tool, enables you to conduct real-time meetings on your desktop. From Acrobat 9 Pro, you can create your own user account on Acrobat.com. You can upload and share most document types—or your entire desktop—in online meetings. This option becomes especially interesting when you want to share files in formats other than PDF or when you wish to demonstrate an action within an application. A real-time online review can save so much time in collaborative discussions—not to mention the reduced travel costs!

Participants join the meeting by logging into a web-based meeting space from their own computers, so obviously they require an internet connection. In a ConnectNow online meeting, you can share just a document or your entire desktop, use live chat, share online whiteboards, and take advantage of many other collaborative features.

Collaborating in an e-mail based review

For the purposes of this lesson, where you'll be exchanging comments regarding the brochure cover you designed in Lesson 2, the process of conducting the review will be simplified. You may not have access to a shared server or a partner to participate in the review, but you can still get to know the relevant features in Acrobat and the interface and tools you'll use to collaborate in a review.

● **Note:** As initiator of an e-mail-based review you cannot send an e-mail to yourself—unless you have two separate e-mail addresses.

Following are the steps of this hypothetical review:

- You initiate the review by opening a PDF document from your Lessons folder in Acrobat Professional and sending it to your selected reviewers as an e-mail attachment.

- You can review this PDF attachment, adding your remarks using the commenting and mark-up tools in Acrobat or the free Adobe Reader. As a reviewer you can either return the annotated PDF file or an FDF file containing just your comments.

Viewing comments

Your task is to review a brochure cover—evidently not sent as an e-mail attachment but as PDF file in your Lessons folder—and add your comments using the commenting tools in Acrobat. First, you'll want to view and assess the comments of other reviewers.

1 If you haven't already done so, launch Adobe Bridge.

2 In Bridge Home navigate to your Lesson06 folder and double-click the file Brochure_Review.pdf, to open it in Acrobat 9 Pro.

3 If the Comment & Markup Toolbar is not already open, click the Comment button ( ) in the menu bar and choose Show Comment & Markup Toolbar.

Attaching a file for an e-mail based review

For an e-mail based review, you can send out a tracked copy of a PDF, which makes it easy to collect and manage all the responses. You can explore this option provided you have an Internet connection, an e-mail address, and a colleague to work with.

1   In Acrobat, open the PDF file you want to send for review.

2   Choose Comments > Attach For Email Review. If this is the first time you've used this feature, the Identity Setup dialog box appears. You'll need to enter your information before proceeding.

3   The Attach For Email Review command opens a wizard to guide you through the process of attaching a PDF file and specifying a master copy. All comments from the reviewers will be merged into this file.

4   Next you need to enter the e-mail addresses of the reviewers. To make this process easier, click Address Book to select addresses from your email application's address book. You can edit your invitation at any time by clicking the Previous button.

5   Click Send Invitation. A copy of the PDF is sent to the reviewers as an attachment. When this PDF attachment is opened, it presents with commenting tools and instructions.

Whenever you receive comments to the review you initiated, the Merge Comments dialog box will appear. You can then merge the comments into the master PDF so that they're all in one location.

When reviewing a document, there are different ways to mark up and comment. In the case of our example comments are made as sticky notes. Any comments added to a file being reviewed are recorded in the Comments List, which is located on the bottom of the document pane.

● **Note:** In Reader, commenting tools are available only for PDF files that have commenting enabled. PDF files in a review workflow typically include commenting rights.

4 To see the list of comments, click the Comments button ( ) at the bottom of the navigation pane.

By default comments are sorted according to the page on which they appear. However, you can change that order to sort the comments by author, type, date, color, or checked status.

▶ **Tip:** To view only the comments of a particular reviewer click the Show button on the Comments List toolbar, choose Show by Reviewer, and then select the name of the reviewer. All comments from other reviewers will be hidden. To display all of the comments again, choose Show By Reviewer > All Reviewers.

5 Change the sorting order by clicking the Sort By button in the Comments List toolbar, and then choosing Author. An Acrobat dialog box appears with some tips. Click OK.

6 Click the plus sign next to an author's name to expand that reviewer's comments. For elaborate comments, the scroll bar on the right side of the comment will enable you to read the entire message.

7 Click the yellow sticky note under the name of Torsten Buck. Acrobat will highlight the corresponding sticky note on the document with a halo.

8 Move the pointer over the highlighted yellow sticky note on the brochure cover. The text of the comment becomes visible.

9 Double-click the yellow sticky note icon to open the associated pop-up window, and then drag to position the pop-up window anywhere you want on the brochure cover.

All comments, except those for text markups, can be moved around the page. You'll appreciate this when you receive documents for review that are cluttered with comments.

Note: In an e-mail based review, hidden comments aren't included when you send your comments to the initiator.

You can hide or show comments by filtering them based on the reviewer. When you summarize or print comments, you can specify whether hidden comments should appear. Hiding a comment that has been replied to will result in hiding the entire thread associated with that comment—that is, all the replies and discussion on the comment.

Replying to a comment

Now, that you've seen the other comments and are part of the review, you'd probably like to put in your 2 cents worth as well. Acrobat gives you a wide choice of commenting and markup tools for giving feedback and communicating your ideas.

Not only can you type text messages into the probably familiar sticky notes, you can also add arrows, shapes, and draw freehand directly onto the file to illustrate your point, or highlight parts of the text and add callouts. You can modify the appearance of your comments by changing the color of the sticky notes or the type style, which you'll be doing as part of the next exercise. An array of stamps helps you to efficiently comment and mark standard business documents and you can also create and customize your own stamps. Provided you have the appropriate hardware and software installed, Acrobat even lets you add audio comments.

What you'll do next is to reply to one of those yellow sticky notes from this e-mail-based review.

1 With the Comments List still open in the navigation pane, select the comment from Torsten Buck.

2 Click the Set Status button on the Comments List toolbar and choose Review > Rejected.

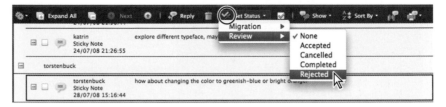

The rejected status is indicated by a red cross below the comment in the list.

3 With Torsten Buck's comment still selected, click the Reply button (🗨) in the Comments List toolbar.

4 A reply box opens where you can explain why you rejected the design. We wrote: **budget for only one spot color printing, let's stick to the yellow, thanks.**.

5 Alternatively you could also open a reply window by choosing Reply from the comment's Options menu.

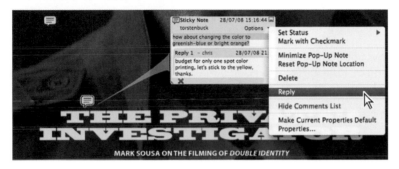

6 Close the reply window by clicking the Close button on the upper right side of the sticky note.

Customizing the appearance of your notes

Finally, you'll add your own comment—this time via the Comments menu—and then change the color of the sticky note in order to make your statement more prominent.

1 In the Toolbar, choose Comments > Add Sticky Note.

2 Double-click the yellow sticky note, which appears on top of the document, and then type your comment. We wrote: **still prefer johnny depp!**.

3 Open the comment's Options menu and choose Properties.

● **Note:** To delete a comment, Ctrl-click / right click the sticky note and choose Delete from the context menu.

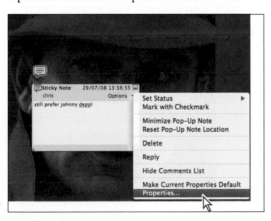

4 In the Sticky Note Properties dialog box, click the Color swatch to open the color picker, choose a bright blue, and then click OK.

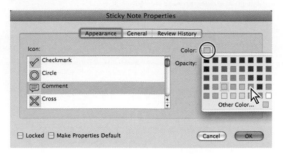

5 Now your note most definitely stands out among the others, and, who knows, maybe they'll even get Johnny Depp for the brochure cover after all.

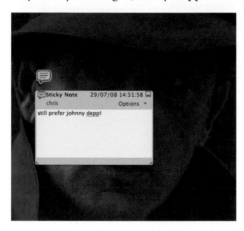

Marking up a document

As you may have noticed already, the Comment and Markup toolbar includes specialized tools for editing text. You can use the Text Edits tool to insert or replace text, underline text or cross it out to mark it for deletion. Your text edit comments do not alter the actual PDF file, they merely indicate where text should be inserted and which text should be deleted or replaced in the source file from which the PDF was created.

1 In the Comments and Markup toolbar (note how it docks to the upper panel) select the Text Edits tool. If this is the first time you've used this tool, the Indicating Text Edits dialog box appears with tips for some standard text edits; once you've scanned through them you can click the Don't Show Again box, and then click OK.

2 With the Text Edits tool still active, select the word YOU in the first feature title: IT'S YOU...ONLY BETTER. Click the triangle beside the Text Edits tool to open a menu of tool options and choose the Replace Selected Text tool.

3 The selected letters are framed and crossed out. Click in the associated pop up window, and type your replacement text (we wrote: **ME**).

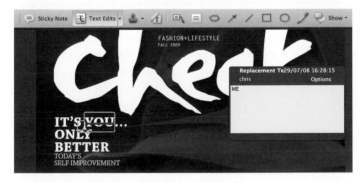

4 For the purpose of this exercise there is no need to save any changes to your review work—just close the Brochure_Review.pdf file.

▶ **Tip:** For major editing work, the specialized tools are faster and easier to use.

Tools like the Highlight Text tool, Cross-Out Text tool, and the Underline Text tool can be used to add comments either on their own or in conjunction with notes. Acrobat provides you with a variety of options for text edits: You can highlight parts of the text and add a note, or cross out selected text by clicking the triangle beside the Text Edits tool to open a menu of tool options. Select the Replace Selected Text tool, and then enter your corrections in the associated pop-up note.

Protecting your work

You can use passwords to restrict unauthorized users from opening, printing, or editing a PDF file. You can use a certificate to encrypt a PDF file so that only an approved list of users can open it. If you want to save security settings for later use, you can create a security policy to stores your security settings.

By adding security to documents, you can limit viewing, editing, printing, and other options to specified users. You can choose if you prefer the users to have a password, a digital ID, or access to Adobe LiveCycle Rights Management.

Security methods

Acrobat provides a variety of security methods for specifying document encryption and permission settings. You can encrypt all or part of a document and limit user actions. For example, you can allow users to input only in form fields or prevent them from printing a PDF file.

Each security method offers a different set of benefits. However, they all allow you to specify encryption algorithms, choose the document components that you wish to encrypt, and set different permissions for different users. Use the Document Properties dialog box to choose one of the following security methods:

- *Password security* provides a simple way to share documents among users when sharing passwords is possible or when backward compatibility is required. Password policies do not require you to specify document recipients.

- *Certificate security* provides a high level of security, eliminates the need for password sharing, and allows you to assign different permissions to different users. Also, you can verify and manage Individual user identities.

- *Adobe LiveCycle Rights Management policies* are stored on a server, and users must have access to the server to use them. To create these policies, you specify the document recipients from a list on Adobe LiveCycle Rights Management.

For more information regarding security, please refer to Acrobat Help.

Managing reviews

In a managed review, a wizard will help you set up your review and invite the participants. The Tracker, as its name implies, helps you to keep track of the review. The Tracker lets you manage document reviews and enables you to distribute forms as well as administer web broadcast subscriptions (also called RSS feeds). No longer do you have to import comments, enable commenting for the Reader users, or manually track reviewers responses.

Even if you did not initiate a shared review but are merely a participant, published comments on your local hard drive are synchronized with the comments on the server. You are notified whenever new comments are published—even when the PDF file is closed, as synchronization continues.

● **Note:** RSS (Really Simple Syndication) is used to publish frequently updated content (e.g. news headlines, blog entries, or podcasts). The RSS format is compatible with XML and RDF formats.

Working with the Tracker

As you might not be connected to the Internet or have e-mail access on your computer, let's just imagine for the purposes of this exercise that you did initiate the brochure review—though your Tracker dialog box will look different from the illustration. Some of the settings for the Tracker can be specified in the Acrobat Preferences dialog box. To initiate a review yourself, please look at Creating a shared review on the next page to get you started with the Tracker wizard.

1 In Acrobat 9, choose Comments > Track Review to open the Tracker dialog box. To open the Tracker in Reader, choose View > Tracker. In the left panel, we were able to select the Brochure_Review under Reviews Sent, as we initiated that review.

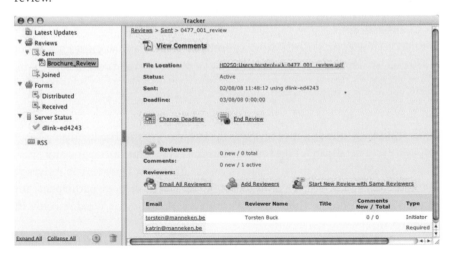

● **Note:** Under Reviews Sent only the PDFs in reviews are listed that you initiated. (Not available in Reader.)

Initiating a shared review

If you are connected to the Internet, have an e-mail account, and use Acrobat 9, you can explore initiating a shared review yourself using the Tracker to help you manage the review.

1   In Acrobat 9, choose Comments > Track Review. A wizard will guide you through this process.

2   When the Tracker dialog box appears, click Create A Shared Review.

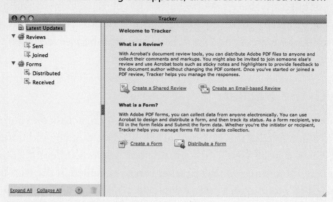

If this is the first time you've initiated a shared review, a dialog box will appear, asking you to create your own user account at Acrobat.com. This account can be set up from either Acrobat or Reader and enables you to upload and share large documents in most common formats and also to share your desktop in online meetings.

If you are already participating in reviews using the Tracker, the Tracker dialog box displays more details about those reviews, as well as forms, server status messages, and RSS feeds.

Once the wizard has guided you through setting up the review and specifying the document location, you can enter an e-mail list of reviewers and invite them to participate.

● **Note:** Your free Acrobat.com account comes with 5GB of storage space.

Since you are already an active reviewer the left panel of the Tracker dialog box displays more details about the reviews, forms, server status messages, and RSS feeds—should you wish to participate in those. The Latest Updates panel gives you a summary of all the latest changes to reviews in which you are a participant. You can turn Tracker notifications on or off inside Acrobat and, for Windows only, in the system tray.

The right panel shows the review details for the item selected in the left panel—in our case the brochure cover review. As published comments on your local hard drive are synchronized with the comments on the server you'll be notified automatically when new comments are available.

About approval workflows

For some reviews you only need to get a document approved, rather than collecting a lot of comments. Acrobat enables you to send a PDF file as an e-mail attachment for others to approve—even in Chinese, Japanese, and Korean!

When participants open an approval request in Acrobat, they can approve the PDF by adding a digital identity stamp.

They can send the PDF to others for approval, or return the PDF to the initiator and other appropriate participants. The initiator can track progress by choosing to be notified each time the PDF is approved. The workflow ends when the last participant adds the final approval. If a PDF isn't approved, the approval workflow must be reinitiated.

To look at the comments from the Tracker, click View Comments to go straight to the sticky notes on the document in Acrobat's main window. At any time during a review the initiator can invite more reviewers by clicking Add Reviewers and entering their e-mail addresses.

2 Ctrl-click / right-click the file Brochure_Review.pdf in the left panel of the Tracker, and choose E-mail All Reviewers from the context menu. This is a quick way to contact all the other reviewers.

3 You can close the e-mail window when it appears, as there is no need to write a message.

4 As the initiator you can discontinue the review by Ctrl-clicking / right-clicking the PDF file, and choosing End Review from the context menu.

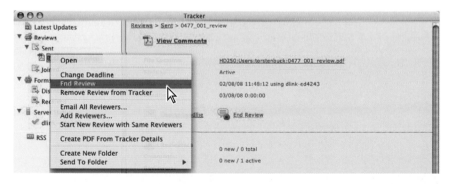

Once a review has ended, participants cannot publish comments to the server. You can restart the review by extending the deadline.

Collaborating in online meetings

● **Note:** Up to three people, including the host, can attend a ConnectNow meeting.

The next exercise will guide you step-by-step through the workflow for an online meeting. Adobe ConnectNow is a personal web-conference tool that you can use to conduct real-time meetings—sharing a document or your entire desktop, and using live chat, online whiteboards, and other collaborative features. As an attendee you join the meeting by logging in to a web-based meeting space from your own computer.

The great thing about this kind of online meeting is that everybody has the same view—which is set up by the person conducting the meeting. As the initiator, you have complete control of what your clients or colleagues are seeing while you walk them through the project.

An online meeting can be highly productive when it comes to sharing ideas, discussing detailed issues and collaborating on a project. As a matter of fact, ConnectNow helped a lot in the writing of this book as the various Adobe product teams were able to demonstrate some of the new features of the Creative Suite live. Version control, platform compatibility, and even having the same programs installed are no longer an issue. You can enable video conferencing, send instant messages, and even permit another participant to take control of the desktop. Interaction takes place in real-time, which makes the meeting more personal and more fun.

Working with Share My Screen and ConnectNow

On the following pages, you'll be guided through the process of setting up an online meeting. The document to be reviewed is a poster for our imaginary movie, Double Identity. This asset has been created in Illustrator CS4 (see the illustration below with some of the vector-based drawing lines selected). To share this artwork from your desktop, you'll use the Share My Screen and ConnectNow features from within Illustrator CS4.

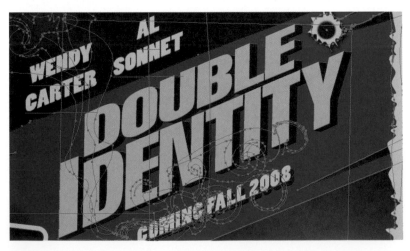

A wizard will guide you through the process of setting up you your online meeting. However, you do need an active Internet connection to be able to work with Share My Screen. If you're not connected to the Internet, you can still follow some of the steps in this exercise and simply scan through others.

1   Switch back to Adobe Bridge, select your Lessons folder in the Favorites panel, and then navigate to the Lesson06 folder. Double-click the file Poster_Review.ai, which should open in Illustrator CS4.

2   In Illustrator, choose File > Share My Screen, which will bring up the ConnectNow dialog box. If you don't yet have an Adobe ID, you need to click Create A Free Adobe ID and fill out a form before you can sign in to share you screen.

Note: You can access Share My Screen from applications other than Adobe Illustrator CS4. To start this feature from Acrobat 9, for example, choose File > Collaborate > Share My Screen.

3   Once you have created your Adobe ID, you need to fill in your e-mail address and password, and then click the Sign In button. *(See illustration on next page.)*

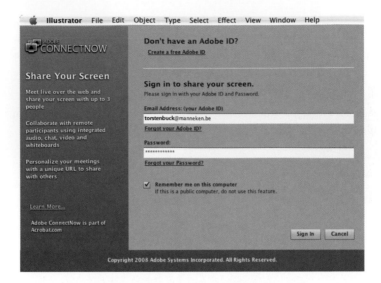

Tip: A customized meeting room URL will make your meeting room easier to remember. You can customize the URL before sending the e-mail invitation, or even later while you're logged in to your meeting room. Choose Help > Manage My Account, and click Change next to Meeting URL.

4 It will take a moment to sign you in. Once you're in your meeting room, you can invite participants by clicking Send E-mail Invitation Now. The recipients will then be able to join the conference by logging into the web-based space from their own computers, as you'll see later in this chapter.

Note: You might need to install the Adobe ConnectNow Add-In. When the Adobe ConnectNow Add-In dialog box appears, click Yes.

5 Close this dialog box, and then click Share My Computer Screen. Once the Add-In application is installed, the screen will advise you that the meeting has been launched.

6 Click Share My Computer Screen. If you have multiple displays, select the monitor you'd like to show in the Start Screen Sharing dialog box, and then click Share.

7 The wizard gives you a quick introduction to screen sharing. Remember, when you share your entire desktop, attendees see everything that happens on your computer screen, including e-mail pop-ups, alerts, and all visible windows and applications. Click OK.

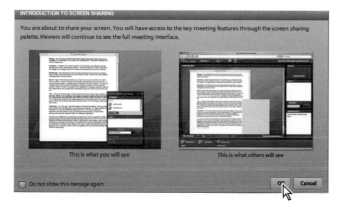

While the meeting is in progress, the ConnectNow screen sharing palette is displayed, giving you access to key meeting features and enabling you to share notes, send chat messages to one person or the whole group, use an online whiteboard to sketch ideas, activate a webcam, and even turn over the control of your desktop to another attendee, which can be very productive for collaborative work sessions and technical support. You can position the ConnectNow screen sharing palette wherever you want on your desktop.

▶ **Tip:** To make your messages stand out, you can customize your Chat pod by choosing fonts, sizes, colors, and emoticons.

8 The open Illustrator file on your desktop is now shared with the other participants. Notice the ConnectNow screen sharing palette, where you could type a welcome message to start the meeting. *(See illustration on next page.)*

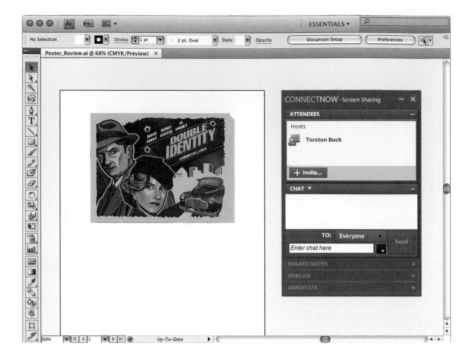

9 When an attendee wants to join the meeting, you'll be notified by a little dialog box in the lower right corner of your screen. Click Accept to admit that attendee to the meeting room. The attendee receives a note to let them know that the host has been notified of their presence.

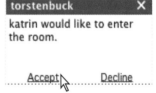

Troubleshooting checklist

This checklist may help if you encounter difficulties setting up or attending an online conference:

- Ensure that you are connected to the Internet.
- Check that your software and hardware meet the system requirements. For a complete list, see www.adobe.com/go/acrobatconnect_systemreqs.
- Disable any pop-up blocker software.
- Clear the browser cache.
- Try connecting from another computer.
- Ensure that you have entered the correct URL.
- Try joining the meeting as a registered user or as guest.
- Confirm that you are using the correct password.

Just imagine how helpful it could be if the tech person could sort things out directly on your computer, even though he's only present online. That's now possible—with Share My Screen you can hand over control of your desktop to another participant in the meeting.

10 In the ConnectNow screen sharing palette, click the triangle to the right of the attendee's name and choose Give This User Control Of My Computer from the context menu.

Being able to work in the application that was used to create the artwork has the advantage that you can quickly react to a suggestion.

As an example, it would take you only a couple of seconds to demonstrate how the poster could look without the female lead actor, which could be a good alternative, don't you think?

● **Note:** To make yourself heard, you can use the microphone on your computer to speak with other meeting attendees using VoIP. Alternatively, use one of the conference numbers provided for traditional teleconferencing.

Attending an online meeting

Now let's change your perspective on this online meeting: you'll no longer be the host, but invited by e-mail to attend this online meeting to review the Double Identity poster. Again, you won't be able to perform all the steps, as you might not be connected to the Internet—nor is your e-mail address on the list of attendees. However, it will be helpful to see this online meeting from the point of view of the participant.

1 Once you've received the e-mail invitation to attend this online review, click the Meeting URL, or type the Meeting URL directly in the address box of your browser.

2 Type your Adobe ID and password, or log in as a guest, enter your name, and then click Enter Meeting.

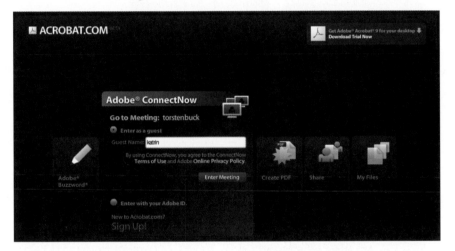

3 It will take a moment to be connected to the meeting room. Once your host admits you to the meeting, your screen will look something like the illustration on the next page. You'll see the Double Identity poster within Illustrator CS4. To the right are the other collaborative features such as Chat.

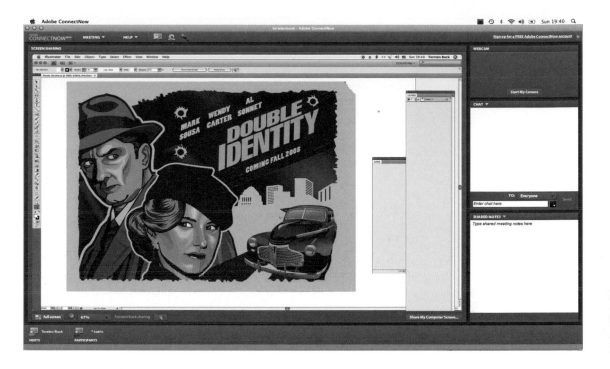

4 Under Chat, we entered in the text box **hi, could we see the poster without the female lead?**, and then clicked Send.

5 By the time we had received a message from the host in the Chat panel a few moments later, the poster had already been adjusted according to our suggestion. What a quick and efficient way to show and tell!

6 To leave the online conference, first say good-bye, and then click Exit Adobe ConnectNow.

Bravo! You finished the online review and with it the last lesson in this book. You've covered a lot of ground; from creating basic assets, to publishing a brochure in both printed and interactive form—from prototyping and building a website and designing for mobile devices, to experimenting with different review workflows. There is so much more you can do with the Adobe Creative Suite 4 Design Premium—this is just the beginning!

Review questions

1 What are the advantages of the shared review using a centralized server?

2 Describe three of Acrobat's commenting or markup tools, and explain where to find them.

3 What does FDF stand for and what is its use?

Review answers

1 Using a centralized server allows all participants to collaborate directly with each other rather than only through the initiator. Not only can they read and reply to each others' comments, but they also receive notifications when new comments are published.

2 Acrobat's comment and markup tools can be accessed by choosing View > Toolbars > Comment & Markup. These tools enable you to make edits, attach notes and even draw diagrams to communicate your ideas or provide feedback for a PDF file being reviewed. Using the Sticky Note tool you can add your comments in form of a yellow note icon that appears on the page with a pop-up note for your text message. With the Text Edits tool you can make a variety of edits such as replacing text, highlighting, underlining, or adding a note to selected text. You can insert text, or cross it out for deletion. The Stamp tool enables you to apply a stamp to a PDF in much the same way you apply a rubber stamp to a paper document. You have a choice of predefined stamps including most commonly used business stamps as well as dynamic stamps with your name and the date you reviewed the document. Additionally you can create your own custom stamps.

3 FDF stands for Form Data Format. FDF files are used to send and share various types of data relating to a PDF file between users, system administrators, and servers. Participants in a review receive an e-mail message with a setup file in Forms Data Format (FDF), which is generally much smaller than the PDF file being reviewed. Once the reviewers double-click this file, the PDF opens in the default web browser with the settings for the review configured so that the comments can be uploaded to the comments repository—again, as FDF files.

INDEX

Key to abbreviations
AA=Adobe Acrobat
BR=Bridge
CR=Camera Raw Photoshop plug-in
DC=Device Central
DW=Dreamweaver
FL=Flash
FW=Fireworks
ID=InDesign
IL=Illustrator
PS=Photoshop

NUMBERS
1-bit colors 275
3D effects (FL) 64
3D images (PS)
    merging 2D images onto 139
    painting onto 139
    support for 13
    working with 49, 136
3D Orbit tool (PS) 136
3D Paint Type (PS) 139
3D Rotate tool (PS) 136
3D Rotation tool (FL) 64
3D Translation tool (FL) 64
8/16-bit WAV audio files 179
16-bit colors 275
256-bit encryption (AA) 95
360° panoramas (PS) 46

A
accordion sections 61
Acrobat.com 24, 93, 291, 302
Acrobat Professional. *See* Adobe Acrobat Pro
ActionScripts (FL) 239, 242
    adding 247
    commands 255
    writing 253
actions (FL). *See* ActionScripts
Actions panel (FL) 243, 248, 253, 255
ACTP 3
addEventListener() command (FL) 255

adjustment layers (PS) 156
Adjustments panel (PS) 276
Adobe Acrobat Pro 92, 290
Adobe AIR 66, 84, 257, 261
Adobe Bridge 114
    adding metadata 123
    Favorites folder 122
    selecting templates 148
Adobe Bridge Home 25, 118
Adobe Camera Raw 48, 49
Adobe Certified Expert (ACE) 3
Adobe Certified Training Providers (ACTP) 3
Adobe Community Help 24
Adobe ConnectNow 93, 291, 304
Adobe Creative Suite 26
Adobe Device Central 22, 106, 266
Adobe Dreamweaver 21, 67, 80, 92, 106, 218, 258
Adobe Fireworks 18, 80, 92, 106, 188
Adobe Flash 17, 61, 236
Adobe Flash Lite 266, 268, 274, 284
Adobe Flash Player 177, 237
Adobe ID
    creating free account 141, 305
Adobe Illustrator 10, 52, 126
Adobe InDesign 12, 30, 150
Adobe kuler 60, 133
Adobe LiveCycle Rights Management (AA) 300
Adobe Media Encoder 66, 106
Adobe Mobile & Devices Developer Center 113
Adobe PDF Print Engine (APPE) 105, 169
Adobe Photoshop 8, 44, 136, 139
Adobe Photoshop Lightroom 48
Adobe Reader 290
Adobe text engine 88
Adobe website 3
Advanced Encryption Standard (AES) (AA) 95
AIF (Audio Interchange File) audio files 179
AIR. *See* Adobe AIR
Ajax 74
alpha value (FL) 246, 250
Animation panel (PS) 180

Production Notes

The *Adobe Creative Suite 4 Design Premium Classroom in a Book* was created electronically using Adobe InDesign CS3. Art was produced using Adobe InDesign, Adobe Illustrator, and Adobe Photoshop. The Myriad Pro and Warnock Pro OpenType families of typefaces were used throughout this book.

Team credits

The following individuals contributed to the development of the *Adobe Creative Suite 4 Design Premium Classroom in a Book*:

Project coordinators, technical writers: Torsten Buck & Katrin Straub

Production: Manneken Pis Productions (www.manneken.be)

Copyediting & Proofreading: John Evans

Special thanks to Christine Yarrow.

Typefaces used

Adobe Myriad Pro and Adobe Warnock Pro are used throughout the lessons. For more information about OpenType and Adobe fonts, visit www.adobe.com/type/opentype/.

Contributors

Torsten Buck has been involved in the development of software for the design and desktop publishing industries in Japan, China and the United States for almost 20 years. A Masters in Computer Science combined with a passion for typography have shaped a career that took Torsten from the development of ground-breaking Asian font technology in Hong Kong to a position as Head of Type Development at Adobe Systems in the USA. Currently he is the Director of Manneken Pis Productions and has authored a wide range of design software training books including several versions of *Adobe Photoshop Elements Classroom in a Book* and *Adobe Premiere Elements Classroom in a Book*, *Creating a Newsletter in InDesign*, and more recently *Adobe Photoshop Lightroom 2 Classroom in a Book* and *Adobe Creative Suite 4 Design Premium Classroom in a Book*.

Katrin Straub is an artist, an MA in media studies, a graphic designer, and author. Her award-winning print, painting, and multimedia work has been exhibited worldwide. With more than 15 years experience in design, Katrin has worked as Design Director for companies such as Landor Associates and Fontworks in the United States, Hong Kong, and Japan. Her work includes packaging, promotional campaigns, multimedia, website design, and internationally recognized corporate and retail identities. She holds degrees from the FH Augsburg, ISIA Urbino, and The New School University in New York and has authored many books in the past 5 years, from the *Adobe Creative Suite Idea Kit* to Classroom in a Book titles for Adobe Photoshop Lightroom 2, Adobe Creative Suite 4 Design Premium, Adobe Soundbooth, and several versions of *Adobe Photoshop Elements Classroom in a Book* and *Adobe Premiere Elements Classroom in a Book*.

John Evans has worked in computer graphics and design for more than 20 years—initially as a graphic designer, and then since 1993 as a multimedia author, software interface designer, and technical writer. His multimedia and digital illustration work associated with Japanese type attracted an award from Apple Computer Australia and was featured in Japan's leading digital design magazine. His other projects range from music education software for children to interface design for innovative Japanese font design software. As a technical writer his work includes software design specifications, user manuals, and more recently copy-editing for *Adobe Lightroom 2 Classroom in a Book*, *Adobe Photoshop Elements 7 Classroom in a Book*, and *Adobe Creative Suite 4 Design Premium Classroom in a Book*.

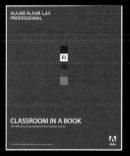

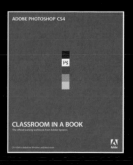

The fastest, easiest, most comprehensive way to learn
Adobe® Creative Suite® 4

Classroom in a Book®, the best-selling series of hands-on software training books, helps you learn the features of Adobe software quickly and easily.

The **Classroom in a Book** series offers what no other book or training program does—an official training series from Adobe Systems, developed with the support of Adobe product experts.

To see a complete list of our Adobe® Creative Suite® 4 titles go to www.peachpit.com/adobecs4

AdobePress

ActionScript 3.0 for Adobe Flash CS4 Professional Classroom in a Book
ISBN: 0-321-57921-6

Adobe After Effects CS4 Classroom in a Book
ISBN 0-321-57383-8

Adobe Creative Suite 4 Classroom in a Book
ISBN: 0-321-57391-9

Adobe Dreamweaver CS4 Classroom in a Book
ISBN 0-321-57381-1

Adobe Fireworks CS4 Classroom in a Book
ISBN 0-321-61219-1

Adobe Flash CS4 Professional Classroom in a Book
ISBN 0-321-57382-X

Adobe Illustrator CS4 Classroom in a Book
ISBN 0-321-57378-1

Adobe InDesign CS4 Classroom in a Book
ISBN 0-321-57380-3

Adobe Photoshop CS4 Classroom in a Book
ISBN 0-321-57379-X

Adobe Premiere Pro CS4 Classroom in a Book
ISBN 0-321-57385-4